A Little God

Courtesy, Africana Museum, Johannesburg

Tshekedi Khama, regent of the Ngwato chiefdom, 1926–1949, leaving offices of British High Commissioner, Cape Town

A Little God

The Twilight of Patriarchy
in a Southern African Chiefdom

Diana Wylie

Wesleyan University Press
Published by University Press of New England
Hanover and London

The University Press of New England
is a consortium of universities in New England dedicated to publishing scholarly and trade works by authors from member campuses and elsewhere. The New England imprint signifies uniform standards for publication excellence maintained without exception by the consortium members. A joint imprint of University Press of New England and a sponsoring member acknowledges the publishing mission of that university and its support for the dissemination of scholarship throughout the world. Cited by the American Council of Learned Societies as a model to be followed, University Press of New England publishes books under its own imprint and the imprints of Brandeis University, Brown University, Clark University, University of Connecticut, Dartmouth College, University of New Hampshire, University of Rhode Island, Tufts University, University of Vermont, and Wesleyan University.

© 1990 by Diana Wylie

All rights reserved. Except for brief quotation in critical articles or reviews, this book, or parts thereof, must not be reproduced in any form without permission in writing from the publisher. For further information contact University Press of New England, Hanover, NH 03755.

Printed in the United States of America
∞

Library of Congress Cataloging-in-Publication Data
Wylie, Diana, 1948–
    A little god : the twilight of patriarchy in a southern African chiefdom / Diana Wylie.
    p. cm.
    Based on the author's dissertation (doctoral—Yale University).
    Includes bibliographical references.
    ISBN 0–8195–5228–3
    1. Ngwato (African people)—Government relations.   2. Ngwato (African people)—Politics and government.   3. Central District (Botswana)—Politics and government.   4. Central District (Botswana)—History.   I. Title.
DT2458.N45W95   1990
968.83—dc20   89-49462
                                                                                                                                        CIP

To my father and
in memory of my mother

Contents

ILLUSTRATIONS ix
PREFACE xi

Introduction: The Twilight of Patriarchy 3

One "A Shape with Lion Body and the Head of a Man":
The Growth of the Tswana Chieftainship, 1800–1925 18

Patronage in the Early Nineteenth Century / 20
Patriarchal Ideology in the Early Nineteenth Century:
  Sacred and Secular / 31
The Centralization of Political Power in the Later
  Nineteenth Century / 36

Two "Full of Passionate Intensity":
Ngwato Politics, 1925–1939 63

The Setting / 64
The Accession / 69
The Regimental Labor Fracas / 77
Hereditary Servitude / 84
The Flogging / 91
The Divorce / 94
The Years of Economic Disaster / 96

Three The Defense of Patriarchy in the *Kgotla* 100

Nineteenth Century Origins of Tswana Law
  and Custom / 101
Twentieth Century Origins of Tswana Law
  and Custom / 107
Law and the Management of Social Change / 124

Four "Lesser Breeds without the Law":
      Subject Peoples and the Ngwato State, 1920–1948   136

      The Nineteenth Century / 139
      The Twentieth Century / 146
      The Birwa Case / 149
      The Khurutshe Case / 156
      The Mswazi Case / 162

Five "Things Fall Apart":
      The Decline of the Ngwato Chieftainship, 1948–1956   175

      The Economic Context / 176
      The Marriage / 179
      The Factions / 198
      The Fall / 204

      Conclusion   210

      NOTES   217
      SOURCES   253
      INDEX   265

List of Illustrations

Frontispiece: Tshekedi Khama, regent of Ngwato chiefdom, 1926–1949, leaving offices of British High Commissioner, Cape Town

Maps:

    Ngwato in the twentieth century   6

    Territories claimed by Tswana chiefs in 1885   47

    Bechuanaland Protectorate reserve boundaries in 1899   48

Genealogical chart: Ngwato Royal Family   56

Photographs (following page 146):

    Khama III, Tshekedi Khama's father

    Village of Serowe, capital of Ngwato

    Ngwato cattle post near Serowe

    The chief's *kgotla* (men's public forum) in Serowe

    Outpost of Bechuanaland Trading Association

    Ox wagons crossing Shashi River in Ngwato

    Bechuanaland Protectorate Police in early 1900s, Fort Gaberones

    Member of Ngwato regiment

    Tshekedi Khama as young man, at London office, on his return to southern Africa

Illustrations

Three of Seretse Khama's supporters awaiting the heir's return from London

Seretse and his British wife Ruth in Serowe

Tshekedi and Chief Bathoen of Bangwaketse greeting British Royal Family, Lobatsi

Preface

One night I sat by a fire at a Ngwato cattle post listening to two kinds of music. One came from the transistor radio belonging to my hosts. It blared rock and roll. In the distance their servant sat at his own fire, playing a thumb piano and singing an old song about, I imagined, the veld. I longed to move closer to the old solitary servant, but in deference to my hosts I stayed at their fire by the noisy transistor. This moment of tension has remained in my memory because it exemplifies many of the moods and problems involved in doing historical field research: the difficulty of perceiving evidence of past indigenous life; the confusing mix of African and Western idioms; the ease with which, in deferring to one's hosts, one risks adopting a view of their society based on their rank within it.

I had gone to southern Africa to research the ways in which the growth of industrial capitalism on South Africa's Rand had affected a neighboring chiefdom. I focused initially on labor migration and its impact on households. My scope broadened as I was drawn to study the nature of the polity that laborers had left when they went to work in the mines, industries, and farms of South Africa. Having lived and worked in North, West and East Africa for nearly four years, I had a keen desire to write a history from within an African society. Having studied British imperial history, I wanted to know in detail the political nature of the small society the imperial power had tried to govern. As time went on, this simple goal broadened into a desire to write a history that addressed the following questions: How do people's ideas change about what is right and proper in public life? To what extent does capitalism preserve and transform political ideas and practices? How do indigenous political life and imperial overrule affect one another? I wanted to learn how a small society and its values weathered incorporation in larger-scale capitalist and industrial societies.

In the course of trying to understand one southern African society, I encountered two formidable characters, one an anthropologist, Isaac Schapera, and the other, a chief, Tshekedi Khama. Schapera shaped contemporary understanding of Tswana society, and Tshekedi effectively spoke for Bechuanaland Africans during a quarter-century. Any student of Tswana society must come to terms with their lives' work. This book is written in full admiration of their talents and accomplishments. To the extent that it is also a criticism, it is because I wanted to read through the political mythology and language they recorded to the political logic lying beneath the explanations.

The inadequacy of a legalistic interpretation of Tswana politics and custom first struck me when I compared the records of disputes I collected in Botswana with the formal statements of judicial principle recorded in Schapera's *Handbook of Tswana Law and Custom*. I found little if any correspondence between stated rules and social outcome. I wanted to extend an anthropological perspective, as I found it in the work of John Comaroff and Simon Roberts, into the past and try to discover the logic of dispute settlement before the chieftainship lost its hold on the center of Tswana life. I wanted to go beyond the reasons by which Tshekedi defended his political acts and to discover the struggles lying behind them: Whose material and political interests were in conflict within Ngwato society? Who won the contests for wealth and power? And why?

Colonial documents, written by and for the elite, both indigenous and foreign, had ignored the common people of Ngwato society. I wanted to supplement them with insights gained from extended residence in the field. And so, for five months, I lived in Serowe, the capital of Tshekedi's chiefdom, and interviewed members of the royal family, their dependents, former labor migrants, European and African traders, and prominent Ngwato commoners. For one month also, I lived in Lerala, a small village near the Transvaal border, and listened to the life histories of nearly fifty former labor migrants and their families. I have had to slight the experience of various other groups within Tswana society because of their relative estrangement from formal political life. The experience of women and of hereditary servants was, for example, difficult to recapture. Often, also, I had to recreate imaginatively the bonds between patrons and clients. I had to manufacture the dialogue—spoken and unspoken—by which factions were built. Nevertheless, my interviews helped me to go beyond the stated motives of historical actors and particularly beyond their legalistic justifications of their actions to define the political logic of a Tswana ruler and his people as they struggled to maintain the independence of their chiefdom, and to mold the relations of power and wealth within it, in the face of British political control and South African economic power.

During my two years in Botswana (1979–1981), I lived on a Fulbright-Hays Award for Doctoral Dissertation Research Abroad. In the field, I was helped by many kind people. Besides the key informants whose names I have listed in the section on sources, the following people "fed" me in a number of ways: Gothe Kgamane, Busi Phasoana, Gilbert Mpolokeng, Carol Kerven, Ted Field, Pauline Peters, Mmipi Raseto, Miriam Lesolle, Mr. and Mrs. Albert Mmola, Thomas Tlou. My translators were James Mpotokwane, Diteko Dialwa, Thuli Johnson, Keitumetse Passman, and Maria Memmo. I am grateful to all of them.

During the last phases of writing my Ph.D. dissertation for the history department at Yale University, I was supported by a research fellowship at the Carter G. Woodson Institute for Afro-American and African Studies at the University of Virginia. Members of the weekly Southern African Research Program seminar at Yale commented on each chapter. Pam Baldwin, widely respected for administering that program, is also a cartographer; she drew for me a good map. The staff at the following libraries generously gave their assistance: the Botswana National Archives, Rhodes House Library, William Cullen Africana Library at the University of the Witwatersrand, the Cape

Town University Library, the Cory Library at Rhodes University; and the McGregor Museum and Duggan Cronin Bantu Gallery; and I especially want to thank Moore Crossey of Yale University Library. In addition, many friends and colleagues have given me valuable advice and help: Hoyt Alverson, Leslie Bessant, Jeffrey Butler, John Coumantaros, Michael Crowder, Eileen Flanagan, Rebecca French, Emily Honig, Carol Kerven, Chris Lowe, Joseph Miller, Athaliah Molokomme, Pauline Peters, Tim Quinlan, Robin Chapman Stacey, Howard Venable. Leonard Thompson and Robert Harms of the Yale history department advised the writing of the dissertation from which this book developed. Jeannette Hopkins was a paragon of an editor. To all these fine critics I owe thanks for their help in allowing me to translate such evidence as the half-heard ancient song into the book that follows.

New Haven, Connecticut
Fall 1989

A Little God

Introduction
The Twilight of Patriarchy

Ksogi ke modingwana, gaesebjwe. (The chief is a little god, no evil must be spoken of him.)
Tswana proverb

Nearly a century and a half separates these two vignettes of Tswana chiefs, both engaging in the world beyond their realms on the fringes of southern Africa's Kalahari desert. One engraving shows the chief of the Tlhaping in 1812 seated on the ground facing an Englishman, seated also "in the African manner," who has just arrived by ox wagon from the south.[1] A dense penumbra of villagers surrounds the chief and the Englishman. The chief's family members and other rich people of the village sit two to three deep in a circle around them. Ordinary people, crowded together, are standing behind. The chief wears a leather cloak, a thick necklace of sinews, and a string of white and purple beads. His greased hair shines with metallic dust. Above his left elbow, he wears five wide rings of ivory. The second is a photograph taken in the middle of the twentieth century of the chief of the Ngwato, a Tswana chiefdom more than 300 miles to the north of the Tlhaping. Leaving the headquarters of the British High Commissioner in Cape Town, the chief, Tshekedi Khama, is alone on the street. His woolen trench coat is cinched neatly about his waist. A snap-brim fedora protects him further against the cold of a Cape Town winter. In his left hand, he carries a battered leather briefcase stuffed with papers. Aware of the photographer's presence, he has averted his head slightly, and he smiles stiffly.

These two pictures point to the great changes occurring on the fringes of the Kalahari since the chiefdoms began to engage intensively in the world beyond the desert. By the twentieth century, the chief had become a far more solitary figure. Yet he had to engage in both British and South African politics, and to this end, he worked in offices to prepare position papers and court cases and to write letters to bureaucrats in London and Cape Town. The changes in fashion indicated changing patterns of trade and also the waning of local crafts and the decline of hunting. Men and a few women now worked to earn money to buy such articles of clothing as fedoras or kerchiefs. They also worked to pay taxes to subsidize the services provided by the chief's offices.

Between the recording of these vignettes, two dramatic events occurred. From 1886 on, gold—discovered on the neighboring Witwatersrand or "Rand," a ridge in the temperate grasslands to the east—funded South Africa's industrial revolution. From the late nineteenth century, the British government established three formal colonies, called High Commission Territories, in the region. Britain annexed not only Bechuanaland, land of Tswana-speaking peoples, in 1885, but also Basutoland, in 1868 and Swaziland, in 1902. In each of these three territories, the British left indigenous government more or less intact; colonial overrule was to be indirect—and therefore cheap. Eight chiefdoms comprised the Bechuanaland Protectorate; one was Tshekedi's polity, during colonial times called the Ngwato Reserve and today the Central District of the independent state of Botswana.

Tshekedi guided the Ngwato through the consequences of these transforming events for a quarter of a century. Ruling the chiefdom as its regent from 1926 to 1950, he presided over the conversion of its political system from one that Max Weber might have called patriarchal—a type of domination based on strictly personal loyalty to a fatherlike ruler who invokes the sanctity of tradition to justify his acts—toward one that was bureaucratic. According to Weber, bureaucracy separates the public from the private fully and in principle by completely depersonalizing administrative management and rationally systematizing law.[2] In the process of trying to shape the local consequences of colonialism and industrialization, Tshekedi employed strategies drawn from both political modes. Some were inherited and others were modern. A similar mix of old and new political language and behavior characterized the tactics of his people as they tried to shape their own destinies within the context of rapidly changing times.

The British overlords of the Bechuanaland Protectorate moved into a hierarchical political order in the late nineteenth century and occupied its highest rung. This order was patriarchal in the sense that its political ideology exalted the leadership of older men who inherited their high rank from ancestors related to the chieftainship. Women, young men, and foreigners generally stood outside the center of power. At best, they were spectators; at worst, they were exploited. The chief was a "father" and the people he governed conveyed their respect by referring to themselves as his children. Closely allied to this hierarchical concept was the ethic of collective responsibility. In the absence of a strong centralized state, senior men were responsible for exacting social conformity from their subordinates. Patriarchal ideology, often transgressed in practice, rationalized a society where the rich distributed rather than accumulated their wealth, and where the power of the state to extract wealth from the people it governed was weak. Political life was acted out in terms of personal relations rather than in terms of depersonalized and rational law.

Patriarchal ideology did not, of course, describe reality. It did not offer a precise legal code to obey. It expressed ideal relations between people as if they were members of one family. The family was an idiom through which political conflicts and alliances were expressed. People were accustomed to describe their grievances in these inherited terms; an unpopular ruler could be

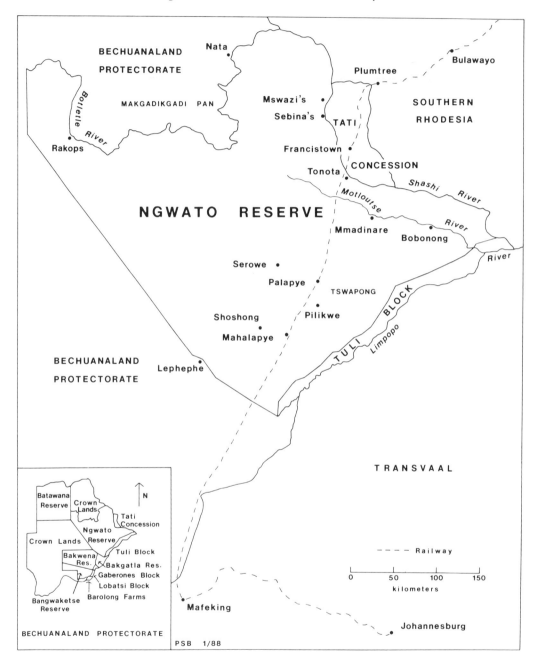

said to have lost his office because he was junior to another claimant, even if there were other, deeper reasons for disaffection. The term *patriarchy,* in short, as used here, connotes relations between men and especially the self-justifying strategies of the elite. In contrast to its contemporary use by feminist theorists, it does not refer specifically to relations between men and women.

Political realities had given rise to the ideals of patriarchy. Most African societies in southern Africa were governed by a chieftainship empowered to settle disputes and to shape public policy. Especially in the nineteenth century, the chief shared these powers with his relatives and his own chosen councillors. These advisers were explicitly recognized to possess, in varying degrees, higher rank than the poorer and less powerful members of their societies. Yet despite this concentration of wealth and power, some degree of popular agreement had to be reached before a policy was enacted. The coercive force available to the political elite was generally too weak to allow a powerful autocracy to arise because, except among those southern African peoples who spent long periods of their youth in national age regiments, households retained considerable autonomy from chiefly control.

While the chieftainship virtually monopolized the realm of formal political institutions, the world of politics extended far beyond that office. Nearly every facet of life and work was shot through with political import. Strategic alliances were set up by hierarchical exchanges of women and cattle, arranged by older men. Through bridewealth payments, as the proverb said, "cattle beget children"; the prestige and wealth of a household depended on its size. The factions based on marriage and clientage made or broke chiefs. The web of exchanges of cattle, women, and grain not only gave power, it also gave life. During prolonged drought, such reciprocity helped people survive starvation. Whenever a patron or client reneged on the expectations generated by an exchange, the web was torn by dissension. Within each village or cluster of homesteads, politics was the work of avoiding this damage by continually mediating, negotiating, and advertising those alliances. Even within the wider political realm, such as the capital village or chiefdom, rank or social status, expressed locally in terms of "seniority," was negotiable. People spoke of seniority as if it were acquired only by birth; in fact, families rose and fell in the social hierarchy depending on their success in building a following of loyal clients.

The chief's court or *kgotla*—a dusty forum in the heart of the capital village, protected from the desert wind by an arc of densely planted posts—provided a political theater in which the patriarchal order worked. Through the *kgotla* one can see evidence of past relationships between the chief and his subjects, on the one hand, and among his subjects, on the other, as they coped with the changing circumstances of their daily lives.

Deriving from "two lights," the word *twilight* expresses the resilience of the old ideological order alongside the new. The mix of dark and light symbolizes the ambiguous meld of popular beliefs about what constitutes the right and proper order of public life, characteristic of a society undergoing profound change. It also aptly characterizes the uneven way that aspects of social life change on the periphery of a capitalist and industrial heartland. Key attributes of Tswana society changed at different tempi: the catalysts to the local development of wage-labor relations were usually weak and did not necessarily occur at the same time that political innovations were implanted from above.

For this reason, the following chapters will reflect the twilight years thematically rather than strictly chronologically. They will focus respectively on the growth of chiefly power, dynastic rivalry, legal change, relations with subject people, and succession to high office. By examining political crises thematically, each chapter will reveal the growth of a certain kind of antipathy to a strong chieftainship. When these diverse sources of opposition coalesced in the middle of the twentieth century, they determined the fate of that patriarchal institution.

This study aims not only to contribute to our knowledge of

the range of political behavior in rural southern Africa in this century, but also, by focusing on the question of changing concepts of political legitimacy, to contribute to the study of rural political consciousness, its aspects that were both inherited and modern, patriarchal and democratic. It is not a biography of the chiefs, but a study of the changing world in which they lived. Nevertheless, because the personal qualities of patriarchal leaders played so important a role in the nature of their rule, Tshekedi's character must be known. The following vignette reflects his participation in this twilight world.

The incident illustrates the mix of political metaphors so characteristic of colonial overrule. It took place in 1930 in the imposing office of the Secretary of State for the Dominions. Even as a young man, Tshekedi angered his British imperial overlords by his pugnacity. One official called him a "pig headed little beast" because Tshekedi, then only twenty-five years old, had pursued a battle to protect the interests of his people all the way to proconsular offices in London.[3] In the office of Lord Passfield—as Sidney Webb, the Fabian socialist, was known when Dominions Secretary—he respectfully claimed the right to veto mining developments in his polity until their terms benefited his "tribe." He argued at length, pinning a map of the Bechuanaland Protectorate to the firescreen in the grand Whitehall office and strewing the carpet with legal documents. Passfield and his staff, in effect the proconsuls of all three High Commission Territories, were impressed but irritated; they reminded him of his obligations under the rule of law. Although a modern industrial project was under discussion, the young chief sought to reassure the proconsuls of his loyalty in preindustrial terms: "[Our tribe] regard[s] the government as their father."[4]

Over the next three decades, Tshekedi would mature from this slight figure, who had only recently won his battle to control a stammer, into a stocky, combative man with remarkable energy for engaging in two particular battles, the fight against his many enemies—dynastic, South African, British—and the campaign to build a modern state on the eastern fringes of the Kalahari Desert. If in 1930 Tshekedi Khama could be considered a nascent patriarch, one who went out of his way to express filial respect for His Majesty's Government, he quickly grew into an exemplar of the patriarchal order itself, a ruler whose personal qualities, relatively unrestrained by codes or institutions, helped to shape the history of his times.

Tshekedi's family heritage had primed him to assume the role of leading, in his own words, "a patriarchal state."[5] He inherited a strong sense of his right to rule, although he was not his father's firstborn or senior son and therefore served his people as a regent during the minority of his nephew, the rightful heir.[6] Like his father, Khama III, Tshekedi provided the polity with charismatic leadership. Both he and his father formulated clear visions of what the destiny of their people should be. They devoted prodigious energy to realizing those visions. Neither man can be dismissed as simply self-aggrandizing or personally ambitious.

Tshekedi transcended the order he exemplified. Not simply a chief, he was also a cattle rancher who followed his father's lead in growing rich in private property. He was becoming an independently wealthy man even as he defended such inherited virtues as communal ownership, collective responsibility, and his own control of the chiefdom's resources. We can therefore speak of his regency as epitomizing the patriarchal order at the same time as he was helping to destroy it.

The Setting in Time and Place

The eight Bechuanaland chiefdoms, together with smaller chiefdoms in South African areas known today as the northern Cape and the western Transvaal, were populated by people called Tswana. The word *Tswana*—like *Nguni, Sotho,* and *Khoisan,* the names of the other great categories of peoples indigenous to southern Africa—describes language principally. Nguni, Sotho, and Tswana are members of the Bantu language family that extends throughout the southern lobe of Africa. Hunters and gatherers who preceded Bantu-speaking herders and cultivators in the region spoke Khoisan languages. Sotho and Tswana tongues are so closely related to each other that their names are often hyphenated or they are both referred to as Sotho. Speakers of these two languages share settlement and kinship patterns that set them apart from the Nguni. Before industrialization, the Sotho-Tswana peoples lived in the interior of southern Africa; the Nguni lived in a belt along the Indian Ocean coast.

The cultural differences observed between the Sotho-Tswana and the Nguni are best explained with reference to ecology. The land settled by Nguni peoples, between the Drakensberg Mountains and the Indian Ocean, was better watered than the inland plateaux where the Tswana lived, and thus the Nguni kept their herds year-round near their homes and fields. Few Nguni except the closest followers of the chiefs lived in settlements large enough to be called villages. Most settlements were extended households, now conventionally called homesteads. Each family group was highly dependent on the herds of cattle whose management it shared. The Tswana lived on arid land occupied simultaneously by Khoisan foragers. Their society was more stratified than the Nguni's; hunting was of central importance to Tswana livelihood and ritual, and people lived during the winter in centralized villages located near sources of water.

Bantu-speaking peoples, Sotho and Tswana among them, were descended from men and women south of the Zambesi River who began to work in iron and till the soil during the first millennium A.D. Certain groups, particularly those who held many cattle, rose to hegemony over others, but these groupings did not necessarily endure long as cohesive units. Partly because land was plentiful, communities tended to divide into smaller groups or chiefdoms named after their putative founders. A man called Ngwato, for example, was said to have founded the chiefdom bearing his name after he quarreled with his elder brother.

From the sixteenth century, with the advent of the Indian Ocean trade in such luxuries as beads and ivory, the tendency of clans or chiefdoms to split apart began reversing. Chiefs could use the luxuries as marks of their own high status and as gifts to reconcile lesser chiefs to paying tribute and fealty to them. By the late eighteenth century, separate communities were joining together to form larger confederations, especially when chiefs were able to secure local monopolies over trade. And yet chiefdoms could still be defined as the followings of a single political leader rather than as territorial entities. By the early nineteenth century, the growth of confederations led to increased competition for resources. The expansion of Shaka's Zulu kingdom, in particular, sent refugees scattering across the region in search of security. This period, called the *mfecane*, encouraged the defensive foundation of great chiefdoms.

European incursions from the Cape northeast through southern Africa further advanced the process of state formation. White settlers occupying land between the Caledon Valley and the northern Cape provoked the native occupants of each region to develop into self-consciously distinct groups. Moshoeshoe's mountain chiefdom of Basutoland is one noted example of a southern African state formed, in a drive for self-defense and profit, from disparate peoples with clan-based identities. Khama's Ngwato chiefdom is another. The process of consolidation occurred slowly. In the late eighteenth century, apparently, a traveler first inscribed the name "Tswana" on a map. By the mid-nineteenth century, at least one acute observer noted, "These people [Tswana] do not use this word of themselves, or of one another; nevertheless they accept of it as the white man's name for them and now begin to use it of themselves."[7]

Within the region, South Africa's late nineteenth century industrial revolution, galvanized by the discovery of diamonds and gold, was separating wage laborers from the land and deepening trends toward the accumulation of material goods and the centralization of political power. People's ideas about the right and proper order of public life began to change. Even in such areas of the hinterland as the Ngwato chiefdom, new classes were arising, forging new alliances, and struggling to control new forms of wealth. People gained access to money by selling their labor or their cattle. Some leapt at the chance to work for wages in South Africa after diamonds were discovered in 1867 and gold in 1886, but the catalysts of large-scale labor migration from the Ngwato chiefdom occurred later and in two phases, the first great impetus from a drought coinciding with a 1933 epidemic of cattle disease, the second during the Second World War when a combination of drought and army recruitment reduced the number of men to unprecedentedly low levels. South African legislative barriers that had kept the export of Ngwato cattle at low levels from 1924 were lifted during the war, then hastily reimposed in 1945, after the war was over.

Rural societies changed their values and forms of organization slowly. As some scholars have remarked, proletarianization was seeping rather than sweeping across rural southern Africa. Inherited institutions and beliefs coexisted with ones more compatible to the industrial era; people used both sets of institutions to advance their interests, even as their sense of their own best interests was changing. The coexistence of two modes of production led necessarily to ambiguity in popular acts and beliefs.

Apart from South Africa's industrial revolution, the other great catalyst of social change was British overrule. From the end of the nineteenth century, colonial administrators deepened their control of the small societies of southern Africa. Up to the 1880s, the South African colonies and republics—the Cape Colony, Natal, the Orange Free State, and the Transvaal—had sought to undercut the chieftainship and to supplant it with magisterial overrule; they did so by issuing proclamations, elaborating an administrative hierarchy, and later, by appointing local councils. By the end of the century, many chiefdoms, such as those of the Zulu, Xhosa and Sotho, had been pacified by the British army. Others were more peaceably subdued by the lure of markets. Administrators were growing to feel that the chieftainship, if properly controlled, could exert a conservative and stabilizing influence.

The British called such a policy indirect rule. The thinly staffed tiers of the protectorate's skeletal and poorly funded administrative structure provided rudimentary services to the "Native Reserves," as the Bechuanaland chiefdoms were proclaimed in 1899. At the local level, Resident Magistrates, called District Commissioners after 1934, exercised judicial as well as administrative functions. Initially staffed by former police officers, each Resident Magistrate's office mediated all of the local chief's relations with the higher tiers of the administrative hierarchy. In principle, after 1919, they heard appeal cases from the chief's court; from their jurisdiction there were two more exalted courts of appeal—the Bechuanaland Protectorate Special or, later, High Court in Lobatse and the Privy Council in London. The Resident Magistrate oversaw the accounts of the tribal treasuries after they were set up to spend local taxes on local development projects in 1938. The next administrative tier, situated in the northern Cape town of Mafeking, consisted of a Resident Commissioner. Responsible for the daily affairs of the entire protectorate, he reported to the southern African representative of His Majesty's government, the High Commissioner, in Cape Town or Pretoria. From 1920, chiefs exerted some influence over the legislation affecting them by speaking their minds in the Native Advisory Council, called the African Advisory Council after 1940, of which the Resident Commissioner was president. The High Commissioner was formally responsible to no one for the legislation that he drafted. By simply proclaiming it, he made it law. The commissioner did report to the Colonial Office until 1925, and to the Dominions Office thereafter, on activities in all three High Commission Territories, Bechuanaland, Basutoland, and Swaziland. The level of development expenditure in the protectorates was exceedingly low not only because of the imperial ethic that dependencies should pay their own way, but also because everyone commonly assumed that the territories would one day be transferred to South African control.

From the 1920s, the rulers of the Union of South Africa were calling their version of this native policy segregation. African jobs, political life, and land rights were, ideally, to be separate from whites'. While increasingly excluded from Union politics, Africans would find themselves represented in rural "reserves" by traditional authorities—chiefs and headmen—organized into councils. This paternalist phase ended in the 1950s, when, in preparation for the creation of Bantustans, the South African government began to meddle in the reserves more overtly and coercively; it imposed compliant but unpopular Africans as Bantu Authorities and allowed them to appoint their own clients as councillors.[8] This decade marks the parting of the ways between the destinies of the three High Commission Territories and the South African reserves—as Britain was preparing the former for independence as internationally legitimate nation-states, and South Africa obliged the latter to retain "tribal" institutions and values as Bantustans or "homelands." In the legislation preparing for the transformation of Bechuanaland into the independent state of Botswana in 1966, chiefs were forbidden to participate as chiefs in national government. Despite this divergence between the fate of the British protectorates and the South African "native reserves," one common theme throughout all of southern Africa in the mid-twentieth century was the coming of closer government from any source. Avoiding the long arm of the law, whether in the form of paying taxes or being subjected to its codes, became increasingly difficult.

During Tshekedi Khama's regency as chief of the Ngwato, the chieftainship was surviving its final phase of relative autonomy from state control. In the 1960s, the departing imperialists would erect the apparatus of nation-state government over the Bechuanaland Protectorate. As a result, the chieftainship in all eight northern Tswana chiefdoms, while retaining its form, would lose its claim to exert primary political authority over its subjects and to serve as greatest patron of all.

A similar process in South Africa was both more advanced and marked by the brutal exclusion of black people from the organs of national power. Through this case study of one Bechuanaland chiefdom, we may be witnessing the kinds of continuities and changes that would have occurred in rural black South

Africa if apartheid policy had not perverted indigenous beliefs and practices by rigidifying them into Bantustans. While the fate of the Ngwato chieftainship became internationally notorious owing to a conjuncture of personalities and events peculiar to that place, the process was general.

Because Tshekedi was a legalistic political strategist, he addressed only those regional issues not yet resolved in courts of law. Believing that race relations in South Africa had crystallized, he preferred to fight for the independence of Bechuanaland and similar polities rather than to become embroiled in Union affairs.[9] Before imperial proconsuls decided after the Second World War to decolonize rather than transfer their southern African dependencies to South African control, he lobbied intensively in Britain and Bechuanaland against incorporation of the High Commission Territories in the Union and battled on behalf of a Bechuanaland Legislative Council and an independent South West Africa. The modern state of Botswana owes its existence in part to his efforts.

Southern African chiefs tried similar tactics of managing their polities' rapid transit from shallow to close government, that is, from government that rarely intruded into the daily lives of the households to one that constantly legislated for, adjudicated disputes between, and taxed individuals and their families. Many communicated with each other about strategies that would allow them to gain the most independence and prosperity. Throughout southern Africa, the designs of European social engineers were matched and elaborated upon by paramount chiefs, who laid the foundations of bureaucracies of their own by hiring secretaries, translators, policemen, and teachers and by paying them salaries. Many sought to create a sense of "tribal" identity by reviving lapsed ceremonies and institutions; for example, Tshekedi's contemporary and former schoolmate, the Swazi king Sobhuza, resuscitated a national harvest ritual called *incwala* as well as age regiments in the 1920s. In varying ways, the chiefs sought to centralize control of their hinterlands, especially for purposes of collecting taxes and preventing secession. They tried to undermine those people, usually rival claimants for the chieftainship, who spoke "evil" of them, and they used codes of law and the printed word generally to extend their jurisdiction over disputes. Their motives were as varied as their personalities. Fierce loyalty to the chiefdom's best interests mixed comfortably with the desire for personal gain. To perceive the chieftainship as an office of exploitation, or as the undisputed and static seat of a "little god," is to miss its rich paradoxical nature and the extent to which both its practices and popular beliefs were changing.[10]

Chapter One

"A Shape with Lion Body and the Head of a Man"
The Growth of the Tswana Chieftainship, 1800-1925

Bogosi boa tsaleloa, ga bo loeloe. (Man should be born for the kingship, not fight for it.)
Tswana proverb

The chieftainship was the "center" holding Tswana society together. The chief allocated scarce resources, conducted assemblies and rituals, and represented his polity in encounters with outsiders. Until the middle of the twentieth century, the chieftainship remained the organizational center of northern Tswana life.

And yet the chieftainship was hardly omnipotent or static. It controlled no independent coercive force, and it was continually assailed by a variety of power seekers. At certain historical moments, these competitors succeeded in shaping and sharing chiefly powers; at other times, they lost their own power and wealth. By the same token, the laws upholding the chieftainship were not unchallenged objects of popular reverence. Law and custom were created, manipulated, and interpreted by contestants for power. The common and misleading image of a relatively changeless and revered institution has derived from what chiefs in this century declared their time-honored powers to be. Tshekedi and his fellow chiefs tried to shape their own and their people's destinies in the twentieth century by claiming that they had inherited leonine powers, that they were monarchs and the sons of monarchs. The aura of timelessness enveloping the concepts of African law and custom must be stripped away to understand how patriarchal government actually grew. One must go back in time before the codes and precepts recorded in colonial legal handbooks.[1]

In the early nineteenth century, a person approaching a Tswana capital from afar first passed through its cattle-post area, then its fields, and then an area denuded for firewood of trees and bushes. In this relatively wild penumbra outside of the village, a traveler was likely to encounter, depending on the season, men and boys herding cattle and women cultivating fields. The traveler might also meet bands of Khoisan hunter-gatherers whose presence was tolerated so near the village only if they were believed not to be cattle thieves. He or she might also see forlorn exiles from Tswana society, like suspected male or female witches or abandoned wives who were compelled to forage in the wild for food. The village itself possessed dwellings so substantial that one early nineteenth century traveler, a man of the Enlightenment, found his first sight of them "a moment, which, in its peculiar gratification and delight, was never surpassed by any other event of the journey."[2] The round thatched buildings were situated within shrub fences enclosing the yard where all the communal activities of family life took place. Although the house that belonged to the chief was no bigger than anyone else's, it lay at the heart of the village near the great open space or *kgotla* where he and his uncles presided over the public life of the chiefdom. The chief's uncles displayed confidence and leadership, sometimes more than the chief himself, and took pride of place in all communal events. So did other rich men. Clothes distinguished the wealthy, those who were rich in cattle, from the poor, those who had none. The rich wore fur cloaks in winter; the poor wore skin cloaks, but for the most part, attire did not betray rank. Nearly everyone covered his or her body and clothes with grease and metallic dust or ochre, walked barefoot, and sported, at most, simple bead necklaces as decoration. This much an acute observer could see in a Tswana village early in the nineteenth century. What the visitor could not so readily see were the ties of patronage linking most of these people to one another, helping them survive the harsh exigencies of life in a "thirstland."

Patronage in the Early Nineteenth Century

The Tswana, unlike the Nguni, who lived in scattered homesteads, concentrated their formal political activities in densely settled villages.[3] Set like islands in the vast Kalahari grasslands, Tswana villages epitomized civilization to the people who lived in them. They signified human power to survive and shape the harsh conditions of life in an unpredictable land. Customs and ceremonies reassured villagers that they could hold back and transcend the surrounding chaos of the wild.[4] The bush was the place where wealth was made by hunting and kept at cattle posts, and where individuals sought wild food, with desperation when droughts lengthened into famines. The village was the place where social order could be recreated after a disaster had sent people, especially the poor, scattering to forage for survival.

Scarcity of water was one major cause of the Tswana pattern of nucleated settlement. The land between the Molopo, Limpopo, and Chobe rivers is dry, and it becomes drier the further one travels to the west. Eyeing this eastern fringe of the Kalahari, where most Tswana chiefdoms were, one foreign visitor dismissed the vast, semiarid plains with apparent boredom as "neither an arcadia nor a desert."[5] Other early observers, particularly those who traveled westward into the Kalahari itself, called the region a thirstland. In the hardveld or eastern zone of present-day Botswana, a scant but adequate 550 millimeters of rain fall in an average year, usually between the months of October and March, but a bad year may see virtually no rain at all. As a result, good harvests occur only once every three or four years. The flat land and low rainfall prevent erosion from being as pressing a problem as it is elsewhere in southern Africa, but planting can be a fruitless task when scattered maize and sorghum seeds bake in parched soil. The land does yield one rather more dependable boon to its inhabitants: the grasses eaten by their free-ranging cattle are sweet and nutritious. Unless a prolonged drought stunts or kills its herds, the eastern Kalahari is good ranching country.[6]

Villages lay near a relatively permanent water point such as a spring. During the dry winter, between June and August, people lived there and participated in communal affairs such as dispute settlement and public labor service. Within villages, family groups lived in clusters, called wards, under the leadership of their most senior male member or headman; senior to all headmen was the chief of the village. During the rainy season, people lived beside their fields outside the village—sometimes within sight of it and sometimes as much as a day's journey away. There they could drink rainwater while they cultivated. In the most distant zone, their cattle grazed. The men and boys looking after the cattle lived in rude shelters near the pans, streams, water holes, and wells that give the land its value. In the dry season, the cattle effectively herded themselves by gathering to drink, even as rarely as every two to three days. In the rainy season, they dispersed across the unfenced veld in search of fresh pastures, and their herders moved with them.

Families foraged, cultivated, and herded depending on the season and their means. Gender determined an individual's work, or, as the proverb said, "a field is a woman's concern, the man's is the cattle *kraal*." (Women cultivated; men herded and hunted.) Together they made all the material goods they needed to sustain them in their daily lives—pots, baskets, skin clothing, mud and wattle homes. They obtained their few luxury goods such as the ochre and metallic dust cosmetics from medium-distance exchanges that were neither rich nor frequent enough to induce them to adopt highly differentiated styles of living. The visual evidence of wealth lay not in elaboration of ornaments or dwellings but in the size of a homestead. People esteemed large households; the few rich households were polygamous, consisting of a patriarch, his wives, his unmarried daughters, his sons, and their wives and children. The more people available to provide food, the more people a household could feed, the higher that household's social prestige. The many monogamous poor, including those who had lost animals or harvests to the vagaries of climate, tried to build herds or survive shortages of grain by borrowing or begging from the rich or their relatives.

The work of survival in the early nineteenth century was intimately related to the work of politics. Throughout the region, people wrested a living from the soil and from the beasts of the veld by effectively following two precepts, each with an important political corollary. First, households were to be largely self-sufficient; they would produce what they consumed, and as a result, they would enjoy considerable autonomy from chiefly control. The management and control of households would remain in the hands of their senior male heads, whether or not a lineage had grown to dominate the chiefdom and collect tribute from its members. Even after a rich lineage had risen to seniority over a village, by virtue of its prowess in cattle raiding or war, it had the power to exact only limited dues, such as labor service, from each household. The political center interfered very little with the production and exchange of goods by families. Second, households were to be linked by a network of exchanges; the exchanges allowed them to prosper as well as to survive hard times. People preferred to loan or exchange their cattle wealth rather than to accumulate it. The strategic distribution of wealth guaranteed survival as best as could be expected in an unpredictable and arid climate. It was the stuff of politics.

These two political realities—that households were fairly autonomous from chiefly control and survived by cooperating with each other—point to a fundamental tension within Tswana society: families were obliged to cooperate with one another, and they were ranked in a social hierarchy. Even though the relative strength of these two tendencies changed over time, the tension between them meant that Tswana people were constantly negotiating alliances to survive. Two of the most visible and prominent exchanges involved cattle and, true to the imperatives of rank, they existed in two tiers: the elite version was called *kgamelo* and the common one *mafisa*.

From notable men outside his family and clan, the chief won loyalty by distributing *kgamelo,* or milk-bag cattle. In the early nineteenth century, the milk-bag system, an elite version of the ordinary cattle-loan system called *mafisa,* originated in the holder's duty to milk the chief's cattle and bring thick sour milk to the *kgotla*; then the chief would distribute it to his wives for themselves and their children, and to the poor. Occasionally the chief would ask the holder to send an ox to the village for slaughter. In return, the milk-bag holder was free to treat the herds as if they were his own—to help provide his son's bridewealth, to slaughter, or to exchange. This liberty had a price: all of the client's property—including his wagons, horses, and small stock—could be appropriated by the chief, and his labor—to hunt and, later in the century, to plow or inspan a wagon—could be called upon whenever the chief needed them or wanted to test the holder's loyalty. The obligation never ended—"the chief's milk pail never dries up"—but in practice *kgamelo* holders tended to be the chief's most loyal supporters; chiefs rarely had to ruin their retainers, whose loyalty was a bulwark against the plots of their royal relatives.[7]

Exchanges—wives for cattle, food and cattle for labor and loyalty—even more than the public face of politics in the chief's court, constituted the essence of political life. People distributed their stock so as to raise their social standing. Throughout the Bantu-speaking societies of southern Africa, people exchanged cattle for wives. The ways in which these exchanges took place—when, how many, with whom—operated "to sustain the influence and advantages of the powerful," as Adam Kuper has recently argued.[8] In the Tswana case, especially among families rich in cattle, people preferred to marry close kin so that, as the proverb says, cattle would stay in the same *kraal*. The less wealthy also preferred to marry their sons to their mother's brother's daughters: cattle ideally moved between brother's and sister's *kraals* or cattle pens. While other southern African peoples tended to construct marriage alliances between second and third cousins or with non kin, marriages everywhere represented a pattern of investment and indebtedness serving to advantage the rich. The economic advantages won by marriage, in turn, had political corollaries, as did the ties forged between family groups by the loan of cattle through *mafisa*. *Mafisa* had a number of virtues; for example, in return for herding a rich man's cattle at his own cattle post, the client milked them for his family and would occasionally be paid a heifer. The rich man not only gained a loyal adherent but also protected his herd from localized disaster by distributing it across the landscape. Such loans or exchanges produced factions that could make or ruin chiefs.

The fluidity of the membership of these factions and, therefore, of social strata is belied by the terms commonly used to connote rank and ethnicity. The words *royalty* (chiefly relatives), *commoners* (those without genealogical connection to the chieftainship), *subject people* (villages paying tribute in the hinterland), and *hereditary servants* (Khoisan herders) give rise to the impression of ranked closed sets. They also convey a false sense of ethnic rigidity. In fact, people continually moved across categories as they negotiated new alliances, usually by marriage and loans of cattle. By distinguishing himself in the *kgotla* and marrying well, a respectable commoner or foreigner might move closer to the chief and become richer than a relative of a late chief who had fallen into disfavor. Up to the mid-nineteenth century, people freely exchanged and produced goods with people of other ethnicities and languages. It is true that hereditary servants were usually speakers of Khoisan languages, and that their physical appearance—short, light-brown-skinned, with peppercorn hair—set them apart from Bantu speakers. Nevertheless, some archeologists have recently argued that there is no evidence that these traits were the basis for invidious distinctions before some Khoisan became Tswana servants from the middle of the nineteenth century: to stereotype their economic activities—

Bantu speakers farmed while Khoisan speakers foraged—is to ignore the movement of people in and out of both productive activities according to the exigencies of survival in an arid climate.[9]

Despite the fluidity of their identity, all Tswana households were located within a hierarchical social system. "Seniority" was the ideological face of the system of patronage distributing resources in Tswana society. The concept of hereditary rank reflected the material dependence of clients on their patrons, and it was expressed in the deference and subordination of juniors. Although the word also connotes differentiation by age, *seniority* principally conveyed distinctions of inherited status. Women, young men, and the poor had no rank. The proximity of a man's ancestors to the chieftainship determined, in principle, his place in society. No man was another's equal. The Tswana used this idea of inequality to explain the natural order of both the sacred and secular worlds; rituals taught the same lesson. As it was the core concept of the Tswana political realm, enacted in customs and ceremonies, rank proved highly resistant to change, and within this explicitly hierarchical social order, households and individuals continually jockeyed for strategic advantage. An ideological commitment to rank coexisted with keen competition to raise one's status.[10] Chiefs and the people they governed all passionately upheld the ideal of rank while they engaged in complicated strategies to lower the status of their rivals.

The *kgotla*, that crescent-shaped forum at the heart of every village, was the place where both the powerful and the weak voiced dissent and tried to humiliate their rivals. But while the space was popular and public, it was emphatically not democratic. The powerful made few attempts to delude the powerless that juniors were privy to the making of momentous decisions. Just as they had no rank, so women, uninitiated men, and the poor were excluded from public meetings, and from the private consultations that preceded them. The *kgotla* assemblies represented the efforts of seniors to advertise or to gain public affirmation of the policies on which they had already agreed, or to break a private deadlock. Whatever the nature of chiefly power or ethnic divisions, this forum remained the pivot of Tswana political life.

People constantly manipulated their own and others' rank. When a band of immigrants was peaceably incorporated by being split between different wards, their "kinship link and their hereditary system of seniority" was thereby severed and they were deftly weakened.[11] Similar motives and effects appear abundantly in tales of Tswana marriages. A chief might marry his rival's sister and, in addition, betroth his daughter to the rival to convert a competitor into an affinal ally. Hoping to win the support of a previously hostile faction, he might marry the widow of its dead leader. At stake in these marital maneuvers was not simply the creation of bonds through which material goods could travel, but people's relative status and, therefore, their access to power. For example, the founding father of the Tawana chiefdom, located northwest of the Ngwato area, was driven into exile by his son after failing to give the boy's mother the funeral rites of a senior wife; this omission had signaled a drop in the heir's own status and therefore his increasing distance from the chieftainship itself.[12] A chief could precipitate a political furor by elevating a junior wife to senior status and her children to heirs.[13] By the same token, betrothal was designed to garner the support of a powerful and wealthy family. Members of the Ngwato royal family customarily married their cousins, and the girl's father and brothers were expected to lead a reliable and influential faction behind her husband. The missionary John Mackenzie observed in the 1860s that "The division of the town out of which each wife comes is always ready to advocate the cause of its representative in the harem, and that of her offspring. . . . [The children] learn to espouse the side of their mother, and the views of the division of the town to which she belongs."[14] If a husband died before a wife bore him a son, her subsequent children, fathered in all probability by one of his brothers, would be the heirs. Frequently, these children would vie with their biological and fictive brothers for factional support. Opportunity was rife, in short, for a number of male candidates to be championed for the chieftainship, each under the claim that he was the most senior. Partly for this reason, succession to high office was neither smooth nor direct in nineteenth century Tswana chiefdoms.[15]

Because the rich derived their wealth also from political dues, a great deal more than prestige was at stake in these marital maneuvers. Political power and economic wealth were interdependent, as is aptly illustrated by the way the Tswana used the word *kgosi*. In the nineteenth century, it referred to both "chief" and "rich man." A *kgosi* might be the chief of a small village or the paramount of a large chiefdom.[16] Both kinds of chiefs derived their wealth from such privileges of appropriation as collecting stray cattle and court fines. The chief's role in settling disputes yielded a fair income. "[C]orporal punishment, excepting in cases of atrocious crime," one early witness observed, "is commuted for a fine; and ... confiscation is often superadded."[17] Stray cattle that no one claimed at the end of the rainy season also became the property of the chief, and a chief took a share of the cattle captured by his regiments. Paramounts also collected gifts and tribute from hunts conducted by regiments of all of the young men of a certain age and from incorporated peoples. All these items—iron and copper, karosses, tobacco, ochre, meat, cattle—signified rank; the distribution of them was a highly political act. In addition, every woman presented to the chief a basket of corn after harvest and contributed her labor to a tribute field attached to the chief's household. Fathers of initiates gave the chief an ox. The estate of each important deceased man also contributed one ox to the royal herd. "The chief will always be the richest man," one early traveler wrote, "for once having arrived at supreme authority, he holds within his own hands the power of attaining property."[18]

In the early nineteenth century, the chief was the first among equals, that is, among relatives and lesser chiefs who profited from similar privileges of appropriation. He appeared and behaved like any other man of means in his society, except that he was usually accompanied by a dozen or so attendants. He enjoyed few ceremonial or sartorial distinctions and his subjects' manners toward him lacked "servility and restraint."[19] Those who were masters of a new craft, such as an iron worker, would charge a chief for their labor just as they charged anyone else. His subjects might even try to rob him. A chief could have a cattle-post thief brought to his *kgotla* only if the thief were "not too powerful."[20]

For practical reasons, the chief best exerted and safeguarded his secular power through the strategic redistribution of wealth, exercising his powers in what Basil Sansom has called a "managerial" fashion by giving servants, followers, land, and cattle to lesser chiefs.[21] He also bestowed formal political office or made those lesser chiefs his confidants or messengers. And, of course, he could gain compliance by threatening to take all these gifts—prestigious positions as well as loaned cattle—away.

The chief influenced the daily affairs of his polity by placing allies in influential positions as land allocators, councillors, or headmen. Because the actual work of distribution was performed by trusted followers, he might on occasion be reluctantly beholden to take their advice—warned, for example, against giving away certain tracts of land or moving his herds to an overcrowded pasture.[22] Unfortunately for the chief, the loyalties of his allies were remarkable more for vacillation than for constancy. The ideological commitment lying behind allegiance appears to have been weak. Within a short period of time, perhaps playing two patrons against each other to see whose rewards would be greater, a senior was likely to stand on both sides of a given issue.[23]

During the early nineteenth century, chiefly authority was emphatically shared by the ranked senior male descendants of previous chiefs. A careful chief ensured that he shared or appeared to share power with his relatives, the group from which his successor would always come. No commoner ever became chief. The chief relied heavily on his deputy, a senior male relative such as a paternal uncle, who ruled for him in his absence and with whom he shared his most precious commodities. The chief's younger brothers shared the task of presiding over public debates with him. Some of them served as official messengers to the hinterland, where they might hear difficult local disputes or, more likely, look after the royal herds.

A chief maintained his hold on his office, and the authority of the office generally, by force but only in extreme cases. He clearly preferred not to use coercion. He could not, in any case, exert force frequently because, unlike the northern Nguni, he had no formal police or standing army. Instead, he was the titular commander of regiments—scattered bands of coinitiates who assembled to do his bidding when summoned by a hilltop crier. These men rounded up stray cattle, destroyed beasts of prey, repaired ward and village *kraals,* cleaned the *kgotlas* and brought offenders to them. They acted as the sole body capable of enforcing the chief's and the headman's directives. Not everyone could be trusted to report for service all the time, and the regiments were known to transfer their loyalties to royal rivals—usually the chief's brothers—who promised deliverance from crisis or simply more plentiful patronage.

In the event that government became uncomfortably exacting, common folk had a variety of means by which they could resist. The most extreme and rare act was to secede, usually by following into the wilderness a patron who promised some kind of protection, generosity, and deliverance.[24] More often, malcontents expressed their opposition indirectly, through absence from their regiments or from the village itself. Some men found life far more profitable and pleasant in the hunting districts and returned only reluctantly to the village when commanded to do so by the chief during a "time of disturbance" when their regiments needed them.[25] Others felt that they would better tend their fields and cattle if they lived near them all year round, instead of having their wives' agricultural labors timed by chiefly fiat and their herds tended by children. Some of the poorest dwellers in remote areas hoped that, by living far from the more wealthy townsmen, they would escape demands for labor or for an item of their meager property. Since the prestige of a household rested on its size and especially on the number of workers it contained, the threat to leave was one powerful weapon wielded by have-nots. A senior whose juniors absconded might find that he subsequently became poorer, less respected, and so less influential with the powerful.

Household heads enjoyed more direct means of trying to influence government than simply trying to skulk into the hinterland; they could throw their weight behind a rival claimant to the chieftainship. This tactic was tried so frequently and effectively that ruling chiefs were often genealogically junior to their failed rivals. As one keen observer noted at the end of the century, "There is at present hardly a tribe in Bechuanaland in which there is not a man who is, behind his back, called 'King of Pumpkins,' in derision at his having suffered a relative of inferior rank to rule over the men of the tribe."[26] According to one study, the vast majority of cases of accession to Tswana chieftainships have never conformed to such rules as primogeniture.[27] Regents are a further example of the scope for machination. Men who were junior in status while senior in years, many regents managed nevertheless to deny the chieftainship to the heir; they became the most senior by successfully aggrandizing power. Royal genealogies could be modified to legitimize their victory. All these forms of dynastic rivalry, while limiting political competition to royalty, did ensure that a chief would redistribute wealth. A chief who had become stingy could find that his backers had switched their allegiance to one of his brothers or cousins.

The less wealthy gained access to this stratum of privilege by becoming clients of the rich, and by begging. As one great chief's wife assured a European missionary's wife, besieged and irritated by incessant requests for gifts, "in our eyes, it is an honour to be begged of—a token of our greatness and ability."[28] A gift was not always forthcoming—as revealed by the plaintive interjection of one praise singer, "I begged for a cow, you didn't give me it"—but the expectations never ceased.[29] Widows and the poor clustered in the *kgotla* to receive gifts of food from the chief. Baskets of grain brought to him by women on their return from the fields were also brewed to celebrate the harvest, given to strangers, and cooked for people who had gathered in the *kgotla* on community business.

While no one articulated an abstract concept of exploitation, it is clear that extracting surplus from the governed beyond the point they considered just was limited by the sheer logic of patronage. As Robert Bates has written, "the bargaining power of the masses, relative to the elites, was strong, and to retain power the elites had to serve the interests of their followers, if only because they would otherwise lose their followers, physically or politically, or other elites would displace them."[30] The effects of changing levels of exploitation on popular conceptions of political legitimacy can be traced by determining how the boundaries enclosing the political community were defined in practice—who was excluded and who was included in the factions that made or broke kings, and how much the governed were asked to pay government for the services it rendered. In the early nineteenth century, while the political community was quite explicitly limited to the chief, his relatives, and their most eminent clients, the simple logic of clientage ensured that no one escaped accountability to the governed, either inside the *kgotla* or out.

Patriarchal Ideology in the Early Nineteenth Century: Sacred and Secular

Proverbs, praise poems, and tales of the Tswana past reflect popular expectations of the chieftainship and of government generally. Chiefs, whether large or small, were expected to be generous with food and productive resources. They were to provide protection against enemies and drought. Government was to be shallow, that is, limited. In the oral tales, these ideal qualities are captured in images both fearsome and comforting, destructive and generous. The diversity of metaphors employed indicates the ambiguity of popular regard for the chieftainship: the chief was a lion to be feared and revered, and a man to be controlled and made generous. The Tswana used the same metaphors during different epochs of their history. Because each image was ambiguous, its meaning could change over time, though its form did not.

The Tswana frequently likened their chief to a lion; the metaphor expressed their fear and respect for the office and for the man. Poets praised the power of a leonine leader, in this case indirectly, "A lion that limps is not worthy of a mane, if it's a coward, it's not worthy of a crest," adding a note of ambivalence, "And *although* you're a lion, and violent . . . I shall praise you."[31] While the people clearly feared him, they also celebrated his ability to "eat" his enemies. Imagery could be used in a cautionary way. To remain a legitimate ruler, a chief had to combine human and leonine traits judiciously. He had to know when to listen to his adversaries and when to strike them down.

More benign, and even feminine, metaphors offer a startling contrast to the images of the chief as king of the beasts of the veld. He was praised also as the "wife," "milk-pail," and "breast" of his people, exhorted to feed and to distribute his wealth among his "children" or subjects. Memoirs of early nineteenth century travelers offer revealing glimpses of the chief as giver of gifts, distributor of bounty. Early in the century, for example, the chief dined daily in the open air, taking pieces of boiled beef from a wooden bowl and distributing them in his fingers to each one of the dozen rich men who always accompanied him about the village. The quantity was insufficient for a meal.[32] The ritual advertised before all villagers the mutual dependence and ideal solidarity of the richest men of the realm. The chief had shown himself to be "first among equals" and a guarantor of feasts, even though he undoubtedly had enemies among the diners and was feeding only the rich. The relatives and clients who accompanied him were parading their own wealth and influence, even though they may have been plotting to usurp the chieftainship. The power of the chief, in any case, depended on the support of the men he was feeding. They were, in one sense, feeding him.

"Lions" and "breasts" clearly reflect radically different aspects of power. Equally clearly, each image expresses a warning as well as praise. The chief was effectively cautioned that his legitimacy as a ruler depended on gaining popular support by judicious distribution of his wealth and by consultation with other influential men. These chiefly clients were, in turn, obliged to grant some material support to their own subordinates. The factions bound together by these patron-client relationships made and unmade "kings."

The sacred world of the Tswana reflected the everyday world of patriarchy. Earthly work and rank crossed over to the land of the dead. Women brought their seeds and hoes with them into the underworld; men carried their weapons to use against the beasts that would prey on their grandfathers' cattle.[33] The dead duplicated the social order of the living. This patriarchal order ranked elder above younger, men above women, genealogically senior clans above more recent ones. In the land of the living, these ranks had been manifest in habits of deference and inheritance. In the underworld, rank determined the scope of the power exerted by the dead over the living.

All living Tswana, not only the chief and ritual specialists, were directly connected to the dead and therefore to supernatural power. They buried their deceased relatives within their courtyards, the men beneath the cattle *kraal* and the women behind their rondavels, or round houses. Within each household, the senior survivor would perform rites of sacrifice and prayer to gain guidance and beneficence for all living family members. The spirits of the dead guarded a social code. From the underground world in the west, they punished and rewarded behavior.[34] But because of the frequency with which villages moved and grave sites were abandoned,[35] the dialogue tended to be between the recently dead and their most senior children. No cult of spirit mediums interceded between them.

The chiefs' own sacred powers were those of their subjects

writ large. Death made their bodies ritually potent in the same way that it had transformed those of lesser rank.[36] Because dead chiefs had carried their rank with them into the other world, their spirits remained powerful. A chief asked his predecessors for guidance as everyone else did, though his questions also concerned issues of communal importance, notably rain and warfare. The scope rather than the nature of chiefly powers distinguished those powers from those of the lesser ranked.

Tswana chiefs celebrated their sacred powers in only a few communal rituals. They presided over the climactic phases of male initiation and led harvest celebrations. In addition, they played an intimate role in the more private ceremonies of rainmaking. Clearly, all of these ceremonies bore great responsibility for popular welfare. Involving the chief in relationships with the dead, they were indeed sacred. But the chief was, even in the realm of the sacred, mainly a manager of ritual rather than a focus of mystical reverence. Tswana chiefs were not divine kings.

While living, the body of the chief served as a metaphor for the polity. In ritual terms, his physical state and the public health were treated as one. To ensure a good harvest, or martial victory, medicines were rubbed into his skin. He was to be chaste from the moment he began making rain, either until the end of the rainy season or until people stopped plowing; the parts of fierce animals were hung about his shoulders and waist.[37] The power of substances applied to his body was in the substances themselves; the power was not inherent in him. In terms of its own logic, the belief that it took death or ceremony to charge a mortal's body with any extrahuman power permitted unpopular chiefs to be replaced without wreaking supernatural havoc on their enemies or the polity at large.

The chief enjoyed privileged but not exclusive access to his own ancestors and to ritual power generally. Ritual experts, considered to have such access, aided the chief in most ceremonies. Some were itinerant doctors, hawking their expertise for profit.[38] Some were rainmakers coming from well-watered country to the east and returning there after having sold their medicinal roots, bark, or leaves and having blessed the seeds and gardens. The chief might hasten the rainmaking process by sending a black ox to the ruler of another chiefdom either senior or renowned for its rainmakers.[39] In such a case, the principle of seniority was being advertised as much as the power of the chief receiving tribute. The sharing of ritual power was apparent also when a village moved to a new site. Ritual experts drew a protective circle around the site and only then did the chief plant markers charmed by ritual experts at the boundaries between the settled and the wild.[40] Nor did chiefs enjoy a monopoly on popular reverence. The chief was not the only, or in all cases the primary, source of rain or health. He was simply an important mediator between the living and the dead. People prayed for rain to a variety of ancestors as well—to the original owners of the medicines, to the past chiefs of other polities.

Although the chief crowned the local hierarchy, the hierarchical system itself—the principle of rank—won at least equal popular reverence. Certain beliefs guarded elite status. For example, a curse was proverbially said to fall on any senior who warmed himself at a fire kindled by his junior, that is, if he lived in a house or village built by one of lower status. Even more pointedly, people believed that ancestors had the ability to curse their relatives from the grave, and that ancestors were particularly prone to harm a junior who had quarreled with a senior and to afflict a person who envied another's wealth.[41] People saved the ritual advertisement of this principle for the most significant occasions in the polity's life: the first-fruits ceremony, prayers for the end of a severe drought, and male initiation (although, because women were not ranked, not female initiation).[42] During the first-fruits ceremony, the communal celebration of the harvest, women brought the first ripe crops to the chief's *kgotla* for ceremonial consumption. The pulp of the leaves was rubbed into each person's body in precise and all-inclusive order of rank.[43] Other ceremonies similarly signified the patriarchal system of seniority as well as the power of the dead over the living. For example, during a prolonged drought, the Ngwato had been known to kill an ox on the grave of their first chief and then to eat it, again in precise order of rank, all non-Ngwato excluded.

The authority of the Tswana chief relied heavily more on secular than on sacred powers. There were several reasons for this. The sacred was imbedded in households and the chief's control of this level of society was not particularly deep. The chieftainship's legitimacy rested lightly on connections to the sacred, partly for reasons of ecology. The aridity of land settled by the northern Tswana tied their villages to streams and springs, and the periodic drying up of these water points obliged these agropastoralists to move often in search of water, continually abandoning their ancestral graves and hence the ritual power of these sites. This itinerancy probably weakened the force of the sacred, at least in its ancestral guise, within Tswana society generally.

The paucity of the Tswana chiefs' supernatural powers is particularly striking compared to that of certain West African or northern Nguni chiefs who swore that only they could control the heavens.[44] Some scholars have tried to elevate Tswana chiefs into "kings" with at least a trace of divinity, citing proverbs referring to them as "small gods."[45] Others have argued that chiefly ritual "dramatized the subordination" of the household to the polity, as if no one disputed that subordination, and as if it was always successful.[46] Neither effort to elaborate chiefly power can override the basic fact that, especially in the early nineteenth century, the sacred roles of Tswana chiefs rarely intruded into the daily lives of the households making up their chiefdoms. The chief was respected more as the pinnacle of the patriarchal system than as a mystical being.

The Centralization of Political Power in the Later Nineteenth Century

As the nineteenth century wore on, however, the chief began to intervene more directly and frequently in the affairs of northern Tswana households. As he began to tax them, to judge their divorce cases, and to invest his wealth in commodities brought by long-distance trade, a more exploitative relationship grew between the chief and some of his subjects. These new powers sprang from sources as diverse as war and the Pax Britannica.

"THE *MFECANE*"

A northern Tswana person listening to a traveler's tales in the 1820s and 1830s would have had every reason to feel that he or she was living on the fringes of chaos. To the south and east, brigands, marauders, and simply hungry refugees had devastated fields and granaries. Zulu regiments had begun to raid for territory and cattle in the 1820s and, as some scholars have recently argued, the Portuguese in Delagoa Bay and the British in the eastern Cape were short of labor and trading for slaves.[47] The resulting violence spread as displaced groups, in turn, stole food and animals from settlements lying in their paths. The entire region was being made hungry by warfare. This awful period has popularly been called the *mfecane*.

For some listeners, the tales would in time be made real. Some of the chiefdoms on the fringes of the Kalahari were broken into bands and scattered westward into the desert. Others escaped devastation by agreeing to pay tribute to the last of the Nguni raiders, the Ndebele, who settled in the western highveld; twelve years elapsed before they were driven away. None of the victims of the devastation formed a state as grand in geographical extent or strategic complexity as the mountain chiefdom of Moshoeshoe's Sotho, and no Tswana chiefdoms forged military alliances with each other. The strategic strengthening of Tswana polities in the face of war occurred in a less dramatic fashion. They accepted refugees and distributed them among existing wards so that the newcomers would not overwhelm their hosts.[48] Canny chiefs used the senior men among the refugees as allies against their royal rivals.

The Ngwato clan illustrates how such defensive strategies strengthened chiefly power. Around 1770 it had broken away from its parent group, the Kwena, and until the 1820s, the Ngwato were simply another Tswana clan or group claiming common descent; the Ngwato moved frequently and were internally divided. In the course of dealing with the upheavals of the nineteenth century, however, the Ngwato chief, like several others in southern Africa, became more and more like a king and his state more and more like an empire. Between the 1820s and the 1840s, the Ngwato had to protect themselves against three bands of marauding outsiders—the Kololo, Phuting, and Ndebele—and even after their recovery, they remained tributaries of the Ndebele, whose soldiers "[e]very year . . . passed through the Bamangwato country, lifting cattle, destroying the gardens and driving the men and women to seek refuge in the numerous caves on the top of the mountains."[49] Then, by gaining access to guns and horses on the southern trade route originating in the Cape, the Ngwato grew powerful enough to repulse the Ndebele—in 1844 they butchered with impunity a party of forty Ndebele tribute collectors. They were able, in consequence, to offer protection to many smaller groups. As a result, they faced the new problem of incorporating other "foreigners" who sought to share their security.[50] Once accepted into the Ngwato, some of these smaller groups were plied with special privileges to win their loyalty. One chief, for example, married his daughters to the new subordinate chiefs. Other foreign groups were trusted to go to the outlying districts to guard the state's expanding borders or to look after wells. The most privileged were, of course, the chief's clients; they received into their custody the cattle that they and other foreigners had relinquished as the price of their security within the Ngwato state. When they were few in number, these privileged foreigners were often placed in a royal ward so that each group would keep an eye on the other's activities.[51] Thus, by coopting foreigners and by using their support against his dynastic rivals, the chief was eventually able to enhance the power of his office far beyond the primus inter pares role that it had once played.

The *mfecane,* in short, taught the northern Tswana the importance of defensive strategy. Hearing of their southern and western neighbors' acute suffering, they learned that survival in the aftermath of the Zulu expansion would depend on both guns and diplomatic guile. The tales of havoc and the sight of desperate refugees had predisposed people to accept solutions that promised security. And so, even on the relatively unscathed fringes of the Kalahari, the *mfecane* allowed chiefs to centralize their powers, and traders and missionaries to gain access to the chiefdoms.

LONG-DISTANCE TRADE

In the aftermath of the *mfecane*, the development of long-distance trade in spoils of the hunt, mainly ivory, gave an even greater impetus to the growth of chiefly power and wealth. A regional trade network in iron and personal ornaments like cosmetics had long existed, but it appears not to have expanded the force or direction of chiefly power enough to give birth to a state. Ivory, on the other hand, supplemented the fortunes that the chief and his headmen had been acquiring in the herds of incorporated peoples and allowed them to become even wealthier patrons. With greater affluence the chief and his headmen purchased the guns and plows that extended their dominion and, in turn, intensified their exploitation of the veld and of the people living within it.

The "Road to the North," a sandy track running between the Cape and Central Africa—to Barotseland, Bulawayo, and beyond—passed through the eastern Kalahari;[52] along this route passed ivory, ostrich feathers, and skins bound for the Cape, and returning from the Cape, guns, knives, hatchets, and breeding stock, as well as less explicitly useful items such as proper Victorian dress, porcelain beads, and decorative wire for women to wind around their legs. First dominated by the Kwena chiefdom, which had also exchanged ivory with the Portuguese in Delagoa Bay for beads and cloth, the route became open later to the Ngwato chiefdom to the north, through whose country ran the road's northeast branch, the route between Mozambique and the Kweneng.[53] From the 1850s, the Kwena chief sought to undermine the northern Ngwato upstarts by interfering in their dynastic quarrels, but by the 1870s the hunting frontier had receded into an area that the Ngwato capital, Shoshong, could more readily control. Although the Kwena chief failed to subordinate the Ngwato, he did receive fine gifts from the royal claimants whom he supported.[54]

Between the 1840s and 1880, ivory was the most precious commodity carried on the Road to the North. As long as game was plentiful, European traders would supply Tswana and Griqua hunters with provisions on credit, to be repaid in ivory and ostrich feathers on their return to the capital. Early in the century, there may have been some elephants left near the Orange River, but the hunting frontier receded northward as the herds were shot out. By the 1850s European and Griqua traders were converging on Shoshong as they made their way to buy ivory in Matabeleland, more than an eighteen days' journey north by ox wagon. They also forged northwestward through the thirstland to Lake Ngami and traded with Barotseland, the furthest outpost of the southern African ivory trade. By the 1870s, however, both the supply of the ivory and demand for the ostrich feathers were dwindling so badly that the fortunes of the Shoshong traders suffered. They revived after the Ngwato capital moved east from desiccating Shoshong to better-watered Palapye in 1889, but the subsequent periods of economic boom would be sporadic, and as the twentieth century progressed, periods of boom occurred less and less frequently.

Three military encounters in the region in the 1890s injected cash into the local economy in exchange for such produce as stock, timber, and water, as well as labor. The first two were the British South Africa Company's military expeditions against the Shona in 1890 and the Ndebele in 1893. The third was the South African War of 1899 to 1902, which brought by far the greatest, although short-lived, wealth to the Ngwato; British purchases of stock alone gave them £25,000 in cash.[55] During times of peace, their exports were reduced, in effect, to offal; in the 1890s these exports were mostly the hides of cattle dead from lung sickness and rinderpest. Like the brushwood and timber the Ngwato also sold to the British, these goods usually were destined for the mines in the south, the hides to become miners' boots and the timber to become fuel or buttresses for mine shafts. After the war, exports from Palapye Road, since the 1890s the nearest railway siding to Serowe, from 1902 the new Ngwato capital, were nearly exclusively cattle. Their destination continued to be the Rand and their prices were continually falling.[56]

New tools decisively affected the wealth and work of those with access to them, allowing the veld to be exploited more efficiently. Firearms permitted the rich to hunt larger numbers of elephants. Plows turned over greater expanses of field faster. Wagons allowed the wealthy to dispense with the Kgalagadi porters who had carried ivory tusks from the Botletle River to Shoshong. A few men purchased their own wagons and so were able to earn cash by riding transport for some of the white traders. In the wake of decades of incessant ivory hunting, commercial flotsam and jetsam remained. Porcelain beads and Manchester cotton took the place of copper and iron beads from Tswapong and blue Kalanga cotton. Tea and coffee, sugar, and flour were imported to please tastes the wealthy alone could afford to cultivate.

Khama III—ruling the Ngwato first in 1872 after briefly unseating his father, Chief Sekgoma I, and then, after finally expelling the old pagan chief from the chiefdom in 1875, until 1923—was famous for his carefully amassed fortune. It derived both from traditional and from modern sources. One ancient form of tribute, the ground tusk of each elephant killed (the tusk that hit the ground as the elephant fell), gave him easy supremacy over all other early entrepreneurs. He could also earn cash from traders by converting two other royal prerogatives: selling the stray cattle his regiments rounded up after the rains and hiring out the services of his hereditary servants to traveling hunters. Shortly after Khama's accession to the chieftainship in 1875, his annual income was estimated to be £3000 and he owned between seven and eight thousand cattle. He shrewdly invested this fortune in improved breeding stock of both cattle and horses and in wagons he hired out and sold; he even grew tobacco for sale, undoubtedly with tributary labor.[57]

The resilience of ties between patrons and clients ensured that many others were touched in some degree by the bounty. During droughts, the chief could truly become the "wife" of the tribe by purchasing from traders grain and seed to feed his people. Similarly, a headman's quality was judged by how generously he spread the benefits of his new wealth throughout his ward—plowing for them and carrying them and their crops to and from their fields in his wagon. But because the wealthy gave priority to their own material needs, the gap between rich and poor did not narrow—the rich plowed their own fields, for example, earlier than they plowed those of their clients, whose harvest was therefore likely to be smaller. Although examples of redistribution abound, the trading boom most benefited families who had inherited the right to collect tribute from hunters.

Clientship relations between cattle owners and Khoisan hunter-gatherers had existed since at least the late seventeenth century when some proto-Tswana herders called the Kgalagadi began to appropriate scarce water points to the west and to subjugate the peoples living on the surrounding land. In the early nineteenth century, after Tswana clans had established dominance over the Kgalagadi, servile hunters became increasingly subject to their new masters' demands for ivory, feathers, and skins, and their land was carved up into hunting and herding zones controlled by these rich Tswana. The value given to spoils of the hunt by long-distance trade enhanced the dependence and exploitation of the Khoisan clients by their Tswana masters. Protection had never been part of the bargain. On the contrary, clientage to one master meant being subject to raids by his rival. A Tswana master might visit them to carry off food they had gathered, or he might command their labor on his fields during harvest. He could even lend or "rent" them to neighboring cattlemen. Legal disputes over the ownership of certain vassals would preoccupy competing patrons in the capital. When the parties in the dispute were chiefs and the dispute led to war, entire groups of vassals might be killed.

The Khoisan hunter-gatherers submitted to these violations probably because the intensity of their victimization was slight in the days before the European ivory trade. Even after the trade began, the hunters, locally called Sarwa, displayed a certain genius for evading control. They kept back produce claimed by their masters and bartered it with Europeans "for a bit of tobacco or a few strings of beads," costing their masters "many hundreds of pounds" in lost property.[58] Many Tswana masters found it less expensive to pay their vassals in gifts; new acquisitions such as calves and goats probably wedded the clients more powerfully to their patrons than any coercive measures had ever done. In this way, some vassals benefited from their work, though they received only a fraction of its value. Poorer individuals also gained direct access to the trade throughout the century, principally by theft and clandestine sales. And of course some "veld people" did resist the Tswana. A few groups used cunning to establish some independence from the chief, but these groups were smashed. In one grisly act of retribution in 1880, Khama burned a Kgalagadi village and killed its leader because he had found him paying tribute to the Kwena as well as to his own chiefdom.[59]

No new institutions were created by this mining of the veld. Rather, old relationships—between chiefs and subjects, masters and vassals—were given new content. Until the twentieth century, the bounds of the political community were not formally expanded to include the veld people; they could not participate in the *kgotla* and were even forbidden to walk along the village paths at night. Whatever resentment people felt against the new exactions or old constraints, no one rejected the chieftainship or its incumbent in an articulate or organized way. They expressed their dissent in the ancient and practical fashion of theft, noncompliance, and desertion.

BRITISH PROTECTION

Missionaries preceded proconsuls in every Tswana chiefdom, not as imperial agents, but as earnest proselytizers. Their political goals and their impact were as diverse as their personalities.[60] The Ngwato case stands apart from other polities where the effect of Christianity was initially muted, perhaps because it was fortunate to have two strong characters, Khama, who converted to Christianity in 1860, and John Mackenzie, who represented the London Missionary Society in the Ngwato chiefdom from 1859 to 1869. The sacred and secular were thoroughly intertwined in the work of both men. By lobbying in Britain and southern Africa for a just alternative to Afrikaner racism, Mackenzie eventually contributed to the annexation of Bechuanaland by the British. Chief Khama used the Christian doctrines brought by Mackenzie first to develop a progressive faction allowing him to depose his father, and then to deepen his control of his own society.

Since the late 1870s Khama had been complaining to British emissaries that Boers were robbing his men of their earnings from the diamond mines at Kimberley, that they stole gifts sent by him and his father to fellow chiefs like Moshoeshoe of the Sotho, and that they were allying with his veld people and dissident brothers to overthrow him.[61] Mackenzie warned Khama that the Afrikaners would subjugate him and his people and rob them of their land. The great chief already recognized the dangers. "There are three things which distress me very much," he wrote to the British High Commissioner in 1876, asking for protection against the Afrikaner republic in the Transvaal, "war, selling people and drink. All these things I shall find in the Boers, and it is these things which destroy people."[62] As a result of these fears and negotiations, the great chief placed himself under Queen Victoria's protection in 1877, even before he "earnestly" asked a British agent to define its consequences.[63]

No shots were fired to incorporate the Tswana chiefdoms within the British Empire. Rather, Khama had actively solicited the vaguely worded protection—the British would promote "peace and order," while the chiefs would retain more or less full sovereignty in internal affairs. In 1885 a British agent had been sent from England to declare Bechuanaland a British protectorate, partly to prevent the Germans in South West Africa from linking up with the Afrikaners in the South African Republic or Transvaal, and partly to prevent the Tswana chiefs from inadvertently signing away their land to mineral-hungry white speculators. Khama exulted in a letter to a neighboring chief in 1889, "I have the people of the Great Queen with me and I am glad to have them. I live in peace with them, and I have no fear of the Matebele or the Boers any longer attacking me."[64] Khama and two fellow Tswana chiefs—Sechele of the Kwena and Bathoen of the Ngwaketse—traveled to England in 1895 to argue that the protectorate should not be handed over to Cecil Rhodes's British South Africa Company. Lionized by the British press, the chiefs succeeded in winning over Secretary of State for the Colonies Joseph Chamberlain from his initial desire to jettison the unpromising territory. The company was given instead a strip of land on the eastern border of the protectorate for building a railway to Rhodesia. Over two decades later, Khama and his followers could see across that border the consequences of South African overrule, and they could still exult at having, for the time being, escaped it: "We understand well the character of the native administration of these [South African] colonies; we know that the natives have no land of their own; many have no gardens to plough; nor are they allowed to chop wood or carry guns, nor have they any cattle; and a native is not regarded as a human being in these colonies."[65]

When the British altered the power relations within the northern Tswana chiefdoms by establishing a protectorate over them in 1885, they did not, contrary to some nationalistic interpretations, squelch most powers of the traditional rulers.[66] The British government wanted above all to avoid the expense that a forward policy would entail. The High Commissioner stressed when the protectorate was established, "we have no interest in the country north of the Molopo, except as a road to the interior."[67] Three years later, the Resident Commissioner elaborated, "the Colony must be content to advance slowly, and to dispense with many desirable improvements until it is in a position to pay for them."[68] The relationship between imperial overlord and subimperial ruler was only occasionally openly antagonistic. After the protectorate was established, a chief invited imperial intervention when his management of domestic politics created costly conflicts and tensions with South Africa, and for the most part, the chiefs manipulated the British presence in order to acquire greater personal power at the expense of their brothers and headmen. Precolonial economic and political independence was indeed lost, but the chief rose within what remained.

British protection allowed the chiefs to alter irrevocably their relation to the land and therefore the basis of their rule. They became territorial monarchs rather than leaders of groups shifting their settlements across the thirstland. They gained inalienable rights to territory whose boundaries remain today substantially those of Botswana's districts. The process took fourteen years. In Khama's case, it began in 1885 when he drew a map to present to the British agent, Special Commissioner Sir Charles Warren, who arrived in the Serowe *kgotla* to announce the vague terms of protection. Far from acceding to all of the great chief's land claims, Warren split his claimed polity in half by provisionally decreeing latitude 22° north as its northern border. Although Lobengula, chief of the Ndebele, the northern neighbors of the Ngwato, should have been pleased by this possible gift, he found its implication disturbing. "The white men are not your neighbors; I was your neighbor. You settle everything without consulting me," he complained to Khama, "In olden times, . . . we never spoke about boundary lines. It is only now they talk about boundaries."[69] In 1899, following a three-year survey commissioned by Chamberlain when he agreed not to transfer Bechuanaland to the British South Africa Company, "Khama's country," as well as those of the other paramount chiefs in the protectorate, was finally defined. Khama had had to give up only

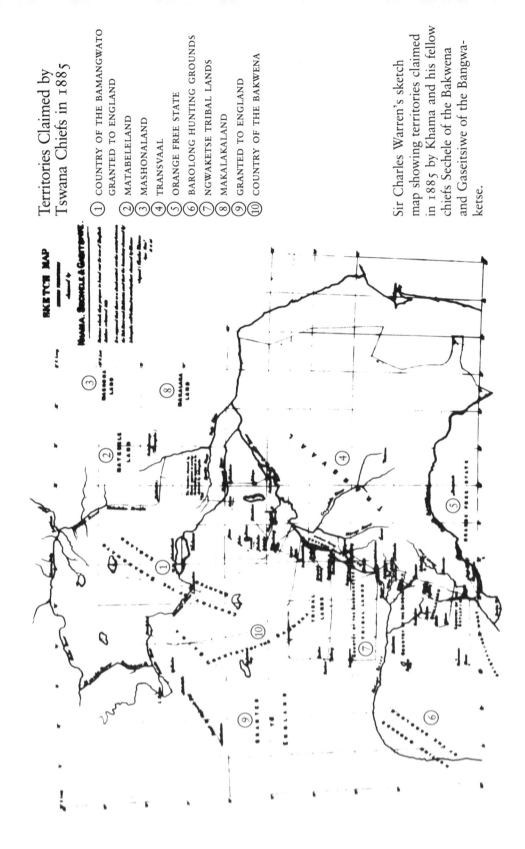

Territories Claimed by Tswana Chiefs in 1885

1. COUNTRY OF THE BAMANGWATO GRANTED TO ENGLAND
2. MATABELELAND
3. MASHONALAND
4. TRANSVAAL
5. ORANGE FREE STATE
6. BAROLONG HUNTING GROUNDS
7. NGWAKETSE TRIBAL LANDS
8. MAKALAKALAND
9. GRANTED TO ENGLAND
10. COUNTRY OF THE BAKWENA

Sir Charles Warren's sketch map showing territories claimed in 1885 by Khama and his fellow chiefs Sechele of the Bakwena and Gaseitsiwe of the Bangwaketse.

Bechuanaland Protectorate Reserve Boundaries Adopted by the British Government in 1899

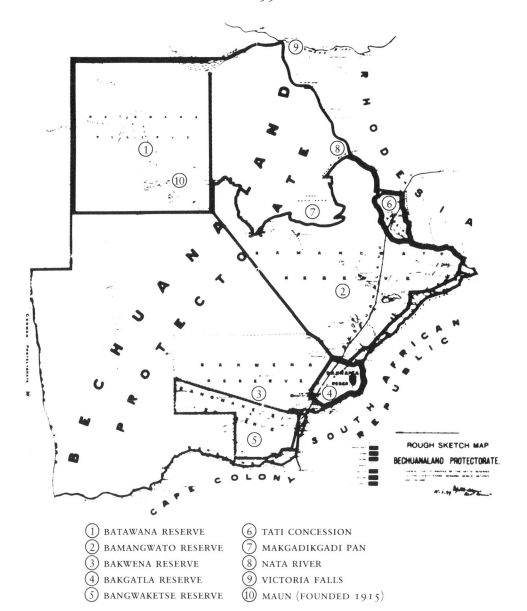

① BATAWANA RESERVE
② BAMANGWATO RESERVE
③ BAKWENA RESERVE
④ BAKGATLA RESERVE
⑤ BANGWAKETSE RESERVE
⑥ TATI CONCESSION
⑦ MAKGADIKGADI PAN
⑧ NATA RIVER
⑨ VICTORIA FALLS
⑩ MAUN (FOUNDED 1915)

Boundaries of the Bechuanaland Protectorate reserves as initially set out by Assistant Commissioner H. J. Goold-Adams in 1895 and adopted by the British government under Proclamation 9 of 1899. Khama received about half of the land he claimed in 1885.

two blocks of land, the narrow strip called the Tuli Block, through which the railroad to Rhodesia had been expected to run, and Tati, whose control Khama had in any case long disputed with Lobengula.

Khama's victory—obtaining land up to the Makgadikgadi Pan and the Nata River in the north and hunting and grazing grounds deep into the Kalahari in the west—bore one small but nettlesome problem: there was no longer any unallocated land where his dynastic rivals could peacefully retreat without dragging in imperial overseers. He felt that they would be in effect locked into his territory, where they could continue to harass him. The Tswana chiefs were fully aware of this prospect. In 1895 they, including Khama, who was at the time being plagued by the secession of a faction led by his brother Raditladi, wrote to the Colonial Office, "In the olden days a chief did not much fear his younger brothers. Rebellion meant war then, and no man risks war unless he has a large following. But now there is no war, and a man does not fear to rebel even though he has no following. He says in his heart, 'I also am a son of my father. The Chief cannot punish me as he would another man. I can appeal to the Government. If I lose, the Government will still give me land, and allow me to take my cattle. If I win, I become an independent chief.'"[70] The British government must have found their logic compelling; after 1895, it ruled that all inhabitants of a chiefdom must submit to that chief's authority.

By introducing taxation, fixed boundaries, and courts of law, the thinly staffed tiers of the British administration both strengthened and diminished the chiefs' powers.[71] The British recognized that their skeleton administration was incapable of governing without the traditional rulers, and so imperial officials rarely interfered in local politics. Between 1885 and 1923 they passed only two proclamations setting limits to what the chiefs could legitimately do.[72] However, with four courts of appeal above the office of the chief—the local Resident Magistrate, the Resident Commissioner at Mafeking, the High Commissioner to South Africa and the High Commission Territories and the Privy

Council in London—any dissident could exploit the appeals process,[73] using the courts to try to make chiefs more accountable and less monarchical.

Taxation, imposed by the British in 1899 and collected for them by the chiefs, allowed Khama to renounce the collection of tribute around the turn of the century.[74] His gesture was hardly altruistic. The market for hunting spoils was poor by then, and the 10-percent fee he was paid for collecting taxes was far more dependable; in 1899, the first year taxes were paid by adult men to the British, he earned about £380, an amount that doubled six years later. He did not employ the strategy of the Kwena and Kgatla chiefs, who sent regiments to labor in South Africa and then taxed them on their return, and who even taxed independent migrant laborers.

In effect, the British were helping chiefs to establish independent fortunes. For more than forty years, from 1885 to 1927, no distinction was drawn between the Ngwato chief's personal revenues and the coffers of his state. This did not mean that chiefs simply exploited their liberties for personal gain; on the contrary, many made conscientious and creative efforts to invest in development schemes that would allow them to resist incorporation into the Union of South Africa.[75]

Tswana paramount chiefs like Khama used some of the tax revenues given back to them by the British to pay a small cadre of salaried bureaucrats—initially about half a dozen clerks, teachers, and accountants—who answered to the chief alone. Together they planned and administered development schemes like schools and, later, livestock improvement camps. The chiefs carefully monitored those aspects of the modern state that they would allow their nascent states to adopt. Salaried functionaries were acceptable to them; formal legislative bodies were not. British taxation served the purposes of modernizing chiefs; the vote did not. With no institutional means introduced to render the governor accountable to the taxpayer, or other such checks on their power, the chiefs were increasingly able to punish their political opponents by banishing them to areas beyond their "reserves" and confiscating their property; the chiefs found that, contrary to their fears, the British rarely listened sympathetically to their rivals' grievances. Presiding over the conversion of amorphous custom into codified Western law, they had acquired precise legal definitions of their powers and of the new boundaries between private and public property.

Paradoxically, British justice and royal rivalry worked together to render communal property private. *Kgamelo* cattle became private property in the Ngwato chiefdom, initially because Khama wished to win *kgamelo* cattle holders to his faction and away from that of his errant son, Sekgoma II. The British backed him in 1907 by declaring that tribal cattle no longer existed and that any interference with this decision would be prosecuted in protectorate courts. Other items of property were being rendered private even without the aid of British justice; as early as 1878, Khama's gardens at the well-watered lands of Chadibe in the Tswapong Hills were considered to belong "especially" to him, and the residents of that village owed their labor to him personally.[76] Khama also sold to his subjects gifts presented to him as a head of state: L. S. Jameson, for example, was said to have given plows to Khama that the great chief then sold for ten goats each.[77] In short, the chief was both gaining new wealth and winning loyal new allies among the people who had formerly held rather then owned their herds.

British overrule encouraged chiefs to make "progressive" innovations, and this greatly enhanced their power; a man's loyalty could now be judged by how readily he adopted the chief's reforms. At the end of the nineteenth century, Tswana chiefs unilaterally swept away a host of time-honored practices. They abolished initiation schools for boys and girls; some decreed an end to life-giving ceremonies such as rainmaking; they also dropped secular customs, stopping the collection of tribute from hereditary servants and freeing them to own property. Cattle could now be inherited by daughters and were no longer to be exchanged for brides. Some abolished polygamy. Many chiefs also prohibited beer brewing.[78] A true ally of the chief could easily be identified by whether his household brewed beer or whether he married more than one wife. The older traditionalists were unlikely to pass these tests, and the chief was protected from the consequences of their anger; he could even grow richer from the fines he levied on their acts of disobedience. The reforms were all couched in the somber moral tones of the Christian church, then in process of being adopted as the state religion in every chiefdom. Although Khama swore that he was not the head of the church, one missionary observed that "in actual fact he knows himself to be [its head], and his people never disguise it for a moment."[79] The losers in all these battles for preeminence were the chief's relatives.

Because the chiefs often displayed publicly their antagonism toward British rule by, for example, lobbying for maximum autonomy under the protectorate government, it is easy to ignore the massive British contribution to their power. For instance, Khama went so far as to complain in a letter to the London *Times* "And now without formal conclave and agreement, when I should have the opportunity of consulting my headmen and putting all important matters fairly before my people, they proceed to place a ruler in my town, so that I myself, before I can buy a bag of gunpowder, have to go and obtain a permit."[80] A focus on such antagonism can obscure that the British often backed down. Khama refused to accept charity from the new overlords, even to the point of preventing the protectorate government from distributing famine relief to his individual subjects; and so the British allowed his headmen to fetch and distribute the grain so that established patterns of patronage would not be disturbed.[81] No case in protectorate courts went against him. And when he refused to join the new Native Advisory Council in 1920, ostensibly because it would not prohibit "liquor, which is the ruin of chiefs,"[82] no one forced him to do so. Khama's funeral paid fitting testimony to his debt to the British. Before burial—in a Christian hillside grave rather than, as customary, in the *kgotla* cattle *kraal*—his coffin was covered with a Union Jack and with a floral wreath paid for by the local traders, missionaries, and administrators.

The households that felt most keenly the enhanced powers of the chief were those of his relatives; they had expected to share the work and benefits of government with him. Aside from chiefs, these disgruntled royals alone used the appeal court system erected by the British. They alone addressed complaints directly to British administrators. They would charge, for example, that chiefs had overstepped their prerogatives by levying taxes directly without obtaining the consent of councillors and confirmation by the *kgotla*. They struggled to capture new institutions and turn them to their own ends. At times the church came to resemble a *kgotla*, with competing members of the elite preaching their messages from the pulpit.

Less exalted ranks of Tswana society employed time-honored strategies for avoiding control, allying with chiefly rivals, deserting or moving away. They continued sacred and secular practices that had been formally outlawed. They paid bridewealth and brewed beer. And even some Christian converts continued to believe in officially discarded faiths; many Kgatla believed at least until the 1930s that the chief was duty-bound to produce rain or to hire ritual experts who could.[83] Organized protest was rare. In one exceptional case, in 1891, a Ngwato regiment constructing a telegraph line went on strike, bluntly explaining their action to a visitor, "It is all very well for Khama and you white men. You have people who will till your lands, and take care of your crops and families in your absence but we have no one."[84] Occasionally, an angry voice at the *kgotla* could be heard shouting complaints against having to pay church levies.

Resistance by common folk, whatever its form, undoubtedly achieved some successes. The means to coerce the population still did not exist despite the Pax Britannica and the creation of an embryonic bureaucracy. Jails and police were few. And so a chief's most reasonable response was to withdraw an unpopular order. After the 1891 regimental strike, for example, the chief only rarely requisitioned regiments for imperial purposes. Protest by royalty, on the other hand, doomed itself to failure by explicitly inviting imperial intervention. British interests in a cheap administration demanded support for the chief against his rivals.

The increasingly secular face of the chieftainship signaled that the Tswana chiefs were, in effect, choosing a new set of standards by which the office and its incumbents should be judged, although they did not necessarily think of the changes that they had introduced in those terms. Even if they had, they would have known that popular expectations would change only slowly. Nevertheless, the reforms following the chiefs' dropping of their claims to be bringers of rain conformed to a pattern. They all signified that the chieftainship was ceasing to be the great patron. Over time, the office would become less and less the dispenser of gifts—cattle, food, land, office, as well as rain. Bureaucratic political office would pledge itself to spend taxes for the good of the political community. It would no longer promise to dispense wealth "by free arbitrariness and lordly grace."[85]

The costs of establishing a tribal bureaucracy were blamed by one observer for diminishing the role the chief could play as a "repository of wealth and dispenser of gifts." Because his income was limited by protectorate proclamations, he was being "deprived . . . of yet another important sanction for his authority."[86] Yet this interpretation gives insufficient importance to the chiefs' willing compliance and skillful manipulation as they sought to consolidate their material and political gains of the nineteenth century. Although they did eventually lose important sanctions for their authority, their wealth in private property was growing at a greater rate than that of their juniors. Given the instability of the regional cattle markets in the twentieth century, the chief and his small cadre of salaried bureaucrats were virtually the only recipients of a relatively dependable income while resident in the chiefdom.

Most of the early secretaries, clerks, and teachers who doubled as modern advisers to the chief were the sons of chiefly clients and only occasionally of royalty. The Ratshosas, the first family to challenge the dominance of the Ngwato chief's brothers among his advisers, were such low-ranking royalty that some disputed whether they were royal at all. Perhaps in order to acquire high status in a modern sense, they had sent their sons to elite African schools in South Africa. Their skills—especially their literacy in English—proved valuable to Khama during his confrontations with foreign powers, and he also used the Ratshosa family as a foil against the intrigues of his agnates, including his eldest son, Sekgoma. Most royalty were so assured of their elite status that they did not bother to invest in the education of sons as did families like the Ratshosas and the chief's clients.

Khama was known as the last of the Ngwato chiefs to govern from the *kgotla*. After the brief (1923–1925) and uneventful reign of his prodigal elder son, Sekgoma II, his role was inherited by his younger son, Tshekedi Khama, who ruled, increasingly, from "tribal" offices. Throughout the northern Tswana chiefdoms, the mode of government was changing from one in which decisions were ideally made by the consensus of senior men to one in which a more solitary chief governed with the aid of salaried bureaucrats who were accountable to him alone.

SOUTH AFRICAN INDUSTRIAL DEVELOPMENT

South Africa's mineral revolution brought new forms of wealth and poverty to the Rand's hinterland. Tswana exporters had no influence over the prices and amounts of goods bought by South African industry, since cattle and men could readily be procured elsewhere in the region. The market for cattle fluctuated in a pattern of short booms and long depressions. South Africa influenced the power relations in Tswana society both by its demand for cattle and labor and by the inconstancy of that demand, and one major result was that wealth remained in a limited

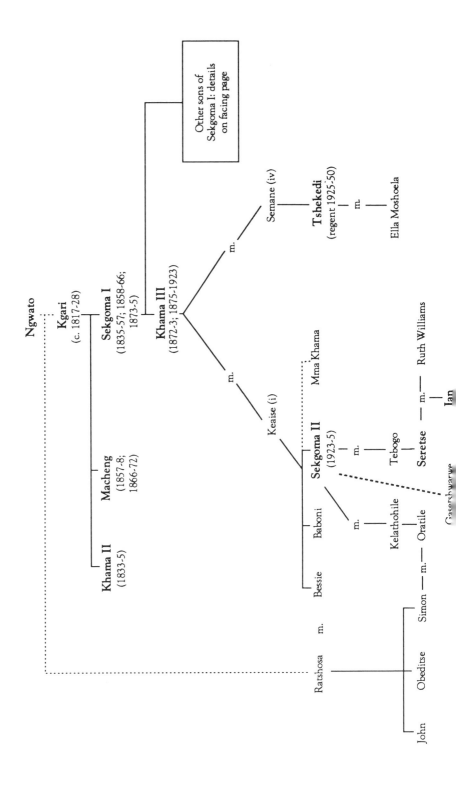

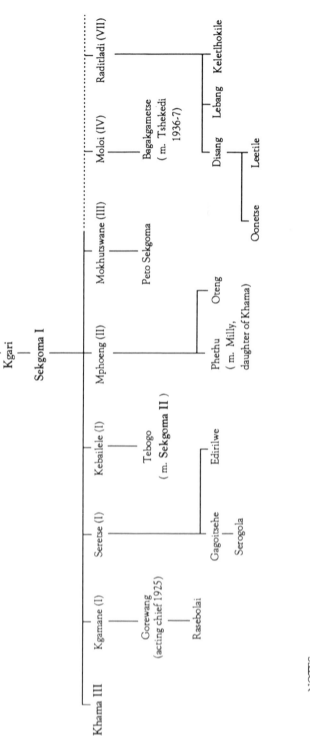

number of hands, and particularly in those of the chiefs. In the short term, the diamonds at Kimberley and the gold mines of the Rand helped to preserve inherited privilege.

After the 1880s, the Rand mining companies bought varying quantities of Tswana cattle. Their meat fed the miners and their hides became boots. But both man-made and natural disasters afflicted the market for Tswana cattle and made it utterly unpredictable. In 1895 a rinderpest epidemic wiped out nearly the entire protectorate herd. The reproduction rate of the remaining cattle could be high, but subsequent disasters kept both their numbers and quality low.[87] Also transport was problematic and costly; railway rates were raised and lowered for the Bechuanaland Protectorate according to the quantity or scarcity of crops grown in Rhodesia, the British colony immediately to the north.

South African cattlemen tried to end the importation of all Tswana cattle and nearly succeeded. After 1919, South African beef prices fell steadily, and ranchers urged their government to impose an embargo on all slaughter stock from neighboring states, in an effort to raise the price of their own low-quality beef and to ensure that Continental beef contracts were filled only with South African cattle.[88] The Union government contrived a compromise in which weight and supply restrictions, which prevented the leanest or lowest-grade beef from being exported, were imposed instead.[89] And so the protectorate's herds steadily degenerated through the reproduction of a "large deadweight cattle population of no use or value to the territory."[90]

Whether or not they could sell their cattle for money, African men still had to pay their taxes to the British. They still wanted to buy things. Just as the tax had been imposed not simply to generate a force of mine laborers, so men now migrated from their cattle posts to wage jobs in mines and cities for more diverse reasons than simply to get cash for taxes. Long before taxes were imposed and the mines had opened, some people expressed eagerness "to work for a year for a cow or heifer" on the farms of the Cape Colony.[91] Missionary observers imagined that this entrepreneurial spirit was diminishing "the repressive power of the petty Caffre [Xhosa] and Bechuana [Tswana] sovereigns."[92]

Mine labor recruiters would make this argument with increasing frequency toward the end of the nineteenth century: "the compulsion proposed is absolute liberty as compared with the tyrannical rule of their chiefs."[93] Both were correct in foreseeing that independent access to wealth was a goal of migration and that it would one day cause social juniors to resent their seniors' monopoly of political power. In the meantime, a man's desire for a herd of his own was clearly an important motive in his decision to leave his village.

Migration from the Ngwato chiefdom had a slower start than in the chiefdoms to the south. Distance from the mines played some role in the tardiness of popular response, but so did the political order or disorder in the respective chiefdoms. In 1876 only 37 migrants traveled from the Ngwato chiefdom to Kimberley, while 942 Tlhaping left the contested territory known as the Keate award. Nearly as many Kalanga—862—left their land to the north of the Ngwato, perhaps because their Ndebele overlords were sending them to earn cash to buy guns and horses.[94]

Khama III exercised firm control over the activities of labor recruiters in his own chiefdom. Initially he sent only "a very few Veldt people."[95] Because they were undoubtedly hereditary servants with no property rights, he probably requisitioned all or part of their wages. He employed a similar strategy with regiments: having sent a regiment to help the British defend the protectorate's eastern border during the South African War, he spent their £1,727 wages on building the Serowe church. The timing of these absences was, in principle, carefully regulated so that they would not interfere with plowing. From 1898 to 1903 Khama stopped recruitment altogether because wages on the Rand had been cut by 10 percent and many of the recruits had died. Drought and the need for tax revenue caused him to lift the ban and, in 1903, six hundred men left Serowe for the mines, railways, and cantonments of South Africa.

The protectorate administration had actively fostered the export of labor. Three years before a tax on each hut was introduced, the Secretary of State for the Colonies, Joseph Chamberlain, had instructed the High Commissioner to encourage all able

Tswana men to work in the goldfields and in railway construction; although Chamberlain did not explicitly urge the imposition of a tax, he did suggest that only needy women and children should receive food relief during the rinderpest epidemic. A few years later, the Assistant Commissioner of Bechuanaland, F. W. Panzera, wrote a mildly threatening letter to the Tswana chiefs: "Mind, the Government do not say that they must work—the Government do not force any man to work if he wishes to remain idle—but if he might work and will not, he must not expect government aid."[96] His approach could hardly have endeared him to Khama, who resolutely spurned all offers of charity that he felt might diminish his powers and his polity's independence. Even the Resident Commissioner tried to convince Khama that the days when migrants were robbed by their employers had ended. He sent the chief warm letters of introduction to apparently honest labor recruiters. "No one knows better than yourself that it is only by labour that South Africa can prosper, and it is in the interests of all that good well paid labour shall be abundant. I hope you will talk the whole matter over with Mr. Macfarlane [Witwatersrand Labour Organization, Johannesburg] and will give him all the assistance in your power."[97] No embargo on the export of Ngwato labor was ever reimposed by the chief. By the time of Khama's death in 1923, the number of migrants had grown so that Ngwato mine laborers were receiving a total of more than £1,700 a year in deferred pay, that is, the portion of their earnings that they collected on their return home. Because Ngwato land was rich in cattle, the amount was low compared with that received by the other chiefdoms and would remain low until the disastrous drought of 1933–1935. The last years of Khama's reign marked the beginning of labor migration's incorporation into the public and private lives of the chiefdom.

The impact of the first decades of labor migration on agricultural productivity cannot be readily assessed. Ngwato grain production remained at a subsistence level even after Khama's death. Subsequent data on pastoral production suggest what common sense would lead us to believe for this period: fewer men migrated when the cattle markets were open; the absence of increasing numbers of men resulted in declining standards of animal husbandry. Chiefs tried to curb the damage to the chiefdoms' herds by requiring every mine recruit to obtain permission from his headman before leaving. In this way, a family that could not spare its herd boy would try to keep him at the cattle post. This desperate attempt by seniors to stem the exodus of their younger brothers, sons, and servants served only to drive untold numbers to clandestine employment in the gold mines of the Rand. Tswana commercial range management was effectively inhibited both by the absence of labor and by the unpredictable market.[98] Since there was little prospect of earning tax money by selling surplus grain—the land was dry, and transport was poor—labor migration was becoming imperative for many Tswana during the early decades of this century.

The ability of junior men to earn money and hold property independently of their rank weakened the oligarchy of seniors but certainly did not destroy it. The wages offered in South Africa were too low to allow a class of vigorous entrepreneurs to grow and challenge the old order. Traditional patron-client relations persisted. Collective endeavor was more difficult to organize and enforce when growing numbers of the population were absent from their villages, but the wards, and labor-sharing arrangements generally, did endure. With them, the ideology of patriarchy also survived, embattled as always by the contrary ways of popular practice.

Over the course of the nineteenth century, the Tswana chiefs had gained greater power and wealth for their office at the expense of the lesser chiefs in their polities. They had made these gains through trade and the judicious distribution of refugees. They consolidated them with the aid of the British and modernized their states by starting to create bureaucracies and by presiding over the growth of exclusive rights to property. The formerly blurred boundaries between owning and holding were to be replaced by sharper divisions between public and private property. At the same time, they began to augment the ephemeral councils of lesser chiefs with educated functionaries who owed their income and authority solely to them, deepening social control that, for the moment, affected primarily royal rivals rather than the mass of the governed. Despite the birth of secular, bureaucratic government, the scope for popular autonomy from chiefly control remained ample. Inherited patterns of patronage proved resilient. The chief remained by far the richest man in his realm. He increased his wealth from inherited herds and servants with revenues from trade and taxes. His subjects could beseech him for gifts from treasuries not only newly abundant but also containing new forms of wealth. In addition, news from the South African colonies boosted the chief's image as a great protector. People regarded him as a bulwark against land loss and debilitating taxes. As long as the chief spent the treasury monies on providing such modern services as schools, hardly anyone questioned his legitimacy or the limited sphere of the political community. He could increase his exploitation of sections of the governed and remain a legitimate ruler as long as he did not, by damaging established relations of patronage, cross the threshold of popular tolerance for closer or more intrusive government.

The ideology of patriarchy, based so emphatically on the distribution of wealth to clients, therefore survived even as chiefs jettisoned the mystical values and rituals of their office. They had done so partly for diplomatic reasons, but also because they were acknowledging and embracing a new era of private property relations. They were effectively ending the ideological underpinnings of their role as Great Patron and were able to do so because the most aggrieved parties of the new order—royalty and Khoisan or Kgalagadi "vassals"—had too-divergent interests to form a coalition of protest. On the Rand's periphery during this early stage of the industrial revolution, the mode of production was being modified rather than transformed. And so the legitimacy of the chieftainship and its patriarchal values was, for the time being, maintained.

Chapter Two

"Full of Passionate Intensity"
Ngwato Politics, 1925-1939

Kgosi thipa, e sega molootsi. (A chief is like a knife that will cut the sharpener.)
Tswana proverb

As soon as Tshekedi Khama, Khama's son, became Ngwato regent in 1926 at the age of twenty-one, his relatives began trying to unseat him.[1] Some shot at him shortly after his accession; others tried to turn British opinion against him in the 1930s, and still others, as it was said, broke up his year-old marriage and poisoned his mother in 1937. Tshekedi himself traced these troubles to grievances inherited from his father's brothers. To a certain extent, he was right. These vicious quarrels did all involve royal relatives who feared slipping away from the center of power. In 1937, before an audience of his people and British administrators gathered in the Serowe *kgotla*, Tshekedi summed up his first decade as chief in bleak terms. "[F]or eleven solid years," he lamented, "my tribe has been engaged in civil wars; their property squandered, not for any material benefit but to defray the ruinous costs of the battles."[2]

Tshekedi had to fend off four publicized challenges to his early regency. Dynastic rivals fought "battles" to define royal privilege throughout his regency. They and other people protested in 1930 against unpaid regimental labor. The third challenge came simultaneously from the most and least powerful groups within the protectorate, the hereditary servants and the British.

Throughout the 1930s, the British acted in principled, though half-hearted, defense of the hereditary servants who performed unpaid labor. In addition, the British banished Tshekedi for two weeks in 1933, effectively reminding him of his dependence on them. The melee was confusing, but becomes less so when seen within its imperial and regional contexts.

The Setting

The British were present in the tribal capital of Serowe not as patrons but as judges. They imposed three levels of courts of appeal that exceeded the chief's own power. Royal contestors could appeal to them—principally to the Resident Magistrate, but appeals could then go beyond to the Special Court of the Bechuanaland Protectorate, and finally to the Privy Council in London. These courts served as public arenas where a domestic political dispute could be taken by the party who had lost his case in the lower court, with each contender striving to convince the British that his version of custom was the correct one. Each man struggled to present a definition of law and custom that would serve his own political and material interests. But the imperial overlords were clearly not impartial judges. Usually supporting the man through whom they ruled, they effectively affirmed and even codified his version of "traditional" law and practice.

The regional economy in the twenties had a similarly conservative effect. Inhibited by depression and dependence, economic change was too modest to destroy the inherited forms and idioms of political life. "Seniority" continued to define one's role in public affairs; wage labor and markets provided most people with such limited material rewards that they were unable to change their inherited status in society. When Tshekedi became regent, most trade was still conducted in barter, taxes could not always be collected, and the rate of labor migration was low.

Cattle were still coin; they embodied wealth and social value with a moral force money could not begin to approach.

Yet these signs of continuity masked important economic innovations that would have political repercussions sooner than anyone, including Tshekedi, expected. A few members of the cattle-owning elite had begun to acquire new forms of wealth. By selling beasts for cash, they were able to invest in new and costly possessions such as permanent homes, education, and later, motor vehicles and water pumps tapping underground streams, locally known as boreholes. The expense of acquiring and maintaining these commodities encouraged their owners to define in more and more exclusive terms who could have access to them. Those with few cattle or none at all were increasingly obliged to sell their labor in South Africa to pay their taxes. Wage-labor relations were growing to affect even hereditary servants. Almost everyone wanted money to buy some item of food or clothing.

The centers of commerce in Ngwato were the dozen or so shops operated by white traders in Serowe. Pervaded by the odor of tobacco, a popular commodity, the shops sold mainly small imported consumer goods—food such as tea and sugar, soap, cloth, and decorative items such as beads, bracelets, earrings, and copper wire. The traders exchanged these goods for a motley array of local produce: grain, when there was a surplus, skins, bones, and even the residue of beer-making for use as animal feed. Sometimes the exchanges worked to the disadvantage of the African; a slip of paper indicating that it was "good for" the purchase of £5 worth of goods might be exchanged by the shop owner, or at least by his manager, for goods worth only £2.[3] This pattern of unequal exchange led some observers to remark that traders could always recover from their losses in the cattle market because they made "excessive" trading profits.[4]

One index of the Ngwato chiefdom's cattle wealth lies in the number of general dealers—white traders all carrying the same goods—who were able to make a living there. Few were obliged to become labor recruiters.⁵ Nearly all were able to maintain their businesses through the decades, even though their profits were irregular—their income from the sale of cattle fluctuated widely as disease infected the local herds and as regional markets closed against them for reasons of politics as well as health. At the worst times, particularly after 1933, the traders perceived themselves to be so financially pressed that they agitated in favor of transferring their freehold farming blocks—Tati and Tuli—to the Union of South Africa, which they hoped would be more responsive to their needs and perhaps subsidize them. For the most part, however, their problems—unreliable speculators, competition from hawkers and mail-order companies—were far less grievous. Several generations of the same families have continued until today to run their family shops in Serowe.

Local white traders inhibited modern prosperity in Ngwato less than regional marketing policies did. When a cold-storage company was established in the protectorate in 1927, it inspected only cattle submitted to it by whites. Although it relented and inspected the Ngwato chief's cattle—"it is wrong to assume that the cattle which will be produced by the Natives will all be of an inferior type," Tshekedi argued—it still operated infrequently in the 1930s and then only with an imperial subsidy.⁶ Similarly, wealthy Ngwato who were trying to establish dairies felt that agricultural officials graded their cream lower than that of whites, who were usually local traders owning land in the freehold blocks. African entrepreneurs were "discouraged" by this discrimination.⁷ A far more damaging case of bias was the 1924–1941 restriction on the importation of Bechuanaland's cattle into the Union. Only heavy cattle were accepted for sale to South Africa, a restriction which, in Tshekedi's words, put the protectorate "entirely at the mercy of the Union," particularly during a time of drought,⁸ when even the fortunes of a rich man—who would formerly have told a local dealer to truck up to a couple of hundred of his beasts to Johannesburg—would suffer.

Economic disaster such as drought, depression, and closed

cattle markets made tax collection difficult and occasionally pointless; only persistent defaulters were prosecuted for their failure to pay. Between 1899 and 1932, each adult man had in principle to pay annually to the protectorate government through his headman a hut tax which grew from ten to twenty-three shillings. In fact, some young men stayed at their cattle posts for so long that they were never registered as taxpayers, and headmen were notoriously lax in paying their own taxes.[9] The protectorate appointed a tax collector for all Bechuanaland Africans on the Rand only after 1933. When Tshekedi became Ngwato regent in 1926, taxation was commonly evaded, but in times of acute general hardship, it was effectively suspended. For those unlucky enough to be obliged to pay, the burden was unfairly distributed; rich and poor alike had to pay the same amount.[10]

Until 1934 few Ngwato contracted to work in South Africa's mines. When the grain harvest was good and cattle markets were open, there was no reason to do so, but during droughts and cattle embargoes, labor migration served the same purpose as "scattering" to the hinterland had done in the nineteenth century: a migrant could eat. He—and almost all of them were men—could also send money home for his family to buy food. Tshekedi's first seven years as regent were seldom afflicted by "starvation"—a reason commonly given by Tswana for migrating—although prosperity was not widespread either. And so the time was not yet ripe for the proverbial warning—"a town without young men has no outer walls."[11] Although public attention focused on contests for power within the elite, rather than on the creation of a new social and economic order, within these contests new kinds of property rights were evolving, which in turn would come to affect "traditional" principles of political legitimacy.

The challenges to Tshekedi's early regency reveal some of the origins of the later mid-century crisis in patriarchal authority. Royalty commanded center stage but the weaker members of Ngwato society, especially commoners and hereditary servants, also continued age-old disputes. At the same time they all adopted new strategies to advance their interests as private property and wage-labor relations began to grow. What repercussions would class formation have on political legitimacy in the twentieth century Ngwato chiefdom?

For the time being, people continued to debate in terms of seniority the right to succeed to high office. The ideal model for succession to the chieftainship states that "the rightful heir was always the living man next in order of seniority to the Chief."[12] And yet the scope for manipulating rank was so wide that each interregnum ordinarily witnessed a struggle between at least two royal contenders, each claiming to be the most senior. Those scholars who have recently begun to call primogeniture an "iron law" governing Tswana succession to high office underestimate the importance of two crucial attributes of political legitimacy among the Tswana.[13] First, although the heir was in principle the eldest son of the great wife, royal genealogy was open to interpretation. Before the introduction of literacy and monogamy, the simple act of determining who was the senior son could be exceedingly complicated. It was a highly political process. A chief usually married several wives and therefore had several houses from among which he would designate the most senior wife. However, a chief's wishes were not necessarily clear or universally respected. When a chief died, factional support could determine which son won his claim to be the eldest son of the most senior wife. This nineteenth century principle held true in the twentieth century—a man inherited the chieftainship not only because of his genealogical heritage but also because of who supported and who opposed him. Second, while the Tswana defined legitimacy in genealogical terms, they judged a ruler according to the quality of life he was ensuring or was likely to provide. Even a chief could be warned "if a child does not do well, we start looking around and ask where he originates from." A bad ruler could fall from seniority. Under British protection, stated principles about succession were tools by which the contenders sought to snare British support, but none represents the legal pattern of Tswana succession because no such pattern existed. In the majority of cases, a chief gained power not only because indigenous rules had designated him to be the most senior inheritor of the office, but also because he was backed by the largest and most influential faction.[14]

The Accession

Tshekedi Khama was twenty-one years old when his half-brother Sekgoma II died and he became entangled in the nest of family vipers. When he rushed home from Fort Hare Native University College, where he was studying for his matriculation examination in South Africa, to attend his half brother's funeral, his sense of urgency must have been heightened by his knowledge that he and his mother would now be seen as craving the vacant chieftainship. Sekgoma's four-year-old son Seretse would be too young to take office for nearly two decades. Even before Sekgoma's death, royal factions had begun jockeying for power in a dispute about what kind of medical care the chief should receive in his final illness.[15] After his death, they competed for the chieftainship itself.

One such faction was descended from a father and sons who had grown wealthy and powerful through both their marriages to Khama's daughters and their skills as literate chiefly aides. Khama had named Ratshosa Motswetle as tribal secretary in 1897 instead of his then errant son Sekgoma II.[16] Ratshosa had married the great chief's daughter Bessie, and one of their three sons, Simon, later followed the Tswana preference for cousin marriage by marrying Sekgoma's eldest daughter, Oratile. Ratshosa oversaw Khama's cattle, supervised land allocation, and handled the chief's papers. For his performance of these roles, Ratshosa earned spite from the less favored; headmen who did not receive chiefly gifts would blame any man who carried out the chief's instructions to allocate beasts to other men. Ratshosa's sons achieved similar eminence and attracted similar spite: in 1919 Johnnie became tribal secretary and was aided by his brother Simon, the headmaster of Serowe's first school; a third brother, Obeditse, served the Resident Magistrate as clerk and interpreter. A rival faction against Ratshosa and his three sons were children of Khama's brothers; one of them, Phethu Mphoeng, led the faction, and the Raditladi brothers followed, in such bitter opposition to the house of Khama that Sekgoma II once accused his cousin Phethu of trying to kill him.[17] With Phethu Mphoeng's position within the Khama family structurally similar to that of the Ratshosas, it is not surprising that they should be rivals. Mphoeng had the advantage of being a "son of Sekgoma [I]," directly descended from the former chief, and he, like Ratshosa, had married a daughter of Khama.

Tshekedi and his mother, Semane, Khama's fourth and last wife—a member of a "fugitive clan," according to one of her enemies[18]—were said to be so distanced from these machinations that Semane preferred her son to finish his education rather than to compete for the regency. This supposed lack of ambition did not prevent a mob of women—led by Baboni and MmaKhama, Khama's daughters by his first wife—from attacking her house when Sekgoma died, ransacking it for "something glittering," the poison that they believed had killed the chief.[19] Another mob gathered to attack the Ratshosa brothers because, so it was said, they had favored treating the sick Sekgoma with European rather than local doctors. The mob dispersed only after one of the brothers fired a gun over their heads. Semane, protected by the Ratshosas, found refuge at the London Missionary Society mission.

The Resident Magistrate, Captain H. B. Neale, tried to stem the rising tide of enmity by scheduling Sekgoma's funeral at 6 A.M. so that there would be no time for beer drinking before it and less chance of a riot. Immediately after Sekgoma's burial, on 17 November 1925, the Resident Commissioner, Jules Ellenberger, announced in the Serowe *kgotla* that the chief would be succeeded by his cousin Gorewang until Tshekedi was mature enough to serve as regent for the child Seretse. Because he was commonly considered to be weak, Gorewang would be assisted by a twelve-man advisory council. Its conduct of affairs was bound to be tempestuous because on it sat two of the Ratshosa brothers and Phethu Mphoeng. With the swift and cunning switch of loyalties so characteristic of Tswana politics, Phethu became a devoted supporter of Tshekedi and an opponent of the principle of the council. In fact, the council was easily abolished when Tshekedi was installed as chief regent because by then it had support from no one except the Ratshosa brothers, who were popularly accused of devising it as a way to continue the influence they had wielded under Sekgoma.

On 19 January 1926, a leopard-skin cloak was placed over Tshekedi's shoulders during a ceremony led, in a judicious display of the shared powers behind indirect rule, by the British Resident Commissioner and one of Khama's half-brothers.[20] Tshekedi made a special point of remarking that he would be led by the wise counsels of the older men of the chiefdom, and that the cloak really belonged on the shoulders of his young nephew. Local Europeans also played a role; Reverend Tile of the London Missionary Society spoke and so did Mr. Kirkham, a trader. "God Save the King" concluded the ceremony.[21] Immediately following the installation, Tshekedi and "about one hundred" headmen visited the Resident Commissioner to ask him to abolish the council.[22] As one council member had earlier explained, "I am opposed to this Council for it was hurried through and formed without consulting either the Headmen concerned or the Tribe."[23] Local administrators, who regretted the lapse of the "more progressive [council] system," warned that peace would be best preserved if its supporters, that is, the Ratshosas, were either retained in office or dismissed privately and graciously.

Immediately upon his appointment, Tshekedi acted to safeguard his newly acquired authority by publicly humiliating the Ratshosa brothers. In front of a *kgotla* meeting, he dismissed Johnnie Ratshosa as his secretary. From Johnnie's perspective, Tshekedi was trying "to rule him through his [Tshekedi's] uncles"; he believed that one uncle, Phethu Mphoeng, was using

Tshekedi to punish the brothers for, so it was charged, engineering his own exile in 1924.[24] But this interpretation gives too little credit to Tshekedi's own drive to consolidate his vulnerable position. His passion for power and his skill at achieving it would soon become dramatically apparent.

Tshekedi was sorely provoked when, after Johnnie's dismissal, the Ratshosa faction issued yet another challenge to the regent's authority. The late chief's daughter Oratile, the wife of Simon Ratshosa, lodged a protest with the Resident Commissioner over the terms of Sekgoma's estate and asked that the case be heard in a European court. She claimed all of Khama's "personal" in contrast with his tribal property—50,000 cattle and thousands of pounds in cash. She had taken one servant girl from her father's widow and one from a chiefly cattle post, claiming that they belonged to her. Tshekedi directed that the girls be returned, and when no one obeyed, he responded in kind, dispatching men to the homes of the brothers to seize the two servants. He demanded that his three challengers appear before him in the *kgotla*.

Tshekedi chose a date, Easter Monday, on which he knew that the brothers would be attending the wedding of a relative, and advertised their absence by inviting the Resident Magistrate to wait for them in the *kgotla*. They did not appear. Neither did Simon come with his regiment to work on Serowe roads that afternoon when commanded to do so by the chief and the head of his regiment. In punishment for this disrespectful behavior, Tshekedi sent a regiment armed with knobkerries (knobbed sticks) to arrest the brothers at the wedding feast. Finding them carrying guns, curious equipment for a wedding, the regiment withdrew. The brothers finally arrived in the *kgotla,* and Tshekedi set out to demonstrate to the crowd the consequences of defying his orders. "I will punish you with lashes; lie down!" he commanded. They refused on the grounds that the "sons" of a chief are never beaten, only fined. Some of Tshekedi's supporters rushed at the brothers with sticks; they knocked Johnnie down. Johnnie got to his feet, was given his hat, and went to the magistrate, who had left, to report what had happened. The other two escaped to their homes and returned to the *kgotla* armed with a rifle and a Mauser pistol. They fired five shots before fleeing. One bullet passed through Tshekedi's jacket and singlet, grazing his skin so that blood flowed. The same bullet wounded two of his aides, one sustaining a severe abdominal wound and the other a shattered right hand. The Resident Magistrate rushed back to the *kgotla* and found "hundreds of armed men" there whom Tshekedi swore he could not restrain. The young chief ordered the brothers to be brought before him dead or alive. They were safely apprehended by the Resident Magistrate, and the next day their old enemy, Phethu Mphoeng, and his regiment burned their houses on the order of the chief, no doubt with delight.[25]

With the brothers about to be arrested and removed to Francistown jail, the Resident Magistrate asked Tshekedi to forgive the one brother, Johnnie, who had not fired at him. Tshekedi agreed to spare Johnnie, stipulating that he should, nevertheless, be banished. The other two, Simon and Obeditse, were sentenced by the Resident Magistrate to ten years imprisonment, a sentence later reduced by the High Commissioner to four years, in light of the punishment they had already sustained through loss of property. Tshekedi continued to harass the Ratshosas economically; after appointing their archenemy, Phethu Mphoeng, to oversee their estate, he sent regiments to destroy their six dairies and eight wells; he demanded that they remove their cattle from Ngwato, stopped the construction of a road to one dairy, and stripped their cattle posts of their hereditary servants, or Sarwa. They argued that the costs of their punishment were cruel and extraordinary: their family herd of four thousand head was sold for only £1042, and their dairies and wells, which had cost £800, were sold for £21.[26]

For five years, the legal repercussions of the shooting incident embroiled the British and their courts in Ngwato domestic politics. The protracted legal battles could hardly have pleased protectorate officials. The Ratshosa case rose all the way from the

Resident Magistrate through the Special Court of the Bechuanaland Protectorate to the Empire's highest court of appeal, the Privy Council in London.

These court cases reflected the ambiguous relationship between African custom and received law. The absence of any clear imperial stand on the status of Tswana law was apparent in the contradictory judgments allowing the cases to be tossed from one court of appeal to another. When Simon and John sued Tshekedi for damages, the additional Resident Magistrate, Captain Robert O'Malley Reilly, appointed especially to try Simon and Obeditse, accepted Tshekedi's assertion that Ngwato law and custom had justified his burning of the houses, and he accepted the collective wisdom of the old men who assured him that in the old days an act of war against the chief would have been punished by death. His perspective undoubtedly derived from his intimate connection with the chief. To fulfill his role as the imperial delegate to the capital of the chiefdom, he had to rely on chiefly guidance in understanding the conflicts within it. His power and authority were intertwined with the chief's. Courts relatively more removed from the arenas of chiefly power made more abstract and Eurocentric judgments. The Special Court of the protectorate, for example, overturned the Resident Magistrate's ruling on the basis of principles alien to the *kgotla*. It argued that there had been no semblance of a trial and no evidence that the burning had been done with the consent of the *kgotla* and the chief's councillors. Tshekedi was incensed by these arguments. In 1930 he journeyed to London, in part to appeal to the Privy Council.[27] To Lord Passfield, the Secretary of State for the Dominions, he argued, "I am a very insignificant person here, but in my own county I am an important person: I am Chief of that Country. I consider that my life should be valued more highly than that of an ordinary person in that country, and I think that the people who made an attempt on the chief of a Tribe or Nation should not be allowed to . . . bring actions against that Chief whom they attempted to kill."[28] Passfield replied that Tshekedi could not deprive the Ratshosas of "the right of access to the Courts if they consider that they have suffered damage." Despite the opposition of Passfield as well as the Imperial Secretary and High Commissioner, the Judicial Committee of the Privy Council did allow Tshekedi to appeal, and upheld his claims under "traditional law." But he won only a partial victory. The Lords of the Council did not approve of the burning and suggested that the High Commissioner should take administrative action to prevent a recurrence. The contradictory nature of these decisions gave rise in the early thirties to imperial concern that the two legal systems should be rationalized.[29]

The Ratshosa case spawned a legal sequel in 1931. Again, a family feared losing power and wealth after its exclusion from the inner circle of the chieftainship. And again, British backing allowed the chief to grow ever stronger than his rivals. When the son of Baboni, Khama's eldest surviving daughter, died, Tshekedi went personally to her home and determined the fate of his 670-beast estate and £364 that had been deposited in a Mafeking bank. "In *kgotla* or out of *kgotla*," Tshekedi explained, "the Chief simply announces the manner in which he has made his decision. ... The Chief like every judge is not bound to do everything in one Court House."[30] In fact, this nearly omnipotent view of chiefly powers offended even his own loyalists. Tshekedi should at least have allowed a senior headman to plead Baboni's case and consulted with royal and commoner headmen, his allies said. He was obviously excluding Baboni's male relatives from decisions about the estate because he knew that she and they supported his rival for the chieftainship, Gasetshwarwe, who was an illegitimate son of Sekgoma.[31] Further, Baboni's late husband was the son of Ratshosa's brother. One of Tshekedi's allies ripped the veneer of principle off the debate and set out to defame the chief's rivals by name: "Ratshosa is very poor, in fact a dog; he owns nothing but his body."[32] The British demanded the public airing of the dispute in July 1932. The Resident Commissioner, Lieutenant Colonel Charles Rey, was so angered by Tshekedi's "difficult and uncompromising" stands on this and other issues that he ordered him to hear the case publicly and issued a vague but prescient warning that it was within the Administration's power to depose him.[33] Tshekedi remained chief nevertheless, and his division of the estate was allowed to remain. His rivals left the match banished and impoverished.

Why did the Ratshosas have so few supporters? Virtually no voices were raised in their defense throughout their careers. That so few people spoke or acted in their favor suggests that they had failed to distribute their wealth among a body of clients. We know that they had spent much of it on commodities. One Ratshosa house in the mid-1920s contained a wealth of consumer goods such as a sewing machine, duplicator, linoleum, books, silver trays, gold cuff links, chamber pots, and a variety of expensive clothing including an academic cap and gown and a wedding dress. The houses holding these riches represented a capital investment themselves. Foreign observers stressed with apparent wonder that "these were not Native huts but well-built houses."[34] Simon also ran a commercially equipped dairy farm, one of eight belonging to his family. Such members of the elite enjoyed the best of all possible material worlds because they continued to claim the unpaid labor of hereditary servants at the same time that they made modern investments.

The brothers were clearly defenders of their own privileges, not populists. Johnnie Ratshosa explicitly regretted the passing of the "olden days when a distinction was made between respectable men of the tribe and wastrels."[35] Simon proposed that the chiefdom's "office bearers be chosen by the tribe from native capitalists."[36] Their education in elite South African institutions, from which the mortarboard and gown undoubtedly came, gave them literacy in English, which, in turn, provided access to the first salaried jobs available in the chiefdom—secretary, interpreter, and schoolmaster. They wielded substantial political power. Simon had been able to take all of Sekgoma's correspondence away to his own home, against the chief's wishes. Tshekedi complained, "whilst they had all the correspondence in their charge

I was under their vigilant eye." Also, some headmen believed that the brothers deliberately kept messages from them from reaching the chief. And by issuing or refusing to issue cattle-sale permits, they controlled the fortunes of ordinary folk. Altogether, the Ratshosa brothers represented a dual threat to elements within the established order: they were early capitalist entrepreneurs who chose to invest their riches rather than to distribute them; and they had achieved their status as the chief's personal clients by virtue of their Western education.

The case clearly illustrates the eagerness with which estranged members of the elite sought to gain British support. The Ratshosas employed a South African lawyer because they could afford to do so and because they knew that destroying a wrongdoer's property is not legal in British law. They understood the ways in which the endemic factional conflict could be skewed in favor of whoever gained the ear and sympathy of the proconsuls. And so Johnnie Ratshosa showed a shrewd understanding of the new forces at play in Ngwato politics when on Easter Monday, unlike his brothers who went to fetch their guns, he ran to the Resident Magistrate for protection and possible support. The British presence was allowing the new capitalist elite to jockey for power without having to dispense their wealth among a faction of loyal clients as in the old days.

The Regimental Labor Fracas

In 1930 a slightly different set of royalty challenged Tshekedi's regency. This time the language was modern and the cause had more popular appeal. The crisis began with a mundane problem—the new Serowe dam was clogged with silt. Tshekedi called out the people of the village to clean the dam but few turned up, whereupon he ordered the regiments to hunt for the recalcitrant workers in the fields and cattle posts where they had gone to avoid laboring. The regimental commander directed two subordinates to collect truants from the Serowe area and from Madinare and to requisition their wagons. One subordinate, a man said to be "of brutal character," gathered nineteen wagons and forty people after threatening arrest and incarceration in a European jail.[37] One old man died after working on the dam; he was undoubtedly a person of no rank since his death is mentioned only once, and then by the Resident Magistrate, G. E. Nettelton.

The case blew up because one educated royal man, Moanaphuti Segolodi,[38] was a shrewd publicist. One week after he met William Ballinger, a Scottish adviser to a black South African trade union, the Industrial and Commercial Workers Union, who was touring the region, he wrote to Ballinger reporting instances of harsh compulsion.[39] Threatened with flogging for refusing to work on the dam, he fled to the Resident Magistrate. The following month, Moanaphuti and his allies began to draft petitions over Nettelton's head to the Resident Commissioner, Charles Rey. This crescendo of publicity called into question the entire system of regimental labor, and in November Nettelton called a public enquiry into the affair.

Tshekedi's enemies argued that he had caused the trouble by acting as a "despotic, tyrant monarch."[40] In their first petition, the eight signatories had written that they were "chained up under the habit of slavery and oppression here in Serowe." Tshekedi had enslaved his people by becoming "absolute master of our own property." He flogged anyone who protested. Appealing to British liberal democratic ideals, the petitioners also decried Tswana "barbarous customs" and asked for "freedom and Peace."[41] They cannily and not entirely accurately cited two recent precedents to support the legitimacy of their protest: a 1924 petition by Phethu Mphoeng against the "cruel customs" of banishment, *letsholo* (a compulsory communal "hunt" or meeting at which the chief's enemy often met with an accident),[42] and flogging; and the 1926 attack on Tshekedi by the Ratshosa brothers, which the protesters curiously swore was "on behalf of the MaSarwas, that they be set free." Segolodi later admitted frankly that "The real object behind [his own] Petition was to remove the Chief."[43] One of his former comrades went even further and expressed a revolutionary hope: "We hoped to have the Tswana chieftainship annulled and that we would be ruled only by the [British] Government."[44]

Resisting the rebels' rhetoric, British officials assumed at best an exceedingly passive role in the affair and effectively supported the chief. Nettelton, the Resident Magistrate, scolded Moanaphuti and handed him over to the chief's messengers after he sought refuge in the government camp.[45] During the public enquiry, Nettelton was more of a silent, and disapproving, witness than a judge. His presence undoubtedly encouraged the petitioners to use civil libertarian rhetoric in their efforts to diminish one another, but he upheld all the disciplinary measures Tshekedi had imposed on his rivals.

After the eight men petitioned the Resident Commissioner against "enslavement," Tshekedi chose a particularly fitting punishment. He liberated all of the Kgalagadi and Sarwa servants of the eight. Not to be undone by the chief's clever twist of their own rhetorical weapon back on themselves, the petitioners' second appeal mentioned that "this 'emancipation' [should] be extended impartially to all," including Tshekedi.[46] Their proposal received no reply, but the imperial officials must have been discomfited by the clear disparity between imperial antislavery language and imperial practice.

Tshekedi blamed the British themselves for contributing to the trouble by failing to allocate money from either general revenue or the native fund to pay the laborers. Since 1929, he had been trying to gain control of the taxes his people paid to the protectorate government, arguing that they should be expended on new development projects. Even though he had suggested building the Serowe dam, Tshekedi believed that the project should rightly be called "government work" and therefore the government should pay the laborers;[47] the regimental workers themselves continually asked when they would be paid, and Tshekedi knew that they resented having to pay tax in addition to working on the dam.[48] Following this logic and a strategy that was devious but ill fated, Tshekedi presented a letter to the High Commissioner accusing the Resident Commissioner of having ordered him to use forced labor on the dam.[49]

Tshekedi was convinced that British socialists had fueled the rebellion against his authority. William Ballinger had returned to Serowe in June 1931 with three like-minded companions—a history professor named Margaret Hodgson, whom he was later to marry, and Leonard Barnes, a journalist accompanied by his own wife—to continue studying "the impact of industrialism on the tribalized native."[50] Resident Commissioner Charles Rey observed with customary spleen that the visitors went about "disturbing the natives by talking to all the scallywags—and all the decent natives hate them."[51] Moanaphuti had met them in Kanye and traveled with them as their interpreter. Their questions were certainly provocative: Were any Sarwa, the hereditary servants, being taught? Did people leave for Johannesburg because they had no cattle? Were people satisfied with working on the dam? They had, Nettelton agreed, interviewed only those individuals who had a grievance against the chief. Tshekedi was so certain that the three socialists had stoked the dissent by insinuating criticism of his rule and by suggesting the mode of protest against him that the next month he engineered the sending of a loyal petition to Resident Commissioner Rey. Signed by 225 headmen, it requested that provocateurs like Ballinger, and also Clements Kadalie, the head of the South African union that Ballinger advised, "be strictly forbidden to enter our territory."[52] The new Resident Magistrate, Captain Potts, telegraphed Rey in July to complain that he had received in total five deputations of Ngwato pressing for the expulsion of Moanaphuti himself.[53]

Tshekedi's assessment of his rivals was blinkered by his knowledge of their forebears, who, like them, were royalty who had been steadily losing their proximity to the chieftainship. Either they or their fathers had at one time or another been banished by the ruling chief for disloyalty and had lost all or part of their property.[54] One Ngwato scathingly remarked, "These are not senior headmen but *lerotse* headmen and their habits are like snakes. They are just persons and their parents were never rulers."[55] Descended from the second ranking royal clan, they had consistently established alliances with losers in the struggle for the center of Ngwato political power. One new petitioner was related by marriage to the Ratshosas, another to the Raditladis; some were allied to Sekgoma's illegitimate son. With the political and economic fortunes of all eight petitioners in decline—Moanaphuti, for example, was trying unsuccessfully to get a job at the Serowe hospital[56]—they probably calculated that they had little to lose in appealing over Tshekedi's head to the Resident Commissioner in the name of "freedom and peace."

Focusing on "inherited grievances," Tshekedi failed to display understanding of his rivals' current problems, peculiar to the world of the 1930s. The petitioners were now marginal to Ngwato society in a more modern sense; they were "new men" by virtue of their education and their investments. Half had been to school; one, K. T. Motsete, had just received a B.A. and B.D. from New College, London.[57] Not surprisingly, Motsete was able to articulate his opposition to chiefly "absolutism" in the most expansive terms: "in olden times the chief was only a 'primus inter pares.' . . . now under cover of British protection which he believes is for himself alone and his rights, a Chief has become a despot who can with the explicit or implicit support of the local Government rule his people with a rod of iron, however much they chafe under it."[58] Motsete further indicted Tshekedi for failing to obtain government funds for local development projects.

Incidents such as Motsete's protest deepened Tshekedi's suspicion of the educated. His own education was far inferior to Motsete's, and he feared the political damage such educated men might cause by using their knowledge of English and of law to address complaints directly to the British overlords and thus destroy his chiefly authority. Therefore, Tshekedi pursued Motsete with a vengeance—searching houses for drafts of letters he might have written for the petitioners, fining him the extraordinary sum of twenty-five cattle for a sexual seduction committed eleven years before. He believed that Motsete would try to humiliate him in front of his people, and so, when the newly returned bachelor of divinity, music, and arts (he became a teacher, not a clergyman) attacked him in front of the *kgotla* for his "cunning," Tshekedi's worst fears were confirmed. He would tolerate only those educated who were devoted to him.

Some of the petitioners were trying to establish businesses in the Ngwato territory. One had begun a dairy, and one was starting to raise pigs and poultry for sale, entrepreneurial efforts of a kind quite rare in Ngwato at the time. Some petitioners ruefully expressed their new goals and ideals. "Outside is the only place for progress," one stressed, "In Serowe there is nothing that one can do for a living. The white man, the instigator of progress, agrees that people should go out."[59] Another elaborated, "We contend that the mode of living today is that an individual is working for his own living, and if he has children he cannot afford [to work] for that man and that other man. . . . at present certain people have got to earn money to educate their children and the Chief should consider other means whereby we could do this."[60] Clearly, by 1930, some Ngwato were keenly seeking to improve their lot in new ways. That the petitioners numbered only eight suggests that the decision to work for money was still a new idea, freely chosen, and not yet a necessity for survival.[61]

Although the chief actors in this drama were royal, there were lesser players as well. Occasionally in the *kgotla* an anonymous voice would blurt out a complaint against the established order. During the public enquiry on the dam project, for example, an undistinguished man sprang up to challenge Tshekedi to explain why "people who are not [London Missionary Society] members" had to pay a "compulsory Church levy."[62] Tshekedi's opponents were not confined to dynastic rivals. Still, most people remained politically mute, showing discontent silently, as in the custom of the past, by, for example, becoming "very careless" about laboring with their regiments.[63] Their expenditure of energy on the regimental labor projects—such as the Serowe dam and a concrete wall across the Metse-Mosweu River in 1931—was notably slight. Ballinger, Hodgson, and Barnes witnessed the work on both projects and could barely contain their frustration at observing the men fill sardine cans "with the mud to be removed, balance [them] on their heads in the native way and solemnly carry [them] for two hundred yards to the bank to empty there. In the course of an hour they would make perhaps four of these farcical journeys."[64] Such bored and deliberately inefficient workers probably felt no attraction to the anti-Tshekedi faction because the petitioners were poor; they would have had little patronage to dispense. Yet popular silence should not be interpreted to mean that most people enthusiastically supported unpaid labor. Although many individuals were undoubtedly restive when taxes and fines were imposed on them, the ground was not yet fertile for the sowing of sedition. Established networks of patronage had not yet been dramatically shrunk by capitalist patterns of investment and by labor migration.

Political protest often, in fact, coincided with drought, and the case of the Serowe dam was no exception. The Ngwato had suffered through a dry plowing season in 1929, and therefore the obligation to serve in regiments was a particularly heavy burden during the latter half of 1930. All men needed to be at their fields ready to plow when the rains began to fall at the end of 1930, but instead they found themselves working on the dam and subject to the bullying of Ngwato regiments. Men without sons or herders experienced the greatest hardship. As one petitioner complained, "I have no hope of saving my cattle from this drought as my wife cannot find water for them. If they go astray a woman cannot trace them. When the regiment found me at the cattle post I had lost sixteen head of cattle."[65] Tshekedi denied that he was blind to these troubles. As early as 1929, he argued, he had proposed that dam laborers be paid.[66] The issue of unpaid public labor itself, in the end, got lost in the far more heated debates over slavery and dynastic rivals.

The debacle ended abruptly with Tshekedi succeeding once again in impoverishing and exiling his enemies. Kesebonye Sephekolo died in Gaborone jail in 1933 while serving the first year of a ten-year sentence. His comrades sank into obscurity, their names never again surfacing in documents or in public fora. Both the Ratshosa crisis and the regimental labor crisis ended with Tshekedi's victory. His rule was strengthened as the British effectively affirmed his cardinal principle: property rights and residence within the chiefdom were contingent upon loyalty to himself.

Hereditary Servitude

The third great domestic crisis of Tshekedi's early years as regent concerned the underpinnings of Ngwato economic life: the relations between Ngwato patrons and Sarwa servants (*malata*), the most subservient relationships in Ngwato society. From 1926 through the thirties, the British tried to bring the society into line with modern conceptions of free labor, but no one in the Ngwato elite really favored the "liberation" of the Sarwa. The Sarwa issue became a cause célèbre when dynastic dissidents used it, as they had in the Ratshosa and regimental labor cases, to drag the great imperial patron into local disputes.

The precise nature of Sarwa slavery is difficult to define. As they were neither bought nor sold, the Sarwa, it could be argued, were not slaves at all. And yet these people—often the short and brown-skinned Khoisan descendants of the hunters and herders originally peopling the thirstland—enjoyed no civil rights. They had not voluntarily placed themselves in the service of Tswana masters and hence lacked the right to withdraw. In the late eighteenth century, soon after Tswana cattlemen had appropriated springs in the Kalahari, the Sarwa who had formerly used those scarce water points found their labor, first as hunters and then as herders, appropriated by the cattlemen as well. For their masters, the Sarwa tracked wild animals, plowed, allowed their daughters to be domestic servants in Tswana homes, and, perhaps most strenuously, drew water by hand from the 15-foot-deep wells to water Tswana cattle in winter. A master had every right to retrieve by force a servant who had deserted. Sarwa families generally lived at the cattle posts in shelters they had themselves erected. Their property was meager, especially since their masters were likely to covet and take the few valuable items they might have acquired, such as a gun. In return for their service, the master gave them food, especially free milk, that they supplemented with wild food and the meat of hunted or stolen beasts. Commonly considered by the Tswana to be wanton stock thieves, they were subject to severe flogging if suspected of theft and caught. No clear definition of their civil rights could appear in a legal system that defined no rights at all. Some Sarwa families had had their unpaid labor claimed by generation after generation of Ngwato masters. The successful assertion of that claim nevertheless depended on the coercive force their masters could muster and their own ability to evade it. The terms of the relationship changed depending on how their masters used their labor.

Dynastic rivals, well aware that slavery was an issue that could attract a good deal of publicity, exploited the use of hereditary servants to gain British attention. The Ratshosa scandal itself had been sparked in 1926 by a dispute over rights to two Sarwa servant girls. The violence of the consequences as well as the publicizing talents of Simon Ratshosa[67] had prompted the Resident Commissioner to launch a small-scale enquiry, which concluded with relief that "no searching investigation could disclose anything really discreditable to British traditions."[68] Immediately afterward the High Commissioner, Lord Athlone, traveled to Serowe to announce the emancipation of the Sarwa. Compulsory service would no longer be allowed and they were henceforth free to live independently of their masters.[69]

Tshekedi subsequently complained to the Imperial Secretary that it was not right that the Sarwa should have been released when none had presented any complaints to the government. The only Sarwa whom he had himself freed, he said, were those owned by his enemies—the Ratshosas and, in 1930, the petitioners against regimental labor. The Imperial Secretary replied in a conciliatory manner, promising no sudden changes. The protectorate government, he explained, had been pushed to interfere by dynastic disputes and, in 1928, by a League of Nations enquiry into Tswana slavery. Perhaps because they feared upsetting the chief and the status quo generally, missionaries and administration officials had been reluctant to see Sarwa clientage as slavery.[70]

Undoubtedly hoping to encourage more Britons to see the problem in the same light, Tshekedi requested Lord Passfield, the Secretary of State for the Dominions, in 1930 to appoint a commission of enquiry into the matter.[71] "If it should appear that the [Sarwa] are not properly treated, we should be glad to be advised so that we may treat them properly," Tshekedi told Passfield, "We feel aggrieved about the publicity which was given to the matter without being discussed with us."[72] The next year a British official, E. S. B. Tagart, spent three weeks touring cattle posts to investigate the issue. Adopting the Tswana concepts of rank, Tagart concluded that, although they were "certainly" not slaves, the Sarwa occupied "a well-defined place in the Bechuana conception of the patriarchal family group": they were forever minors, never to be freed from paternal power. The greatest obstacle to their liberation was, Tagart wrote, the scarcity of paid employment in the chiefdom and in the entire protectorate.[73]

The frequency of official reports on slavery in the Ngwato chiefdom gives a clue to their relentless ineffectuality. Tagart's "Report on the Conditions existing among the Masarwa" in 1933 was followed by the London Missionary Society's "The Masarwa" in 1935 and by J. W. Joyce's "Report on the MaSarwa in the Ngwato Preserve, Bechuanaland Protectorate," written for the League of Nations' Advisory Committee of Experts on Slavery in 1938. Ngwato patrons feared that official reports and investigation would encourage insubordination among the servants. Tshekedi, for example, complained to the Resident Magistrate in 1934 that the Sarwa were now deliberately killing "our cattle and when asked they would say they are now free people, and as they have worked for the Bamangwato for many years without pay they were only using what was theirs."[74] He was adamant in insisting that any Sarwa who left Ngwato without his master's permission would have to be returned.[75]

Tshekedi was blaming the high-minded meddling of the British for the trouble, but the roots of Sarwa "insubordination" actually lay elsewhere, and reforms instituted in Sarwa-Ngwato relations were also born of economic circumstance as well as imperial rhetoric. By the 1920s, when a few Sarwa had begun to acquire property like plows and cattle, Khama had given them the right, in principle, to pass such possessions on to their children, since they had, in fact, earned this property—by receiving cattle as rewards, selling cream or puppies born to their master's hunting dogs or skins from animals that their own dogs had killed.[76] Most hereditary servants remained outside the money economy itself and, unlike the Tswana, paid no taxes unless, as a few did, they earned wages. Indeed, there was an unspoken agreement at all levels of government that requiring payment of taxes would encourage Sarwa to leave their masters in search of scarce wage employment elsewhere.

The conditions of Sarwa servitude remained harsh despite Khama's reform of the late nineteenth century decreeing that they had the right to bring disputes to the *kgotla*. Most Sarwa still received no pay, only the right to milk and to the meat of dead beasts and occasional gifts of clothing. The master continued to act as a lord: he could take Sarwa children from their parents to serve as domestic servants in Serowe; he gave them land and could take it away; he could fine them for disobedience.[77] The discipline to which Sarwa were often subject was the master's *sjambok* or cane. Such violence repaid insubordination, cattle theft, and desertion. It could end in murder that might not always be reported. As a result of Khama's reforms, if a master abused his Sarwa, the servants now could appeal to the chief, who might decide to keep them for himself or assign them to a new master. In Tshekedi's view, the Sarwa, as a result of such reforms, had become primarily his subjects rather than property associated irrevocably with a certain herd, master, or piece of land. Yet few Sarwa exercised the right to appeal for reasons possibly having as much to do with distance from as with lack of confidence in the justice of the *kgotla*. Their masters also avoided taking cases concerning Sarwa to the *kgotla*, though their reasons were different: they considered it pointless to bring servants to court for cattle theft since so few had the means to compensate the owner, and the masters were often burdened with the fine.

Despite the reform that Khama had granted, the Sarwa remained subject to the random and violent imposition of frontier justice. In 1930, for example, a Ngwato cattleman named Rajaba Monageng thrashed one of his three Sarwa to death for deserting his cattle post and for stealing his calving cow. Rajaba was brought to trial but only, he told me in an interview, because the family of the deceased reported the crime to the Ratshosas, who in turn told the District Commissioner. These Sarwa clearly had no confidence in appeals to the *kgotla*. Rajaba's attitude may be extreme, but it is worth quoting him to reveal the disdain with which some masters regarded their hereditary herders; "I thrashed them very hard [325 lashes] to teach them a lesson—they must learn to do as I told them. . . . [I have] never beaten dogs like I beat those Mosarwa [sic] and [I] never would."[78]

At times the Sarwa counterattacked against their tormentors. Some fled north of the Nata River and became bands of cattle thieves who responded to Ngwato overlords "in a warlike manner."[79] After their traditional source of livelihood had been shot out by hunters, many Sarwa had turned to stock theft to get meat to eat. One Resident Magistrate was worried about Sarwa in the Nata Crown lands who he heard had repulsed Tshekedi's hunting companions who were trying to force them to return to Serowe. He wrote, "it seems to me that the sudden release of large hordes of more or less savage MaSarwa who have been kept under control and authority of their lords and masters, the Bechuana, may wander around the country stealing and killing cattle when they feel inclined, and if they collect together in big communities as they appear to be doing on the Crown lands at the Nata; the Government will have a difficult business in hand."[80] During most of 1929, half the prisoners in the Serowe jail were Sarwa stock thieves.[81]

At the same time that game was becoming more scarce, wages were luring Sarwa to work for Khurutshe and Kalanga farmers—a process that may well have heightened ethnic tensions within the chiefdom—or for European farmers in Tati, who paid them 10 to 15 shillings a month in 1931, half what they paid a Ngwato but at least twice as much as a Kalanga would have paid.[82] With wages of this kind the Sarwa were obliged to pay taxes and would, they hoped, become exempt from being called to labor by a Ngwato headman. A tax receipt could also be a ticket to a miner's pay, free of further tax deductions, and small but increasing numbers of Sarwa were being attracted to the mines. In 1935, only fifty to sixty Sarwa were known to go each year to the Transvaal, but the migration of Sarwa workers over time has probably been greatly underestimated by scholars.[83] In 1931 one European expressed surprise when Sarwa at a cattle post 60 miles northeast of Serowe addressed him in Afrikaans as "baas"; Sarwa migrated further than many realized. Some masters tolerated these trips as temporary absences and protested only when a cattle post was left with Sarwa women and children and no men. Quite apart from chiefly directives, some Sarwa were, in effect, freeing themselves by exchanging hereditary masters for contractual ones. Some Sarwa were becoming genuinely independent by migration, and in areas where, with access to markets, they were settling in villages, plowing, and buying stock with earnings from the sale of skins and cream. The geographical extent of this change should not be overemphasized, but the character of it was extensive. Sarwa who lived in remote cattle-post villages cultivated only with a hoe and for immediate consumption. As late as 1917 Tati Sarwa had neither tilled the ground nor assisted their masters in doing so.[84] Only fourteen years later they plowed there extensively, living in their own villages, sometimes under Kalanga headmen.[85] In the Tati area and especially in the land east of the railway between the Shashi and Motloutse rivers modes of living were rapidly changing.

The Sarwa who remained in service now found themselves subject to increasing demands. No longer simply herders, they had become cultivators and domestic servants as well. A master with sons often absent at either schools or jobs in South Africa and needing to remedy the new labor shortage, found it "easier than in former days to summon his MaSarwa from their village ... to plough for him near the capital."[86] Few, if any, extra benefits rewarded the Sarwa's extra labor. Masters who were trying to commercialize their pastoral production were particularly stingy; a dairyman could now be unwilling to share with his Sarwa the milk that had formerly been part of their reward.

Tshekedi spelled out the logic that undermined the old system of patronage: "I as chief, pay yearly a sum of about £1000 for the keep of the Masarwa who herd my cattle. If I paid [them directly] for their services in cash, I would see that they worked better, and fewer men would do the work for less than the keep of the many costs me."[87] As a commercial rancher, Tshekedi believed he would now profit more by paying individual herders than by serving as patron for entire families, that is, buying their food and incurring all their debts whether for clothes, marriages, or court fines.

The cash economy allowed the old political elite to convert their cattle wealth into capital investments while continuing to exact customary labor service, with their servants working harder for relatively fewer rewards. The master's children, now released from having to spend their entire childhood working for their parents at home, in the fields, or at the cattle post, were free to go to school or, later, to labor abroad in preparation for making a greater material contribution to their parental home.

The British could decree the liberty of these *malata*, as they did, but the scarcity of local opportunities to work for wages limited their economic independence. And despite the political clamor of the twenties and thirties for an end to involuntary servitude, the greatest advantages Sarwa gained continued to be those they wrested for themselves by stealing cattle and by absconding. The transformation of Ngwato ranks into classes was only beginning.

The Flogging

Imperial support for the chief did have limits. These limits were determined by Britain's strategic need to keep South Africa within the Empire, and thus, when a collision of South African racial politics with events in the Ngwato Reserve brought international attention to the chiefdom in 1933, as such a collision would do again fifteen years later, the British demonstrated how frail was their support for a "tribal" ruler.

The incident that reached newspapers worldwide was provoked by the dangerous mixture of race and sex.[88] It developed into the flogging of a white man by an African, an equally dangerous assault on white racial supremacy. A young white native of Serowe, Phinehas McIntosh, had aggressively pursued African women and slept with a number of them. In response Tshekedi asked the Resident Magistrate to remove him from the chiefdom. When the magistrate took no action, Tshekedi tried McIntosh in the *kgotla* on a charge of assaulting a Ngwato man in a dispute over a girl. The chief ordered the white culprit to be flogged, thus upsetting the racial hierarchy in his own chiefdom.[89] The Resident Magistrate informed Tshekedi that he was in direct conflict with the protectorate law decreeing that a chief had no right to thrash a European, and the magistrate sent a protectorate policeman to serve a warrant for Tshekedi's own arrest. Resident Commissioner Rey, Tshekedi's nemesis, already at loggerheads with him over proposals to reform chiefly administration, suspended the young chief from his office and confined him to the Palapye police camp. One week later, a Royal Navy detachment of two hundred sailors and marines arrived in the Ngwato Reserve by train from Cape Town. An "administrative" enquiry was held at Palapye; there were no lawyers or jury present and the judgment was delivered by Admiral E. R. G. R. Evans, commander-in-chief of the Africa station of the Royal Navy and Acting High Commissioner during the absence of Sir Herbert Stanley. During the enquiry, marines aimed their machine guns at the crowd of African spectators and helmeted men with fixed bayonets stood near Tshekedi. During his own shrewd cross-examinations of McIntosh and the Resident Magistrate, Tshekedi tried to raise the question of whether the young wagon builder was not truly, by virtue of his way of life, a white Ngwato, and whether the section of the Proclamation of 1891 prohibiting him from trying whites truly applied to him as a hereditary chief. When reading out his judgment, Admiral Evans added insult to the young chief's losses:

You admit flogging a European after judging him in your *Kgotla,* knowing full well that you had no legal right to do this, and no jurisdiction over him. Your duty as Acting Chief was to set a good example. You have not set a good example. . . . it appears that you are an extremely capable acting chief, quite able to deal with your people and to lead them, but it appears that your over-mastering passion is your selfishness and the study of your own personal rights and privileges.[90]

Evans concluded by banishing Tshekedi: "for the deliberate and flagrant violation of the Protectorate law well known to you, I shall suspend you from the exercise of your functions of Acting Chief at His Majesty's pleasure, and you will not be allowed to reside in the Bamangwato Reserve." Tshekedi was sent into exile in Francistown, in the freehold farming block of Tati, for less than two weeks and was officially pardoned by King George VI, after having written a letter of submission, on the ground that he had abandoned his claim to try Europeans.

Tshekedi had indeed won enemies in South Africa and the protectorate by flouting both administrative and racial hierarchies. South African logic was explicitly stated in a telegram of appreciation that Oswald Pirow, the Union's Minister of Defence, had sent to Evans; it had been necessary, he argued, to take decisive action against Tshekedi because Africans were getting above themselves and threatening trouble in the mines and elsewhere in South Africa.[91] The protectorate administration, on the other hand, was riled by Tshekedi's persistence in addressing himself directly to the Secretary of State instead of through the Resident Commissioner. Rey, the Resident Commissioner, believed that Tshekedi had deliberately contrived to raise a constitutional issue in order to oppose the two forthcoming proclamations intended to limit chiefly powers. Rey was undoubtedly wrong about Tshekedi's purpose. The incident had blown up because the British had not responded to Tshekedi's initial call for imperial help in dealing with a white who was cohabiting with women of the chiefdom. In consequence, it raged beyond anyone's control, fueled by emotions provoked by the explosive mixture of violence, sex, and race; as an article in an Afrikaans newspaper warned, "If we allow a white man to be whipped by natives, we can expect worse things."[92] But the incident scarcely served anyone's interests.

Lessons could be drawn from the affair that foretold a subsequent, more serious crisis. The British had been shown that bold interference in tribal government would close Ngwato ranks against them—no Ngwato agreed to replace Tshekedi during his brief banishment and even Simon Ratshosa proffered his sympathy. Tshekedi, for his part, had learned that his rule was highly vulnerable to regional politics. The threat of Bechuanaland's transfer to the Union was grave, particularly after General J. B. M. Hertzog's Fusion government came to power in 1933, pledged to incorporate the High Commission Territories in the Union. The flogging incident graphically suggested that transfer would damage, if not destroy, independent chiefly government. As one chiefly partisan later argued, "if the Union takes our land, the chief will be reduced to the position of foreman."[93] During the 1930s, the Ngwato commonly believed that the chieftainship was their only protection against the physical insecurity that incorporation in South Africa would bring. This belief endured as they saw South African policies—restricted markets and low wages—contribute to their steady impoverishment.

The Divorce

The inherited grievances in the chiefdom reached a crescendo in 1937 when Tshekedi was divorced. Only thirteen months earlier, in February 1936, he had married Bagakgametse, the daughter of his father's brother, Moloi. He had been courting her ever since he became chief. She was educated, having been sent to school in South Africa, but one of her greatest attractions was her genealogical relationship to Tshekedi. She was not only a preferred marriage partner according to the royal preference for patrilateral parallel cousin marriage, but the match might also heal some of the breaches in the royal family by transforming agnatic, or brotherly, competitors into affines, or allies. The marriage lasted only a year. Soon after the wedding, Tshekedi left Serowe to visit his cattle posts at Nata, and while he was gone, Leetile Raditladi paid a social visit to Bagakgametse, by his own testimony simply sharing her company while she listened to the radio or while he tried out a book of songs with her friend, a new schoolteacher named Ella Moshoela. When Tshekedi returned from Nata, he made two shocking discoveries. His wife and his mother were living in intense mutual suspicion, and his mother's health had begun to weaken. Tshekedi feared, even before she died in 1937, that she had been poisoned. Even worse, Bagakgametse was pregnant with a child whose father was, he believed, Leetile Raditladi.[94]

Behind every crisis that had preceded this rupture in his personal life, Tshekedi saw the same pairs of malign hands, belonging, he believed, to his relatives—the Raditladis and the Ratshosas and the fellow travelers who were related to them by marriage. To exorcize these dynastic demons forever, he now determined that their leaders must be banished, an act that in terms of protectorate law, was for him to recommend but for the British alone to carry out. He demanded a public enquiry into the whole sordid chain of events. Never before had so delicate a matter—the breakup of a royal marriage—been exposed to formal public scrutiny. Although he was an intensely private man, Tshekedi had undoubtedly calculated that only the glare of publicity and, most important, public humiliation and banishment would end the incessant challenges to his rule.

Disang, Leetile Raditladi's father, complained bitterly that the chief had no right to try a case in which his personal interests were at stake. The District Commissioner's court would have been a far more neutral and suitable forum, Disang believed, but his faith in the objectivity of protectorate courts was misplaced. The commissioner, Vivien Ellenberger, present as an observer, sided with Tshekedi on virtually every point and went so far as to write in his official report to the Resident Commissioner in Mafeking that Leetile was "a bad young man."[95] He recommended that the three Raditladis—Leetile, Disang, and his brother Lebang—be banished and also that they be heavily fined. Their final ruin was achieved in 1939, a year after Tshekedi had married Ella Moshoela, not a relative, with whom he would have a long and stable marriage and five children. Because Tshekedi's own public enquiry had an explicitly political agenda, Disang was right in believing that it would fail to clarify what had actually happened. Nor did his own performance help matters; his memory lapses and simple protestations of innocence made him less than a credible witness. Tshekedi won the round in this particular dynastic feud and, in large part for this reason, enjoyed relative peace for nearly a decade until the late 1940s.

Dynastic quarrels were usually quarrels about rights to property, and this case was no exception. Tshekedi even explicitly accused Bagakgametse at the enquiry of having married him "for property."[96] The Raditladi case reveals clearly the kinds of possessions the Ngwato elite had been able to acquire before the Second World War. Leetile owned a piano; he had sent it by rail to his new home in Mafeking. His father, Disang, divided his own herd between five cattle posts, at least one of which had nearly two hundred head, and admittedly he had "paid a lot of money" to have a well dug at each one.[97] Since people as rich as Disang had their own brands, they could buy and sell cattle without the chief's permission.[98] Disang, in addition, plowed 52 acres, which had been cleared of stumps, undoubtedly by the labor of MaKoba servants whom he did not pay because "they lived on our property."[99] In a peculiarly inverted way, the case also reveals that elite fathers were now expected to buy clothing and an education for their sons; Tshekedi had in the *kgotla* reprimanded Disang for failing to provide these for his eldest son.

As in the previous episodes of these dynastic quarrels, the most tantalizing question concerns the paucity of the rivals' supporters: Why were they so few? In contrast to the old days when large numbers of people seceded in the wake of their patrons, these royal rivals were alone. Again, a full answer must take into account the devious personalities of the actors themselves. And, again, the material investments of the elite must also have played a role in limiting the numbers of their followers. Their investment in things rather than in people continued to make their challenges more quixotic than genuinely menacing to Tshekedi's rule. They threatened the system of patronage when they bought such items as pianos with their inherited wealth rather than distributing it to clients, and in so doing, they undermined the patriarchal order far more effectively than if the bullets fired in the *kgotla* in 1926 had actually found their mark.

The Years of Economic Disaster

Dynastic rivalry was only one of the pressing problems confronting Tshekedi during the first decade of his regency. In the early thirties, in addition to suffering the consequences of the worldwide depression, the Tswana chiefdoms experienced a series of natural disasters that crippled local plans for economic development and the ability of many households to feed themselves. A drought withered crops in 1932 and for four years discouraged many people from planting. The Resident Commissioner observed, "Things are in a shocking condition at Serowe—no grazing for the cattle, the big dam dried up, very little food, diseased dogs howling all night and most of the day."[100] Adequate rain did not fall again until 1936. People also had difficulty purchasing enough grain to survive because cattle sales—virtually the sole local source of cash—had been thwarted when in response to a foot-and-mouth epidemic that began in 1933, cordons were set up to prevent the disease from spreading. With clean cattle unable to move across the cordons to markets from increasingly congested pastures, their condition deteriorated and their weight dropped. The South African embargo on underweight cattle, established in 1924, remained in effect until 1941 when the war in Europe had provoked a shortage of beef in the Union. People who would formerly have sold beasts to get grain and other supplies to survive a drought were forced to sell their labor instead. With wage-paying employment scarce within the entire protectorate, they were compelled to turn in increasing numbers to the South African Rand. The number of men officially recruited from the Ngwato Reserve for the mines by the Native Recruiting Corporation rose dramatically—from negligible in 1930 to twenty-four hundred in 1935,[101] and untold numbers of men and some women slipped over the border to jobs in South African industries and farms.

In the early phases of the crisis, tax collectors, respecting people's plight, did not press those who fell in arrears. The government's need for revenue became so acute that, in 1934, the Resident Magistrate gave suspended sentences to hut-tax defaulters in the hope that they would find work and be able to pay taxes. But the following year Tshekedi and the District Commissioner together decided to sue the defaulters.[102] Tshekedi put his highly touted principle of collective responsibility to work and made headmen, themselves notoriously lax in paying taxes, directly liable for part of the arrears. By 1939, he had collected more than £7,000 for imperial and "tribal" coffers in this way.[103] His efforts forced clandestine cattle sales at low prices and obliged less well-off men to search for employment in South Africa.[104]

Tshekedi took issue not with taxation but with the circumstances giving rise to low wages. He pleaded with the administration "to alleviate our hardships by providing a suitable market for our produce instead of placing us in a position whereby we are forced to sacrifice our cattle mainly to find taxes."[105] Because the tax was not graduated it hit hardest those men with few cattle. Poorer men probably paid the lion's share of the costs of establishing a bureaucracy, but the few services that bureaucracy, in turn, provided were primarily for the benefit of richer men; agricultural development was virtually neglected by the protectorate administration in favor of services for commercial ranchers.[106] Occasionally one finds expressions of resentment against this imposition that was driving men to labor and even against the administration itself; in the Botletle River area in 1935, for example, rumors circulated that the protectorate administration was distributing food relief and then sending the people who accepted it to the mines.

Between the early thirties and the Second World War, the cash returns to migrant labor came to exceed income from the sale of livestock, and as a result, the number of workers going to South Africa from the protectorate during that period increased fourfold.[107] The collapse of the livestock export industry was systematically related to the rising rate of labor migration in all the protectorate chiefdoms. In Ngwato, which had had with Ngamiland the highest rate of cattle sales and the lowest rate of migration, these disasters of the early thirties changed the domestic economy particularly dramatically.

The first decade of Tshekedi's regency can give a false impression of constancy: "traditional" social relations appear undisturbed by the development of industry elsewhere in the region. There are two reasons for this appearance of stasis: first, the subjects that dominated public discourse—dynastic rivalry and hereditary servitude—suggest that the chiefdom was stuck in its ancient ways; and second, for most of Tshekedi's first decade, the catalysts of social change—the export of cattle and labor— were weak. Capitalism was growing at an uneven rate: the development of local wage-labor relations lagged behind the growth of private property.

The highest and lowest strata of Ngwato society were the first ranks to be deeply affected by the growth of private property. Members of the elite invested their wealth in education, in commodities, and in banks, while their servants avoided increased demands for their own labor by absconding, stealing, and searching for wage labor. The great middle rank of Ngwato society remained enmeshed in old patron-client relationships and reciprocities; its members' ability to produce subsistence and surplus was strained by labor migration and taxation but they were still holding on to their sense of physical security. They were not excluded from communally held land. Thus, they remained politically silent. "Traditional" political forms and idioms survived even while they were being given new content by the presence of British overlords and by the prize of new riches to be won.

Chapter Three

The Defense of Patriarchy in the *Kgotla*

Foko ja kgosi le ageloa mosako. (Always build a fence around the chief's word.)
Tswana Proverb

In 1938 Tshekedi Khama was engrossed in reading a new book, *A Handbook of Tswana Law and Custom*.[1] Compiled by the chief Tswana anthropologist, Isaac Schapera, the book was printed on alternate pages so that it could be annotated by administrators of the Bechuanaland Protectorate in the course of their duties. On these blank pages, Tshekedi penned his thoughts about Tswana law,[2] carefully recording an image of the Ngwato past and of the present as he wished it to be seen. He even suggested that Schapera rewrite the volume for the "moral instruction" of youth.[3] Sensitive to his people's reputation as well as to challenges against his own power and views, he bristled at Schapera's suggestions that royal relatives had to be consulted in tribal administration or that Tswana men regarded their women as servants. Tshekedi wanted to ensure that the content of the newly codified, though previously unwritten and flexible, custom was appropriate to the dilemmas that he and his society were encountering in the twentieth century.

Tshekedi clearly believed, as did British administrators, that law was an effective tool for controlling social change. He taught by word and deed "traditional" and "modern" lessons in the settling of disputes. He neglected certain issues. His power had limits. The southern African political economy set boundaries on his ability to legislate social change or stasis. Further, the governed themselves showed a genius for evading government.

Tshekedi's well-documented rule is a case study in the origins, as well as the effects, of African customary law. In his marginal comments—denying the subordination of women and foreigners, his need to consult his relatives and the abuse of chiefly authority—was he inventing tradition? Was he, with the aid of Schapera and the protectorate administrators, engaged in creating customary law? Martin Chanock, who has recently argued that African customary law was a product rather than a precursor of colonial overrule, would probably say that he was.[4] But Chanock's analysis begs the question of how Tshekedi's creation was related to Tswana political ideas and behavior, past and present. As Simon Roberts has further reminded us, law in the chiefdoms of the Tswana derived not simply from the machinations of chiefs, but also from "the normative Tswana lifeworld as ordinary members experienced it."[5] African customary law, Roberts argued, was not discontinuous with the precolonial past, neither was it simply an ideology imposed by chiefs for purposes of domination.

The question of how customary law evolved is important not simply because it demonstrates that some African traditions were invented recently, but because it reveals the resolution of disputes as a strategy. The chief and the people Tshekedi governed used the *kgotla* to guide their individual and collective destinies, to defend or attack patriarchal values during changing times.

Nineteenth Century Origins of Tswana Law and Custom

To reduce precolonial Tswana law and government to formal rules and institutions is to force them into alien molds. In the *kgotla*, whether at the heart of a large village or in a small ward, there was no judge to impose an enforceable norm on litigants. There were no legal codes. Rather, in the *kgotla* people negotiated for advantages before their kin and neighbors. The merits of each case were decided, not on the basis of a conceptually distinct category of rules but with respect to the status and political allegiance of the respective parties.

Coercive force was exerted only occasionally. When summoned by a crier on a village hilltop, bands of age-mates would assemble from their village wards, or fields and cattle posts, to constitute an occasional army or police force. These regiments would, for example, back the chief's right to control the movements of his people, punishing them for leaving the village for their lands before he publicly proclaimed their right to depart. They were most likely to discipline eminent subjects who could afford to build a faction hostile to the chief; if a senior man seemed loath to leave his lands or cattle and participate in *kgotla* or other communal life, he was likely to be suspected of treason. The regiments might be told to destroy his fields or confiscate his cattle. The mass of the people were not worthy of such force.

Precolonial Tswana states tolerated a low level of social control. As one early witness of *kgotla* justice observed, punishment might be pronounced by the chief in accordance with the majority view of his councillors, but it was rarely inflicted.[6] Similarly, a decree—such as the prohibition of beer brewing—might have to be repeated several times if people were inclined to disobey it. Without a police force or standing army, the means of regularly enforcing such rules simply did not exist.

Normally, the *kgotla* controlled behavior in a far more subtle way. Its decorum advertised the prestige of the powerful. Its invective humiliated the poor and out of favor, stripping them of any honor. One royal Ngwato later looked back on the unashamed days when status mattered, lamenting, "Today the people are all of the same rank like Europeans, we have lost our customs of obedience and reverence, we are a people that honoured other people."[7] The public management of demeanor was a weapon of the powerful, and the *kgotla* was the theater where this political drama was acted out.

In Tswana villages, the clusters of homesteads called wards also helped to achieve social conformity with a minimum of coercion. Failure to cooperate with other families in one's ward would be met with concrete sanctions such as late aid in plowing or no aid at all. Unless one were wealthy and could secede with a band of clients, opportunities for surviving on one's own scarcely existed. The system of land allocation—by the chief to his overseers to headmen to household heads—perpetuated ward unity and interdependence; one's neighbors in the village were, in principle, also one's neighbors at the lands and at the cattle posts. The head of the ward was in precolonial times its wealthiest member by virtue of his inherited cattle or gifts of cattle from the chief, and so the junior members of the ward could also be his clients. Discord within the ward could set at risk the basis of its members' subsistence.

Kin and neighbors conducted and settled disputes among themselves. The chief rarely interceded in the details of his people's lives. If a family proved unable to resolve disruptive conflict among its members, the ward *kgotla* would listen to the problem. In both fora, the principle of collective responsibility was upheld.

In exceptionally disruptive and significant local cases, the problem would be sent on to another, higher *kgotla*, providing a set of listeners with different and wider factional interests. This *kgotla* was situated in one of the Ngwato capital's four sections. Each section provided not only a basis for regimental organization and the canvassing of tribal opinion, but also, in effect, a court of appeal for wards within the capital and for villages in the outlying districts. In accordance with the Tswana custom of creating pairs of allies, each section court was presided over by one junior and one commoner headman.[8] Each headman judged cases that concerned members of the other's rank. This pairing, in principle, avoided exacerbating rivalries among royalty. It could also check royal claims with commoner power. Before the reign of Tshekedi's father, Khama III, cases brought by common folk would stop at the section *kgotla*.

The supreme *kgotla*, the large round open space in the capital, primarily judged cases "between two chief men of one clan or division of a town." In the early nineteenth century the chief was said to interfere in disputes and pass judgment on them only if asked to do so. Great men quarreled in the supreme *kgotla* about valuable property such as water points, hunting grounds, and hereditary servants: "The vassals with all their belongings are the subject of litigation and endless jealousies; and it needs all the skill of a chief to settle these matters between greedy and plausible rivals. When a decision is come to, the poor people in the country are hastily 'lifted' by the successful litigant, to be brought back again should he afterwards lose his case."[9] In light of the wealth of legal maxims celebrating the omnipotence of the chief, it is well to remember that his customary jurisdiction usually extended directly over such great and "greedy" rivals, but only indirectly over the mass of the people who were the relatives and clients of the headmen. He was preeminently the judge of judges who were therefore left free to settle disputes according to their intimate knowledge of the parties involved.

Eminent men affected the course of justice. Influence with the chief and headmen could procure a pardon, although Tshekedi would later pen in the *Handbook*'s margins that he "entirely disagree[d]" with Schapera's claim that damages were rarely collected from the chief or his relatives.[10] Especially in the nineteenth century, the chief's decisions on disputes among headmen or lesser chiefs were determined by the extent to which he trusted them as allies or feared them as potential rivals. A man remained chief only by winning the support of the majority of influential smaller chiefs in his realm. He had virtually no independent means of enforcing sanctions against antisocial behavior. He could deploy only the regiments, but they were headed by his potentially disloyal agnates. Enforcement was, for the same reasons, equally as problematic at the level of ward government. The image of the early and mid-nineteenth century *kgotla*, then, is one of a flexible and loosely defined body with particular sensitivity to the imperatives of patronage.

Tswana experience cannot, of course, be reduced to the calculations of rulers. The values of patriarchy were indeed popularly held. During the colonial period, between 1885 and 1965, for example, no one explicitly rejected the chieftainship, the *kgotla*, or esteem for rank. People were taught to respect these values in everyday practice and in ritual rather than in specialized legal or educational settings. No one explicitly taught obedience to law during initiation ceremonies of males; rather, boys learned the "songs of the law" that had taught obedience to fathers. These songs also expressed the challenge posed by sexually potent young men to their elders' control of access to women. As Jean Comaroff has noted, initiation of males and females imposed "images of normative right upon those of youthful insurrection."[11] Tension between the various levels of the social hierarchy was carpeted over, though not entirely concealed, by a gerontocratic ideology that no one explicitly challenged. This "world in which symbols of male identity were . . . instruments of control" was the "lifeworld" that the *kgotla* expressed and defended.[12]

By the end of the nineteenth century, the power of the chief was rising. Khama's expanding jurisdiction and his legal decrees ate into the formerly localized and small-scale basis of dispute settlement. With his enhanced power, Khama was able to embark on a program of tribal legislation so innovative that people came to distinguish between traditional law and Khama's law. Christian teachings had inspired many of these legal innovations.

Khama's conversion to Christianity in 1860 won him a whole literature of naive and fulsome praise from Protestant missionaries.[13] One may argue inconclusively about the relative force of personal conviction and strategic manipulation of European allies in Khama's decision to accept the London Missionary Society as the sole Ngwato religious sect and to declare Sunday a day of rest; Tshekedi angrily penned, without explanation, in the *Handbook*'s margins that Khama had certainly not abolished bridewealth payments in 1875 because the London Missionary Society had pressured him to do so.[14] Other changes in Ngwato custom appear only partially to be Christian reforms. Khama's abolition of initiation ceremonies and rainmaking in 1877 and his discouragement of polygamy presented such profound challenges to the existing social order that they must also be seen primarily as tests of loyalty to Khama rather than as simply religious reforms. Other fiats were more clearly attempts to serve the common good but were not necessarily Christian in origin, as, for example, laws regulating the sale of corn and breeding cattle to Europeans, aimed to prevent markets from luring the Ngwato to dissipate their scarce agricultural resources. Finally, Khama's reforms also served to allow him to manipulate the transfer of wealth between generations; by introducing female inheritance, he increased his control over both his sons and sons-in-law.

These laws foretold the deepening of government control of family life. Formerly, the paramount chief heard no cases involving women and very few appeal cases. Starting with Khama's reign, *only* the chief could decide inheritance and divorce disputes. He also began to judge cases on appeal from common folk rather than continuing to allow the sectional courts to deliver the final judgments. In cases that bore significantly on his concepts of Tswana values and on his own powers, the paramount chief could now use the *kgotla* generally, and the dispute-settlement process in particular, to educate subjects and to manipulate circumstances that might threaten his position. Khama staked his authority on the reforms in a situation of acute political instability. Backed by the British, he had managed to extend chiefly jurisdiction farther than it had ever before reached.

Not that Khama's coercive powers had grown so dramatically that he was able to disregard popular opinion completely. His personal wealth had prospered from the wagon trade, and he shared this wealth with clients whose loyalty could consequently become far more emphatic than that of his own relatives. He still depended on both clients and royalty—men clustered squatting or sitting on low chairs along one side of the *kgotla*, their European dress advertising their eminence[15]—for help in deciding cases and in enforcing those decisions. Khama had not acquired independent or unlimited means of coercion. British protection aided but did not ensure the chief's growing supremacy. It offered Khama a two-edged sword. While helping him to centralize further his own power, the British also introduced a rival legal and political system that began gradually to usurp his own authority.

Twentieth Century Origins of Tswana Law and Custom

Khama was the great innovator, decreeing dozens of changes in his people's habits. His son Tshekedi explicitly made very few changes to inherited practices[16] but preferred to justify his acts by invoking custom rather than by presenting himself, the regent, as a great "tribal innovator." Nevertheless, customary law was relentlessly created during his regency. Its creation had three main catalysts: British overrule, the social changes brought by labor migration, and dynastic rivalry.

The struggle for dominance between European or "received" law and customary law was prolonged; the victory of the law of the nation-state over the law of the chiefdom is recent. The British overlords sought to establish the primacy of their authority at the same time as they ruled through intact chieftainships. By establishing courts of appeal higher than the chief and by introducing a High Commissioner who could make law simply by proclaiming it, they brought to the northern Tswana chiefdoms an unprecedented paradox. Without intending to, they affirmed and even enhanced chiefly power, even as they were undermining it.

The early years of this paradoxical relationship—that is, during Khama's reign—were the least tense. The British administration did not have the inclination to employ imperial officers when a few local clerks and police officers could provide a serviceable administration.[17] In 1885 when the protectorate was declared, Khama agreed to allow the Queen's officers to make laws governing only the relations between black and white. He was willing to let whites judge themselves if they left his authority over his own people intact. "I am not baffled in the government of my own town," he stressed in his agreement, "or in deciding cases among my own people according to custom."[18] Khama's firm though elliptical warning must have pleased the imperial envoy, Sir Charles Warren, who advised his government to protect the road to the interior through Khama's country cheaply by leaving the Tswana chiefs to govern "in their own fashion." Others warned that British intervention in quarrels among chiefs and even between chiefs and European "trespassers" would bring only trouble and expense.[19]

For six years this happy state of laissez-faire persisted. Even when the Bechuanaland Protectorate was formally established in 1891, no one troubled to define accurately "the extent of jurisdiction exercisable by Her Majesty over the Natives."[20] The protectorate was governed according to the Roman-Dutch law of the Cape Colony as of 10 June 1891 and by the proclamations of the High Commissioner thereafter. The two Assistant Commissioners were duty bound to find out the opinion of the chiefs and their people on any proposed law, but legislation could be initiated only by protectorate officials. While cautioning that "any native laws or customs" regulating civil relations should be respected, the Order in Council of 1891 establishing British administration gave wide discretionary powers to the High Commissioner. For years he barely used them. There was simply no reason to interfere with law and custom in a backwater with virtually no economic value.

Received laws did proliferate after 1891 in accordance with the bureaucratic imperative to establish orderly, efficient, and dispassionate administration. In 1896, murder cases were removed from the chief's *kgotla* for trial by the Queen's resident officer, in part because murder was often connected to witchcraft, in the eyes of the British an alarming and primitive belief.[21] The next category of legal case was removed from the chief's jurisdiction nearly thirty years later: from 1926 on, a couple who had married under civil law could be divorced only in a magistrate's court. The following year, the practice of witchcraft became a penal offense and only the Resident Magistrate could judge it. A limited number of statutes also restricted the activities of residents of the chiefdoms: Africans were forbidden to cut green wood, for example, and no one, black or white, could buy a shotgun without a permit from a British official. For the most part, such laws simply set a few limits on the jurisdiction of *kgotlas,* and so they failed to disrupt the customary legal process as it was experienced by the mass of the Tswana.

The Bechuanaland chiefs knew, however, that these apparently minor innovations were highly significant. They marked the beginning of the gradual withdrawal of criminal and some civil cases from the jurisdiction of the *kgotla.* They marked the decline of chiefly power. In 1927, the year after Tshekedi had become regent and when he was only twenty-two years old, he and two other Tswana chiefs traveled to Cape Town to express their "anxiety and unrest" and confusion about the legal situation to the High Commissioner, Lord Athlone. "Why take the power from us," Tshekedi asked, to divide property upon the dissolution of Christian marriages? He went on to challenge the Empire's right to interpose itself between the chieftainship and its subjects. Reasserting his own right to collect taxes from all his subjects, including those on freehold farms, he declared "even if a man is outside my Reserve he is still under my control." Tshekedi also objected to the freeing of the Sarwa from servitude, because abolition would circumvent his control of labor relations and the movement of his people. "The only difference [between a Sarwa and a Ngwato] is that [the Sarwa] are under the Bamangwato just as the Bamangwato are under me. So far as the Masarwa are concerned I look upon them as equal but like servants.... if a Masarwa wants to leave his master and the latter objects, I [as chief] would deal with the matter. The Masarwa is entitled to come to me and make enquiries." Aware that British feelings on the issue ran high, Tshekedi was cagey in his remarks. Denying that the Sarwa were slaves, he admitted only that "It would be very foolish on our part if we asked to be allowed to live with slaves." The three chiefs' anxious tones reveal that they correctly perceived their authority to be threatened.

In reply, Athlone pledged his intention to consult the chiefs whenever one of his proclamations would change their customs. He reassured Tshekedi in particular that "no sudden changes" were planned for Sarwa relations though he hoped that "the Masarwa should in due course enjoy the same liberties as the Mangwato and that they should be helped to progress gradually until they reach the same degree of civilization as the Mangwato." Despite having their fears assuaged on these points, the three chiefs could not have been pleased with the High Commissioner's warning, "you should remember that you cannot always remain as children." From this fatherly word of caution, he went on to stress that the protectorate government "proposes in every way to uphold the personal liberty of the native inhabitants of the Reserves" by allowing discontented servants to leave their masters. He also refused to allow the chiefs to try cases involving witchcraft, to divorce a couple married under European law, or to collect taxes in the European or freehold farming blocks of the protectorate. Athlone concluded by expressing the hope, doubtless infuriating to someone with Tshekedi's pride, "The Chiefs will understand from what I have already said that both they and their people are bound to become more and more civilized, until one day they will become more like the Europeans."[22]

At the same time as these limits were imposed on the jurisdiction of *kgotlas,* a new appeal structure was being erected: from 1891, the resident officer could hear appeals from the chief's *kgotla* in very serious cases; from 1919, he would receive appeals from the chief's verdict in any kind of case, hearing them in company with the chief, yet another example of a deeply conservative "reform." And yet the Assistant Commissioner of the Southern Protectorate noted in 1904 that he was "very seldom" called upon to determine any questions of African law and that he heard very few appeals from the chief's court.[23] This pattern undoubtedly held true in the Northern Protectorate as well. Since

The Defense of Patriarchy in the *Kgotla*

few, if any, early administrators appeared to understand the logic of customary law, this tacit agreement was probably all to the good. I have found no evidence that the District Commissioner, or even the High Court, served as a popular court of appeal during the entire colonial period. Given the power of the chief over every aspect of public life in Ngwato, few people were willing to risk incurring his displeasure by appealing over his head. In any case, up to 1940, no Ngwato District Commissioner reversed a *kgotla* decision by declaring its jurisdiction illegal.[24] Such intervention would have incurred profitless costs in time and money. The fiscal conservatism of the British Empire, particularly in such backwaters as the Bechuanaland Protectorate, was entrenching the late nineteenth century indigenous political order.

Those few who did appeal were almost exclusively close relatives already estranged from the chief who had good reason to believe that they and their descendants would always reap chiefly retribution. Hence they had nothing to lose. As Chapter two revealed, the most notorious royalty, the Ratshosas, initiated in 1926 a series of appeals that by 1930 reached, unsuccessfully, all the way to the Privy Council. The Ratshosas were followed closely in notoriety by the Raditladis, who sued Tshekedi for their inheritance in the District Commissioner's court and lost. Like politics, courts of law remained dominated by royalty and their prominent clients.

Because the protectorate's authority derived so emphatically in practice from the chiefs, it is not surprising that the appeals failed. Received law did, however, help to make Ngwato state politics—which were, of course, mainly "palace" intrigues—open to the public and judiciable by a higher, though not impartial, tribunal. On occasion, the higher tribunal could be hostile to the chief, as when the High Commissioner banished Tshekedi for two weeks for ordering the flogging of a white man.[25] The Ratshosa appeals and the flogging undoubtedly contributed to the urgency with which British administrators were preparing to diminish and control chiefly power.

Throughout British Africa by the 1930s imperial officials were trying to anglicize the substance and procedure of African law because they believed in the superiority of their own institutions. As the High Commissioner, Lord Athlone, complained to the Secretary of State for the Dominions, Lord Passfield, in 1930, "we must substitute civilised methods for autocratic rule, and semi-barbaric methods, which have occasionally been practised in the past."[26] Three years later Alan Pim argued, in an extensive command paper on the economy of the impoverished protectorate, that African institutions "should gradually be brought into conformity with the requirements of a civilised Administration resting on a money economy."[27] Lawyers, as well as observers like Pim, alarmed at the economic stagnation of this imperial backwater, had been winning the attention of metropolitan proconsuls away from the local administrators and the missionaries who stressed the importance of preserving African legal agencies and ideas. Some imperial advisers, most notably Lord Hailey, openly hoped that legal innovations sponsored by the British would overcome the resistance of African laws and institutions to the "gradual advance towards individualisation of property in land which may lead to improvement in production."[28] Ideally, modern law would liberate Africans to hold and acquire new forms of wealth. Schapera's *Handbook* fitted well with these efforts to use rules to govern African societies more closely. So did the Natives Tribunal Proclamation and the Natives Administration Proclamation of 1934.[29]

These two proclamations defined the powers of the chiefs for the first time and made their tenure of office subject to the administration's approval. As the chief architect of the proclamations, Resident Commissioner Charles Rey, explained in the first blush of pride in his creation, they were to serve as a model for all British territories in southern Africa.[30] They were designed to provide for direct rule "when the tribal machinery may break down." In drafting the proclamations, he and his fellow administrators had intended to interfere as little as possible with the smooth functioning of Tswana law and custom.[31] The "great guiding principle of indirect rule" was to be maintained. Of course, Rey's assessment of when the political machinery was in fact breaking down was bound to differ profoundly from that of the Tswana chiefs. The Ratshosa case, for example, had in Tshekedi's eyes threatened to damage the chiefdom only after the imperial government had inhibited his own ability to discipline his rivals. In this sense, Rey's proposals were highly political and potentially disruptive, even while he probably believed them to be merely efficient. Rey's simple stipulation that the tribe must be consulted fully before any tribal appointment was made could excite a chief's fears that his enemies would usurp that consultation and depose him.

The Natives Administration Proclamation called for the establishment of a tribal council. The chief would appoint councillors, according to "custom." As Bathoen Gaseitsiwe, former chief of the Ngwaketse, pointed out, the proposal itself transgressed custom, since chiefs had formerly relied on informal access to anyone whose advice they needed, rather than on a formal council. Bathoen, who became an elected member of Parliament after independence in the 1960s, remembers that he and Tshekedi feared dropping lower and lower in the administrative hierarchy, becoming in effect "very subordinate government officials."[32] While their fathers had communicated directly with the High Commissioner, they feared that they would now have to get permission from the District and Resident Commissioners for everything they did. They believed that the master plan was to diminish their powers and then appoint a Native Authority in their stead. Time, Bathoen remarks today, has proven their worst fears correct.[33] Behind their resentment that their powers were being illegally diminished lay the perennial fear of incorporation in South Africa. Tshekedi was particularly alarmed by similarities between the proclamations and the South African Native Administration Proclamation No. 38 of 1927. In 1934 he wrote a cautionary letter to the High Commissioner pointing these similarities out.³⁴ Tshekedi's defense of the powers and privileges of his office was matched by his ardent desire to see Bechuanaland remain free of South Africa.

The Natives Tribunal Proclamation set out to formalize and regularize the administration of justice. Each chiefdom would have a two-tier hierarchy of tribunals below the supreme *kgotla*. The chief would nominate members to the senior tribunal from among members of the tribal council. The senior tribunal would nominate a headman to preside over each of the junior tribunals; and this headman would in turn nominate a headman to act with him in trying cases.³⁵ All would be salaried. Each level was to keep written records of its proceedings. The cases that they were allowed to try were strictly defined, as were the penalties they could impose.

By recognizing these three *kgotla* levels whose decisions were legally binding, the proclamations dealt the harshest blow to the ward courts, not to the chief. Adjudication was being raised above the level where one's family and neighbors could determine the outcome of a dispute. With the ward *kgotlas* supplanted by more aloof administrative courts, government could, in principle, penetrate social relations to new depths of control. In this sense, the British reforms and the opposition to them were equally damaging to the autonomy of households.

Each party saw autocratic tendencies in the other. Bathoen remembers that both he and Tshekedi believed Rey was jealous of their powers. While Tshekedi feared the growth of the Resident Magistrate's local power, Rey had confided to his diary soon after his arrival in October 1929 that the chiefs "practically do as they like—punish, fine, tax and generally play hell. Of course their subjects hate them but daren't complain to us; if they did their lives would be made impossible."³⁶ Both points of view contained some truth.

Still, imperial faces had to be saved. The "protectors" were not above threatening to transfer their recalcitrant wards to the Union of South Africa. In the Serowe *kgotla*, the Resident Magistrate, G. E. Nettelton, angrily harangued all the chief's men for refusing to participate in the scheme, "I have heard much of the chief's loyalty and desire to remain under the British government. I should be sorry to doubt the genuineness of that loyalty or the reality of that desire."[37] His threat, coupled with the recent display of military force by the British navy as it struggled all the way to Serowe to avenge the flogged white man, may have chastened some of his listeners, but they remained unmoved: "we will refuse as a son to a father. We have no thought of fighting against our father, who is bound to listen to his son and explain to him."[38] Rey was infuriated by Tshekedi's act of "insolence and defiance" in writing, over the Resident Commissioner's head, directly to the High Commissioner about the proclamations, and vowed to depose the chief if he continued to oppose them.[39]

The furor provoked by the two decrees was legally resolved only when Tshekedi and Bathoen tried to turn the legal weapon to their own advantage.[40] In 1936, in the Special Court at Lobatse, the two young chiefs sued the High Commissioner for unlawfully altering Tswana law and custom; they lost. During the course of the trial, Tshekedi and Bathoen proved conclusively that there was no legislative or practical precedent for this interference with their powers; that is, the proclamations contravened Colonial Secretary Joseph Chamberlain's promise in 1895 that colonial rule should closely follow the traditional system of government. The presiding judge, Justice E. P. Watermeyer, had had to look elsewhere to prove the extent of the Crown's sovereignty inside the protectorate. He found the proof in the Foreign Jurisdiction Act of 1890,[41] an act that effectively gave the Secretary of State for Dominion Affairs the power to determine questions of the Crown's jurisdiction in a foreign country. Not surprisingly, the secretary of state, Malcolm MacDonald, advised against Tshekedi and Bathoen: His Majesty's powers to legislate and to administer justice were not limited by treaty or agreement.

The administration's victory was symbolic. Although the

proclamations remained, Tshekedi did not enforce all parts of them, and he was not punished for his sins. A Ngwato praise poet celebrated his victory,[42]

> When the tribes were gathered yonder,
> and all the chiefs went to be shaved,
> ours, he was not shaved,
> ours did not have his hair cut,
> Tshekedi it is who stays as he was.

No one found the proclamations workable, but they could not be annulled because they had already become law. According to Bathoen, a compromise was reached privately. After discussions including the new, conciliatory Resident Commissioner, Charles Arden-Clarke, and the two chiefs, a new proclamation was issued in 1943 based on both the 1934 version and "custom": although the European District Magistrate gained the power to revise the *kgotla*'s decisions, the list of offenses beyond the *kgotla*'s jurisdiction was radically pared down, and the composition of the tribunals and councils was not specified.[43] The compromise was finally achieved by vagueness, allowing each party to appear to have won.

Two elements of imperial logic are immediately clear. Protectorate officials had wanted to forestall all opportunities for the chiefs to provoke conflicts with which imperial authority would eventually have to deal. This logic is apparent in the proclamation clauses that excluded from chiefly review any cases involving treason or sedition, the corporal punishment of women, banishment, forcible removal from the lands, hut burning, and so on. Many of these prohibitions can be seen to refer to a past cause célèbre such as the Ratshosa case; others were clearly intended to prevent similar crises in the future. One further premise animated the reforms. Customary law was to be made irrevocably subordinate to and separate from received or imposed law: no *kgotla* could decide a case involving a civil marriage or willed inheritance: sentences had to be reported to the Resident Magistrate and on occasion approved by higher officials. If customary law was seen to be "incompatible with the due exercise of His

The Defense of Patriarchy in the *Kgotla*   117

Majesty's power and jurisdiction or repugnant to morality, humanity or natural justice or injurious to the welfare of the natives," it ceased to be law.[44] The law of the nation-state, though not yet dominant, was clearly ascendant.

While British overrule acted as one clear catalyst of legal change in the twentieth century, another less visible factor was changing the relationship of Tswana people to government and to each other. This second catalyst was labor migration. At the same time that chiefs worried about the eclipse of their monopoly of formal political life, they were disquieted by changes brought to their societies by the absence of many wage-earning men. They feared that migration would decrease birth and marriage rates and, by driving women to town in search of money to buy food, would pollute the morals of the rising generation.[45] Young miners who returned home did not, they believed, care for tribal work or pay their chiefs sufficient respect: "[i]f this is allowed to go on," Chief Kgari of the Bakwena warned, "the tribe will gradually die."[46] Some of the people they governed were similarly concerned about the new freedoms wage labor abroad afforded, especially to younger men and women. Jobs on the Rand offered them the means to escape their duties to their households, wards, and even to the chiefdom itself; "they neglect all tribal laws because they say they are men of themselves and can earn their own living."[47] The process that scholars call proletarianization was popularly experienced as a new wave of individual irresponsibility.

Migration brought into the *kgotla* an increased caseload at the same time that it allowed certain of the parties involved to slip away from the *kgotla*'s jurisdiction. The social debits of labor migration were many. It brought about desertion from cattle posts and the abandonment of families. It spread tuberculosis. Migrants and their wives frequently accused and counteraccused each other of adultery. A returned migrant often found that his property had been squandered while he was abroad. The absence of able-bodied young men ate into the effectiveness of the regiments as they were ordered to perform public works. A mine labor contract under a false name or the simple and illicit expedient of crossing the Transvaal border to find work on one's own provided a neat way of avoiding the payment of fines as well as of taxes. Pay was so low that, according to Tshekedi's hyperbole, "not one of them . . . returns from the mine with anything. The money that they earn at the mines is spent in food."[48] Some migrants remitted too little money to their families to compensate for their absence. Kin phrased their quarrels increasingly in terms of money.

In time, these debits would translate into profound threats to the stated values of the patriarchy. Because the workplace functioned outside chiefly control, the *kgotla* would become a forum where only some of the affairs of a person's life would be negotiated. Wealth and power would be acquired by social juniors independently of their patrons. Collective responsibility would be riven by an individual's freedom to move beyond the chiefdom and acquire property on his own. Old men would lose control over young men, and men would lose control over women. The chief was not the only one who would come to lament the passing of a social order. The entire gerontocratic hierarchy would come under threat. The lessons of respect for and domination by older men, taught during initiation, would bear less and less relevance to daily life in which junior people could independently acquire and hold property.

Martin Chanock has recently argued that African customary law was created and enforced in response to such gender and generational conflicts. Africans created rules in response to the subversion of patriarchal hierarchies by colonial capitalism and to the permeation of social relationships by money. This process was more advanced in Central Africa, the focus of Chanock's study, than in the Bechuanaland Protectorate. In northern Tswana societies, the land was too arid to support the development of commercial agriculture. And so most farmers did not need to intensify their control of agricultural laborers such as wives, children, or hereditary servants. Nevertheless, the Central African and Bechuanaland cases are located on the same continuum.

After the introduction of colonial legal codes and courts, customary law evolved throughout the region as a product of the interaction between African interests, "the western legal form, the colonial state, and its economy."[49]

Although labor migration dissolved social bonds, chiefs and others hoped that it would also bring into their chiefdoms money that, when taxed, could fund projects for developing a strong state, one independent from South Africa. For this reason, chiefs were ambivalent toward it; rather than try to prohibit migration, they tried to control it, setting limits to the numbers of young men who could be recruited each month by the Native Recruiting Corporation (N.R.C.), prohibiting the migration of women, and requiring the N.R.C. recruiter to obtain a headman's written permission before putting a young man on the train for Johannesburg. Labor migration did extend one boon to the dispute-settlement process. It allowed hitherto penniless thieves to be fined so that their victims could be compensated. If a man had no property, the chief had the authority to send him to the local labor recruiter and to attach a portion of his wages. Tshekedi even used recruitment for the African Auxiliary Pioneer Corps during the Second World War for this purpose. In these ways, he and other chiefs sought to turn all effects of labor migration to their advantage. And yet, for some of the same reasons as in the nineteenth century—the vastness of the thinly populated landscape, the lack of a standing army or police force—the chiefs failed to control the movements of their people.

The greatest debit of all from the standpoint of economic development was the low wages paid to black laborers in South Africa; migrants could purchase no capital equipment to improve agricultural productivity. The chief was the first and for a long time the only person in his polity who could afford to buy a tractor, sink a borehole, or "breed up" his herds with imported stock. The mass of migrants carted home blankets and clothes in their tin trunks.[50] If they were thrifty, they could afford to buy a beast.

Unreliable markets and low prices further inhibited the development of cash cropping and commercial ranching. Bechuanaland cattle were effectively closed out of Rand markets between 1924 and 1941, and the open periods between those dates were so few and brief that they hardly inspired confidence among marginal ranchers. Again, only the chief and about thirty of his men, the sons of his close relatives or lesser chiefs, traded cattle on the Johannesburg market with any frequency.[51] Only the chief contracted independently with traders to send large shipments of cattle down to the gold mines on the Rand.

Although the chief alone could be called a commercial rancher during the colonial period, his fortunes too suffered from the boom and far longer bust cycles that buffeted the export trade of the eastern Kalahari after it began to send ivory tusks to the Cape in the 1840s. Demand for all Tswana produce fluctuated with South Africa's prosperity and, in addition, the level of remuneration was often artificially low. Throughout the history of their participation in long-distance trade, the Tswana chiefdoms had exported raw material drawn from the veld—ivory, hides, cattle. After gold and diamond mining began in South Africa at the end of the nineteenth century, men went across the border in much the same way. They also were in a sense extracted from the veld. Their low wages were determined by the unfree labor market on which the mines' prosperity was founded. Behind them, the migrants left only wives and older relatives to till fields and look after cattle in their absence. As the domestic labor force shrank, so did the size of cultivated fields, and the chiefdoms became net importers of food.

The effects of the reforming decrees by "tribal innovators" can be assessed only against the background of this stagnation in productive relationships. Apart from the chief's efforts, there was little local capital accumulation and investment. Land remained communal. Only a handful of wage-labor jobs were created within the chiefdoms.[52] Patron-client relations remained the dominant form of social and productive investment.

The legal innovations carried out by Tshekedi occurred within the context of procedural and social transformations brought about by labor migration and British overrule. To fully divine the effects and origins of his innovations, it is necessary also to understand the political rivalries inside the chiefdom. Influence exerted by political interests over dispute settlement is easiest to trace in cases concerning royalty. Although factional allegiance shaped commoners' disputes, too, there is no way now to recapture the identity and nature of these factions. Because royalty protested loudly to protectorate officials whenever their "traditional" prerogatives were denied, splendid records of their grievances do exist. So, too, are there records of how customary law was manipulated by the chiefs to their own disadvantage. Both sets of cases illustrate vividly the divergence between the ideal principles of Tswana law, as recorded by Schapera in his *Handbook,* and its practice.

Nineteenth century legislative innovations derived in part from the imperatives of maintaining power in the highly competitive indigenous political arena. The same was true of Tshekedi's twentieth century regency. He did not, as his father had done, explicitly make many new laws. He did use the occasion of settling royal disputes in the *kgotla* to reassert the primacy of his own authority and cripple his opponents. Less explicitly, but just as emphatically, he too was creating customary law. This process is particularly clear in cases involving the definition of rank.

The principle of "seniority" was supposed to govern dynastic rivalry. In fact, the winner of a contest for power usually won acclaim as the highest in authority and first in precedence as a result of his victory. The definition and rewards of seniority may be seen to have varied according to the relative strength and purposes of the powers in conflict, as in a 1939 case, when the District Commissioner—"*mokgotla la* England"—heard an appeal case from the supreme *kgotla*. It was a rare event.[53]

Such an appeal usually concerned royalty, since royalty alone publicly rejected a chief's authority or, as Tshekedi penned in the *Handbook*'s margins, "History reveals that any tribal feud is always headed by a 'Kgosana' [royal family member] claiming a position in some form or another."[54] The circumstances of this case were not, however, peculiar to royalty; they could occur whenever a man had married two women but only one of them according to Christian rites. In such an event, which one was the senior or legitimate wife? And whose children were to receive the lion's share of their father's inheritance?

The family in question were descendants of Khama's rebellious younger brother, Raditladi, and of the two marriages of Raditladi's eldest son, Disang. The brothers' rivalry had continued into the next generation and into the twentieth century. (Tshekedi, as noted earlier, believed that one of Disang's sons, Leetile, had had an affair with his wife.) When Disang died in 1939, he left seven children by two wives and also substantial debts with Serowe traders. Because his estate—155 cattle—was only slightly larger than the sum of his debts, Tshekedi took it upon himself to pay the debts and to allocate the few remaining beasts exclusively to the children of the first wife, even though Disang had divorced her and had not, in any case, married her in the Christian church. The loser was MmaLeetile, the second wife or, as she called herself, "Disang's proper wife, he married me according to law." MmaLeetile was the sister of the three Ratshosa brothers, two of whom had wounded Tshekedi in the *kgotla* shoot-out in 1926; her heritage was no doubt a crucial factor in turning Tshekedi against her children. She also bore the stigma of having been the preferred wife of a man who had troubled Tshekedi by communicating grievances against chiefly rule to William Ballinger during Ballinger's 1930 visit to the Ngwato chiefdom and who had supported the government's legal and administrative reforms in 1934.

In principle, Tshekedi was aiming to redress Disang's extravagant "favoritism" of his younger children by designating Oonetse, the eldest, as his heir. Thus, he disregarded a letter Disang had written dividing the estate. Tshekedi justified his act, not surprisingly, in the name of "native custom," arguing that Disang did not write the letter in the presence of his eldest son or of his brothers. He further justified his allocation of some cattle, contrary to custom, to the second son of the first wife, by explaining that Disang had ignored his command, issued in a past *kgotla* case, to take care of this younger son, and "as my judgment has been ignored," he felt he must enforce it after Disang's death. Because there was a dispute, Tshekedi claimed that he was acting within his rights by intervening in the division of the estate.

Disang's brothers, Lebang and Keletlhokile, protested when Tshekedi sold the cattle and paid the debts: "This is not native custom. It has never been done by any Chief before him." Customarily, Lebang swore to the District Commissioner, the eldest surviving brother—that is, him—would have sold the estate and paid the debts, and only if he failed would he have called in the chief. Instead, "I was treated as though I had no authority and was a herd boy." Keletlhokile, the first Ngwato ordained as a London Missionary Society minister, complained further, "It is not Setswana custom that the children of another woman could inherit the property [two huts] belonging to another house." Strictly speaking, Keletlhokile was right. And yet no one was abiding by custom. This amorphous body of precedent suggested that it was Lebang who should direct the disposition of the estate if all the children were minors, which they were not, and also that the eldest son of the great wife should succeed to his father's status.[55] With the replacement of polygamy by Christian marriage, no authority clearly redefined the concept of "great wife." Schapera's *Handbook* does not address the issue. The District Commissioner, admittedly eager to avoid prolonging a dispute riven with such ill-feeling, confirmed all of Tshekedi's major rulings and dismissed the appeal.[56]

Into the breach between customary and received law the chief had slipped, affirming the primacy of his own authority. In so doing, he also, virtually by coincidence, affirmed the principle of seniority. Under the system of indirect rule, the *kgotla* served as a conservative political forum, defending relations in the language of custom and inherited status while giving the victory to those who held political power. Tshekedi's legal creations were shaped by both his public and his self-interest. His success in enforcing these fiats was determined by his imperial backing, the state of the regional economy, and the extent to which his people could be made to obey.

Law and the Management of Social Change

At the same time that the Serowe *kgotla* was a highly political stage where royal rivals fought and were publicly exalted or disarmed it was also a universally respected forum where Tswana values were advertised. If one attempts to disentangle the ideological from the more practical political lessons one is left with a set of principles safeguarding the patriarchy: the fundamental unit of discipline and accountability was the family group or ward; the power exercised by the chief and delegated by him to his subordinates was supreme; the *kgotla* was the sole legitimate public forum; the seniors by age and rank commanded respect and deference. These four principles were so deeply imbedded in Tswana life that people never explicitly rejected them, whatever their actions might signify.

The principle of collective responsibility emerges in case after case. A man's wardmates or members of his family group shared with him responsibility for his misdemeanors. They were liable to be fined or publicly rebuked if they failed to remind him of his communal obligations. An individual could not independently decide to marry or divorce, seek work, sell cattle he had not earned, reallocate his land, or abandon his ward. If he did so, he would be reprimanded when the case was brought to the *kgotla*. The head of the family group might even be fined for failing to control its members. A headman could be made to pay the taxes of defaulting residents of his ward. The *kgotla* could caution a man not to reject his wife without consulting both his ward and his wife's parents. It could fine a man's male relatives for failing to take to the hospital a wife he had beaten.[57] Each such case brought home the lesson that a person could not act unilaterally to sever or damage the relationships constituting his immediate social space.

The Defense of Patriarchy in the *Kgotla*   125

Respect for the *kgotla* as the basic unit of public authority was a lesson the dispute-settlement process sometimes taught quite didactically. Proper decorum was carefully guarded by rules forbidding insults and swearing. Anyone who indulged in abusive language was effectively abusing the judge and should be reported to the chief or fined.[58] Taking the law into one's own hands also won a public rebuke. A woman might decide to punish her neighbor by taking from him a beast that had trampled her crops. The *kgotla* would tell her to return the beast and criticize her for usurping its authority.[59] Similarly, a man might refuse to pay a fine because he rejected his conviction for slander. The *kgotla* would chastise him for his obstinacy and his failure to choose the proper mode of appeal, and he would be told to pay.[60] Respect for rank was, sometimes quite pointedly, taught in the *kgotla*. A man might be fined a cow for being "rude, insolent and disrespectful" to his seniors.[61]

The didactic function of the *kgotla* was achieved by punishment as well as by publicity. Tshekedi, for example, was known to be a "very severe" judge who failed to graduate fines according to a person's wealth.[62] During moments of crisis in the chiefdom, discontented people would publicly voice their resentment at fines imposed unfairly and for political reasons in the past. These moments were also times when more punitive fines were likely to be imposed. Tshekedi abused the power to fine most flagrantly when he told K. T. Motsete, the bachelor of divinity recently returned from London, who had insulted him in the *kgotla*, to pay twenty-five cattle for a seduction committed eleven years before. Such fines earned Tshekedi the reputation of discriminating unjustly against the educated, even though he had argued in the *Handbook*'s margins that teachers and the educated were treated with *very* great respect by all his people, including the older and more conservative members of the chiefdom.[63]

While the *kgotla* reaffirmed inherited values by lesson and by penalty, it also selectively adapted them to the circumstances of modern life on the Rand's periphery. It was, after all, the right of the patriarch to modify the patriarchal order so that its core principles and institutions would endure. Two of the most significant innovations of the colonial era—the grant of civil liberties to women and to hereditary servants, and the privatization of property—were so affected.[64]

The liberties granted to women and to hereditary servants in the twentieth century were not gifts but practical measures. The wealth of the chiefdoms was no longer as dependent on the labor of either group as cultivators and herders, respectively, as it had been in the nineteenth century. With the rise of wage labor, and with the subsistence and wealth of many families now dependent on the money remitted by male migrants, it was no longer so necessary to control those workers who were beyond the pale of rank.

Although women remained jural minors, from the 1880s on they began to gain new rights. Khama decreed that women were now to share in their fathers' wealth. Men were to give cattle to their daughters on marriage, and also to bequeath cattle to their unmarried daughters. Perhaps a decade later, Khama reversed a prohibition against women appearing independently in his *kgotla*. He ruled further that an abandoned wife became entitled to heavy compensation if she had not provoked her plight. One innovation stood opposed to these gains. No woman or girl could leave the Ngwato territory by rail without the chief's permission, a constraint that, unlike the liberal reforms, was easy to enforce. The Ngwato chiefs stationed representatives at railway sidings to prevent women eager to earn money in Johannesburg, but without passes, from boarding the trains. Tshekedi bristled when people interpreted these restrictions to mean that Tswana women were oppressed. In the *Handbook*'s margins he wrote, a woman "is entitled to full consideration in the management of her home and it is not uncommon, in a dispute arising in a household, to hear the expression 'lelwapa ke lame' *i.e.* I have full powers in matters pertaining to the household." Besides, he noted ironically, "the general inferiority of women to men . . . [exists] even amongst civilized people."[65]

The Defense of Patriarchy in the *Kgotla*   127

In the realm of public authority, however, there was no place for women despite the civil libertarian reforms. Until the early 1950s, women could not attend *pitsos,* the assemblies in the chief's *kgotla* to discuss matters of pressing public importance, although many expressed the wish to do so by at least the 1940s. No tribunal member was female. In principle, a royal woman was considered a possible regent if there were no senior royal male to push forward as a candidate against a despised contender, but in fact no woman ever did serve as regent.

Even if some royal women had been able to gain places in the public councils, it is improbable that other women would have benefited. Women simply enjoyed no economic independence from men. An unmarried woman could be given her own plowing field by her father, but it reverted to him on her marriage, when she left to plow land allotted to her husband.[66] A woman who had acquired her own cattle—usually a gift from her father—kept them at her husband's cattle post and needed his permission and help to sell them. She would give part of the proceeds from their sale to him. Before Khama's reign, widows and daughters inherited nothing. Khama's encouragement of female inheritance could be molded later, like all chiefly rulings, to the political crisis of the moment, and so, during the 1939 episode of the Raditladi dispute, Tshekedi interpreted his father's dictum to mean that female inheritance was a gift, not a right.[67]

Though Khama had ruled that women could bring disputes to the *kgotla* and speak there in their own defense and as witnesses, as legal minors they were subject to the control of father, husband, or brother. Were women disadvantaged during the dispute-settlement process? On the contrary, the judicial process often operated as their protector, even while it did not grant them legal independence. If a woman's brother tried to eject a woman from their father's cattle post or if her uncles robbed her of her own animals, the *kgotla* would step in and affirm her rights to own and inherit property and to share the family's resources. Even in divorce proceedings, the *kgotla* did not necessarily favor men. If a man left his wife to live with another woman, she could report the matter to the *kgotla,* and both the concubine's ward and his parents' ward could be fined for encouraging or allowing his desertion.[68] A deserted wife might be given all of her husband's property. A neglectful or abusive husband, especially one who was believed capable of inflicting bodily harm, could lose his wife, just as a woman who deserted her husband could be told to leave the marriage, losing all her belongings in the process.

In short, the quality of a person's performance of domestic duties had greater influence over the settlement of disputes than did gender. Since women had no corporate existence, their welfare could not be dissociated from the family unit to which they belonged. When the unit failed to provide for their subsistence and to protect them from bodily harm, the *kgotla* ideally stepped in as protector. Women were treated like children, as in need of paternal protection.

The following case can easily be read as a story of the failure of the *kgotla* at the ward and family levels to intervene quickly between a violent husband and his wife.[69] The delay was caused, however, not by the defense of the husband but by the defense of the institution of marriage. In 1940 Tshekedi heard the story of the violent marriage of Ramasimo and his wife Sekgarametso. For years, Ramasimo had assaulted his wife daily, even during her pregnancy. His brutality was so widely known that his own ward pointed out the "worthlessness of their . . . son." Sekgarametso's family was said to want the case heard by Tshekedi "so that if you [Ramasimo] kill her, [the cause] will be known." This apparently callous expression probably cloaked the family's hope that the chief would indeed grant a divorce. Neither family group wished to usurp chiefly authority by explicitly requesting or favoring an end to the marriage. They simply laid the details before the chief. Although the *kgotla* authorities were reluctant to violate the institution of marriage by readily dissolving it, unreformed brutality could provoke the grant of a divorce. None of this woman's faults—for example, staying in the village to brew beer rather than moving to the lands to plow, refusing her husband's gift of a shawl, swearing before her parents-in-law—mitigated her right of self-preservation, though each of these misdemeanors did win mild rebuke from the tribunal members. The case was, in short, one in which it was impossible even for the husband's family to argue for the maintenance of the marriage. Tshekedi, therefore, allowed Sekgarametso to return to her parental home.

The Sekgarametso case offers a stark contrast to another in which Tshekedi refused to allow a couple to separate; the wife's father had explicitly challenged chiefly power by unilaterally withdrawing her from the marriage, saying elliptically that he feared only the chief and thunder. Tshekedi punished him by preserving the marriage.[70] Even cases like this one among insignificant commoners could be charged with high political tension and import.

The question of the legal status of women was rarely explicitly addressed during the period from 1937 to 1950. I have found only one case of this nature, when in 1940 the chief of a regional court, Phethu Mphoeng of Madinare, declared, "We now judge according to the decisions of Chief Khama [III], . . . those of Sekgoma [I, Khama's father] are out of date,"[71] as he proceeded to allow a widow to separate her residence and her inherited property from those of her husband's younger brother. Formerly, the brother would have been responsible for her, but the relations between them had deteriorated to the point of witchcraft accusations. One observer warned, "Personally I think that sort of thing would corrupt all women, if the chief gave Nchaben [the widow] cattle." Nevertheless, the chief decided that their animosity demanded a separation.

The *kgotla* system upheld male supremacy less by treating men more generously than women, than by insisting, as in the case of Sekgarametso, that the family group or ward was the fundamental unit of social justice. It continued to extoll ward responsibility and unity even while the ward was being drained by labor migration and thus becoming less able to protect women from neglect and desertion. The 1940s saw a dramatic increase in the rate of labor migration, eventually changing the shape of

Ngwato settlement and Ngwato production. Women not only had to take over male tasks such as plowing, but they also had to cope with the consequences of the fact that wage employment was available almost exclusively to men. Their economic dependence on men increased at the same time as the likelihood that they would be deserted by the men whose children they bore.

In addition to partial reforms in gender relations, so limited in effect, the patriarchal order was further adapted, in principle, to changing times when the chief decreed new liberties for the hereditary servants of the chiefdom. Khama first included them in a grant of civil liberties and partial citizenship in the late 1870s by decreeing that Sarwa were not to be bought, sold, or transferred from one man to another. Around 1900 he abolished their compulsory payment of tribute and allowed them to acquire and keep their own property. These grants were partly a matter of convenience. Khama argued, for example, that the *kgotla* could at least collect damages from a Sarwa criminal who owned stock.

The role played by the *kgotla* in enforcing legal innovations becomes clearer when we learn what kind of cases the *kgotla* tended not to hear. Within my sample, only one case explicitly concerns a Sarwa. Of course, it is not clear which figures in other cases may have had Sarwa ancestry; given the general use of the term to describe peoples of the veld, that ancestry cannot always be rigorously defined. We can be concerned here only with people publicly labeled as vassals. What does the paucity of cases concerning these hereditary servants reveal about the dispute-settlement process?

Vast expanses of land separated the cattle posts, where most vassals lived, from the wards in Serowe to which each post was attached. In the hinterland, hereditary servants enjoyed a certain liberty to steal cattle if undetected, but they could also become victims of frontier justice. In 1935, one chiefly client burned a Sarwa settlement that harbored, so he believed, the thieves of his cattle. The incident was publicized only because the assistant District Commissioner happened to come upon the burned re-

The Defense of Patriarchy in the *Kgotla*   131

mains of the village.⁷² A century of legal inequality had undoubtedly inhibited the Sarwa's confidence that the *kgotla* would give them an equal hearing. Tshekedi swore that he never turned a Sarwa away from his *kgotla*, but lesser chiefs were known to spurn Sarwa coming with grievances. By the mid-1940s, Sarwa were at least beginning to be integrated into the *kgotla* system at its highest level.⁷³

The case of Bakgomohi, a headman in Kgalagadi district, where he had been put in charge of Tshekedi's cattle, illustrates the slow entry of the Sarwa into the mainstream of Ngwato society. Bakgomohi had recently moved his family group near one cattle post where Baitshenyetsi, a Sarwa, was employed as a herder. Soon afterward, in 1944, Bakgomohi contravened the order of a senior headman by telling Baitshenyetsi that he had no right to cultivate by hoe, and so the Ngwato headman took the field and its corn as his own and destroyed Baitshenyetsi's melons. Tshekedi reaffirmed the Sarwa's right to plow, and he reprimanded Bakgomohi for his greed but did not punish him or withdraw from him his positions of authority. Since no one defended Bakgomohi's action in the *kgotla*, it would appear that the case was heard to advertise publicly the Sarwa's rights. Tshekedi also used the incident to chastise a greater client for abusing his power over a lesser client and for, in effect, demeaning chiefly authority. One cannot assume, therefore, based on this slim evidence of Sarwa participation in the *kgotla*, that veld people had equal access to a fair hearing.

A third liberating measure introduced by Khama concerned property. Khama ruled that daughters and wives could inherit property from their household head, but thereafter the *kgotla* was the site of no further innovations regarding either property devolution or the definition of private property. I suspect that these innovations were articulated exclusively in the magistrate's court in the course of dissolving civil marriages or of dividing a willed estate.

The chief was more likely than the magistrate to manage property for explicitly political purposes. The fate of Disang Raditladi's estate in 1939 illustrates the extent to which individual property could still be subsumed within communal property when it served a chief's interests. Tshekedi ordered that all of Disang's belongings be requisitioned, including his wife's and children's personal property—their cattle, wagons, horses, and gun. All these goods were sold to pay debts incurred by Disang. The chief was investing the right of ownership exclusively in the household head because it was politically convenient to do so.

In the less exalted ranks of Ngwato society, the *kgotla* played no role in redefining wealth as the property of the individual who had earned it.[74] Cases explicitly concerning ownership were rarely brought to the *kgotla* under that guise. Disputes about property were considered to be disputes between people about the rights and duties of their relationships. The customary principles governing the allocation of property remained for the most part unchallenged, and debate centered, rather, on who was the senior son and which marriage was legal, issues that provided the framework for most property disputes. Occasionally an unprecedented dilemma would arise but its resolution was framed strictly in customary terms. For example, following the Second World War, the relatives of deceased soldiers had to decide who should receive their military pay. In one case, a dispute arose because the soldier's widow had left his family group and returned to her own people. Should she receive the money? The *kgotla* ruled that since she had behaved as if she were divorced, she had no claim to the pay.[75] Social relations determined rights to property.

Except in politically charged cases, the *kgotla* did not play an active role in the privatization of property, and the process itself did not enter public discourse at all. Neither did the contraction of patronage excite any ideological stands. Tshekedi frankly admitted that because modern subjects gave fewer gifts to their chiefs, "young chiefs today do not provide for their subjects as the old chiefs did," and no one explicitly challenged him.[76] Why was the *kgotla* silent on these immensely important issues? Why did law come first to persons and only later to property? The less wealthy were more likely to accuse individuals whose generosity failed to live up to their expectations than to blame a process. In any event, modern times had given even the poor the means of acquiring their own property; they could try to redress with wage labor abroad any material suffering caused by the waning of patronage. Nor was it in the interests of those who were acquiring private property to bemoan a process that was benefiting them. Most important, the process of exclusion was occurring in a piecemeal and gradual manner. Despite the hopes of imperial advisers like Lord Hailey, people had not lost their land to private ownership. Neither had they lost their herds to stock restrictions imposed by a state unresponsive to their needs. They knew both these processes far too well. They could see them happening just over the border. The two issues of land loss and taxation rather than more abstract ones relating to property were the great galvanizers of articulate and anguished protest against changing times.

As Tshekedi penned his thoughts on the blank pages and margins of Schapera's *Handbook* in 1938 and, more importantly, as he decided cases in the *kgotla,* he was indeed creating custom, although he undoubtedly did not perceive his role in those terms. Nor was he the only inventor of Tswana tradition. The process of inventing tradition had been going on at least since the late nineteenth century and was simply continuing in Tshekedi's *kgotla.* As the chief's wealth and power had grown, so had his jurisdiction over his people's disputes. In the twentieth century, the British protectors struggled to modify local legal procedure by bringing it into line with their own formal and centralized legal institutions. Tshekedi, like other Tswana paramounts, was encouraged to revamp stated norms by introducing and enforcing civil libertarian decrees.

Tshekedi achieved his most stunning successes on two fronts, most notably, managing to marginalize his dynastic rivals and denying them any inherited role in the administration of the chiefdom—a right which "does not exist and never did" as he wrote in the *Handbook*'s margins.[77] Second, he kept alive the communal idiom. He gave his people a sense of continuity and control. Still, Tshekedi enjoyed greater success in advertising and, to a certain extent, in enforcing patriarchal values than he did in controlling and managing broad social change.

The economic preconditions for fulfilling the civil libertarian aspects of the indigenous and British protectors' reforms did not exist. Subordinate groups—particularly women and hereditary servants—remained economic dependents. Few wage-labor relationships developed locally, and most people did not produce a surplus for sale. Some men and a few women tried to free themselves from the binds of their inherited status by becoming labor migrants, but their wages in South Africa were too low to allow them to achieve any enduring independence. Thus patron-client relations persisted, and so did the related ideology of seniority, justifying privilege by age and rank.

While status relations were being defended and reformulated, contract relations, mainly among the privileged, were just beginning to evolve.[78] Clearly, before the Second World War South African industrial development had wrought transformations within its periphery that were too limited to shift social relations within Tswana chiefdoms from ones based on status to ones based on contract. Generations of legal scholars have handed down this paradigm, from status to contract, as exemplifying the great transition from precapitalist to capitalist society.[79] The Ngwato case represented a mixture of the qualities often depicted as representing the poles of the two social orders: siblings cooperated *and* competed; fundamental social value was given both to honor *and* to control over economic resources; people felt loyalty to their nuclear *as well as* to their extended families; and some social relations remained flexible while others were becoming more rigidly defined by codes of law or chiefly judgments. Polar attributes are inadequate to describe these relations on the periphery of a recent industrial revolution.

While it continued to be revered as the sole legitimate political forum, the *kgotla* was in the process of becoming a partial legal system. It was unable to address grievances among absent wage laborers, and it was silent on issues of private property. The twentieth-century Tswana legal process, like so many amalgam systems, based on both "traditional" and "received" or foreign procedures and norms, provided no constraints on the aggrandizement of wealth and power by a few. Civil libertarian decrees rested largely on the plane of rhetoric as the old political elite grew rich in new ways. Before long, the contradiction between collective and hierarchical rhetoric, on the one hand, and individual endeavor, on the other, would throw into question the legitimacy of the chieftainship itself.

Chapter Four

"Lesser Breeds without the Law"
Subject Peoples and the Ngwato State, 1920-1948

Lesepa legolo lamoeng, lepitikwa ke dikhukhwane. (A stranger's excrement is great, a citizen's is rolled away by the beetles.)
Tswana proverb

Tshekedi Khama, struggling to give birth to a modern state, was bedeviled by his backlands. He spent his entire regency trying to transform a loosely defined polity of formerly tribute-paying peoples into a state populated by obedient taxpayers. Around the turn of the century, Tshekedi's father, Khama III, had begun the long and arduous process by converting tribute into tax and encouraging the small scattered villages of his domain to settle more closely together. Like the other Tswana paramount chiefs, Tshekedi also followed the imperatives of indirect rule and the logic of his father's efforts to create a prosperous state, one independent from South Africa, by imposing ad hoc levies on his subjects. In addition, he doubled the number of his representatives in the hinterland.

In the process of introducing more expensive controlling government, Tshekedi provoked his subjects, especially those he called "subordinate tribes," to defend themselves.[1] Some tried to do so by making themselves into communities worthy of self-determination and imperial respect. Marshaling and manufacturing historical and legal precedent with varying degrees of success, they attempted to convince their British overlords of their right to exercise, or to be free of, subimperial domination. They tried to make themselves into tribes. One nearly succeeded.

Throughout colonial Africa, governors and governed worked to propagate the myth that the fundamental unit of African social and political organization was the tribe.[2] That belief happily allowed colonial administrators to govern cheaply and efficiently through so-called tribal leaders. Precisely who was a tribal leader and what was a tribe constituted unwelcome dilemmas. The governed threw up a variety of candidates as well as a variety of tribes for them to lead.

People were redefining their ethnic identities as weapons of resistance against closer, more controlling, government. They were not, of course, creating their twentieth century identities ex nihilo. Ethnic differences—of language, settlement patterns, custom—had always existed; only in the twentieth century did subject peoples begin to use these differences to frame demands for independence. Seeking British imperial recognition, they rallied under the banner of separate ethnic identity to defend themselves against coercion and new forms of poverty—landlessness, high taxation with few visible rewards, local unemployment, and the low wages earned by labor migrants. Seeking political power for themselves, ethnic politicians tried to acquire and manipulate churches, schools, and lawyers to plead their case. To the exasperation of colonial administrators, imported institutions were once again turned to the service of indigenous political interests. Did these "tribes" contribute in any way to the patriarchy's twilight years?

Unlike the other great Tswana chiefdoms of eastern Bechuanaland, that of the Ngwato contained subjects with widely diverse ethnic backgrounds.[3] The dominant Ngwato "clan," or those claiming a common descent from the founder ancestor, was a minority group.[4] In 1946 the clan comprised only 18 percent of the population of the Ngwato chiefdom, or tribe, as it was called in colonial times.[5] Outnumbered by the Kalanga of the northeast, they were the second largest ethnic group in the chiefdom bearing their name. The BaNgwato lived almost exclusively in

Serowe, though some Ngwato wards had been sent out to become part of large regional settlements, usually to support one of their members who had been appointed to serve there as the chief's representative.[6] The distinctions between the Ngwato clan and its subject peoples were in no way rigid. A group of newcomers was integrated into the capital by being made part of an already existing ward or being allowed to found one on its own. A talented and loyal "foreigner"—that is, one who could not trace his ancestry to the Ngwato clan—might rise to become the chief's right-hand man. If a foreigner adopted the Tswana language or married a Ngwato, his children could, in time, become known simply as Bamangwato or citizens of the chiefdom.

Throughout Tswana history, subject peoples rarely rebelled. Isaac Schapera tabulated 107 major internal disputes occurring in all eight Tswana chiefdoms between 1750 and 1945 and discovered that only 14 of them explicitly concerned a subject community.[7] Praise poets, those partisan Tswana historians, have preserved memories of numerous dynastic disputes and few disloyal acts of subject peoples. They spoke of a "lion," or chief, quarreling with an "elephant," his brother, more often than they spoke of the "children," or followers, of a rebel chief being made to weep. Rebellions occurred in the hinterland far less frequently than rebellions in the capital village because Ngwato overrule was essentially weak or sporadic. Without a standing army, the Ngwato chief was unable to acquire or rule distant peoples with a massive display of military force.

The openness and fluidity of identity stemmed from the economic independence of the two categories of peoples—Ngwato and foreigner—from one another. The wealth of Ngwato households was not based on tribute paid by subject peoples; only the Sarwa, on whom Ngwato wealth had depended, suffered continual exclusion. No such denigration applied to incorporated foreigners. Since the establishment of the Ngwato chiefdom, free aliens retained all their previous liberties upon agreeing to pay tribute to the Ngwato chief. Relations between subject peoples and the capital were preeminently political and strategic affairs.

Low status rarely appears to have harmed anyone's welfare. Rather, it implied distance from high political power. A junior—that is, a younger man or one related distantly or not at all to the chieftainship—usually commanded no great attention and certainly no deference in the *kgotla*. Low rank implied a relative lack of social esteem, as was apparent in the few rituals, such as first fruits, initiation, and rainmaking, when the Ngwato clan advertised its precedence. Low rank also limited the range of suitable marriage partners through whom a family might hope to improve its fortunes. Primarily, however, low rank provided a vocabulary of insults for hurling at aliens when they were disloyal.

The nineteenth century roots of ethnic and regional relations within the Ngwato chiefdom were, therefore, relatively peaceful. Why the entire nineteenth century yielded few cases of organized resistance to Ngwato hegemony, while between 1920 and 1950 alone three highly publicized instances of resistance occurred is a question to be explored.[8]

The Nineteenth Century

The Ngwato clan began to extend its influence over the northeastern fringes of the Kalahari Desert in the late eighteenth century. The clan's myth of origin says that it had only recently split off from its parent group at that time. In the following decades it would consolidate its power, first as a bulwark against the Ndebele to the north and, later, as a result of riches gained from occupying a long stretch of the trading road to the north from the Cape. The Ngwato clan rose to dominate others because it controlled a strategic and well-watered area.

The relationship between a precolonial capital and its periphery ideally brought reciprocal benefits. Less powerful peoples received protection upon payment of tribute. Sometimes the tribute—skins and ivory, for example—had commercial value. Often, however, the value of the tribute—such as decorative ochre—lay only in its use. Safety as well as material benefit were the dominant motives of the tributary relationship in the nineteenth century Kalahari.

The hinterland of Ngwato dominance was neither acquired nor ruled by the massive expenditure of military force. The way for its relatively peaceful construction had been opened by the more violent incursions of the *mfecane*—by the Kololo (circa 1826–1828), the Phuting (circa 1831), and the Ndebele (1837–1844). As a result, peoples in the hinterland were apparently prepared, and at times even eager, to accept Ngwato protection. Virtually no oral traditions in the area of Ngwato dominance preserve memories of subject peoples having been "crushed," to use the Zulu metaphor. Rather, refugees from various kinds of turmoil—famine and disease, witchcraft, domestic quarrels—would ask the Ngwato for permission to live under them.

Subject peoples may have found it politically convenient to drop stories of forced subjugation from their histories, but the few admitted exceptions would seem to prove the rule that the incorporation of alien peoples was primarily a peaceful process. Sekgoma I rarely sent regiments out to conquer.[9] His son, Khama III, proudly asserted that in constructing his state, he had had to attack fellow black people only once.[10] Some Tswapong today swear that they acquiesced to Khama's demand that they pay tribute not because he had defeated them in battle but because they were afraid of the powerful war medicine he had acquired from a rainmaker. There were also more mundane reasons for their acquiescence. Khama sent a regiment, some old Tswapong men say, and stopped the Ndebele from killing their people in raids and tribute-collecting expeditions.[11] A less violent suzerain had replaced a more violent one.

Even though the Ngwato never adopted the ruinous smash-and-grab tactics of the Ndebele, they could and did display their power over subject peoples who threatened their sovereignty either by attempting to trade independently, or by striking an alliance with an enemy, such as the Ndebele, or the Boers, who could rob the Ngwato of land or cattle. The might of the

Ngwato, and their willingness to display it, rose and fell with the prosperity of the wagon trade on the Road to the North, and especially with access to firearms and ammunition. Immediately after repulsing the last Ndebele tax collectors from Shoshong in 1844, the Ngwato chief took over their tax-collecting role and threatened certain subordinate groups with guns so that they would pay tribute to him instead. Some subordinate groups, hoping to find refuge from this extortion, considered fleeing south to the Kwena, the major trading rivals of the Ngwato, but Chief Sekgoma refused to let them go because they would deprive his trade network of its wood and iron products. "Since he has got guns," David Livingstone observed, "he compels them to pay him tribute."[12]

At least one village was destroyed for contriving to trade independently of the two regional overlords. In about 1880, Khama killed its Kgalagadi headman for paying fur and skin tribute to both the Ngwato and the Kwena.[13] As an example to other subject peoples, the headman's village was burned and its property confiscated by a Ngwato regiment. His people were sent to live among Khama's loyal servants at his cattle posts on the distant Botletle River. Such a display of power was brutal, but quite rare. I have found no other of its kind in Ngwato history. Far more commonly, the overlord destroyed the plowed fields of recalcitrant subjects. If they showed signs of resisting the chief's will, he might call out a regiment and order their removal to a new area—such as the capital, where they could be kept under close watch. They would forfeit their hard labor of the season, but there is no evidence of large-scale loss of life. An individual leader was usually the sole victim.

Before the British finally defeated the Ndebele in the 1890s, the Ngwato depended on the peoples who lived between them and the country of Mzilikazi, the Ndebele chief, to warn them of attack. Occasionally a subordinate chief would ally himself with the Ndebele, and the Ngwato would lose cattle posts and suffer the destruction of villages. Such a chief had undoubtedly calculated that he would win greater liberty for himself by striking an alliance with what appeared to be the stronger side. Around 1862 a Talaote chief, Kedikilwe, fled from Shoshong, then the Ngwato capital, to Mzilikazi's capital in an attempt to contrive such independence.[14] He failed to win any support for this plan among his fellow countrymen, and his tactic was doomed. When the Ndebele arrived in his chiefdom, demanding to be guided to the Ngwato cattle posts and paths, the Talaote of one village demurred, saying that they wished to serve Mzilikazi only as vassals and herdsmen. The Ndebele retaliated by attacking and destroying their village.

This effort to establish some independence from two regional powers earned the destruction of the Talaote village for the same reason that the Kgalagadi headman was crushed two decades later. An independent people were a threat to wealth and security. Ngwato praise poets sang of their cowardice and disloyalty: "to say you respect the duiker," or totem of the chief's family, "makes us laugh," ran one derisory line aimed at the leader of a subject people who tried to ally with the Boers in 1887.[15] The enmity and suspicion apparent in the poems did not necessarily survive in popular imagination, but an epithet for traitor could be resurrected long afterward and flung back at the aliens if they again proved to be disloyal.

Sometimes the enemy with whom subject peoples could ally was dynastic rather than foreign. Macheng, the Ngwato heir who served as chief from 1857 to 1858 and 1866 to 1872, once gained in the Tswapong Hills an ally who harbored him when he was fleeing from his rival and successor, Sekgoma I.[16] This regional ally was killed for his act of disloyalty to the victor. To this day, his death is recounted as one of the two memorable episodes of Tswapong history and as the justification for Tswapong compliance with Ngwato rule: "We could not compete with or question the Ngwato for Machuchubane [the ally] was murdered when he questioned Ngwato power in Moeng, when he attempted independence."[17] Despite these tales of death and subjugation, Ngwato overrule does not appear in general to have been harsh. If a subject people paid tribute and eschewed alliances with dynastic rivals, the Ndebele or the Boers, they could live so uneventfully that their histories are virtually bare.

The relatively peaceful relations between the Ngwato and their subject peoples suggest that extraction of tribute was neither frequent nor heavy. Small societies coexisted peacefully with the Ngwato also because they themselves needed protection against the Ndebele and, further, because they feared Ngwato reprisals for treasonous activities such as guiding Ndebele soldiers to Ngwato cattle posts and paths. Unlike the Ndebele, the Ngwato lacked the military organization to be continually harsh as rulers.

An equally plausible explanation for the ties of loyalty, tenuous though they were, would be that particularly during the prosperous second half of the nineteenth century, the subject peoples profited from a connection to the wagon trade that they could acquire only through subservience to the Ngwato chief. As one old man from the Tswapong Hills remembers,

> Khama came to Sikwa [a local chief] and said, "Sikwa, I would like to help you." Khama promised Sikwa a gun. He brought the gun and for every animal Sikwa killed he had to give Khama the side on which the animal fell after being shot. Then we changed to give Khama a front limb. Every Morwa [a southerner] is our senior because we have long surrendered to Khama. Then came an ox wagon with a tool box and loaded all the animals we killed. Then he brought us a horse to chase wild animals.[18]

The guns, horses, and sometimes even wagons that the Ngwato chief, grown rich on the ivory trade, could dispense, as in the case of Sikwa, contributed to the prosperity of the tribute-paying peoples and to the local power of their leaders.

During the nineteenth century, Ngwato control was light. Hereditary rulers retained jurisdiction over their people even after incorporation. On presentation of one ox to the Ngwato chief, the foreign chief became a tribute-paying client and his people became Ngwato subjects, though they were regarded as of inferior status.[19] In principle, Schapera assures us, the Ngwato did not interfere with the internal affairs or customs of these immigrant communities, though subjects from the hinterland did enjoy the right of appeal against their chief's decisions.[20] Until the end of the nineteenth century, each subject community had a Ngwato "listener" appointed to represent it in the capital. The role of this commoner headman was not coercive. He and his fellow ward members housed visitors from the district and relayed messages between it and the chief. He collected tribute for the chief but received none for himself, either in kind or in labor. During famines, the listener would distribute within his district any grain and guns that the chief could spare.

When Khama III reformed this system in 1896, he initiated the first step toward closer regional government. He tried to disperse his subject peoples more evenly across the country and eventually sent five resident headmen to govern them in the hinterland. In attempting to redistribute his subject people at the same time as a caravan under Cecil Rhodes was trekking to remote Ghanzi in the dry west, he was clearly trying to stake his claim to land he feared he might lose to whites if it were vacant. He also believed that Ngwato herds would recover faster from the devastating rinderpest epidemic of the preceding year if they could graze on fresh pastures.[21] In instituting closer government, he was also attempting to prevent the communities surrounding his capital from making a separate peace with his enemies, whether they were dynastic, such as his notoriously disloyal son Sekgoma, or European, such as the Boers. Khama had good reason to fear that his polity would dissolve if he failed to contain dynastic rivalry. He sent one faction of royal rivals into exile in Rhodesia in 1895 because they had been trying to undermine his rule in the hinterland under the guise of evangelization. When one of the dissidents later testified, "The Chief did not want the outlying villages evangelised, he thought they were being spoilt,"[22] he was alluding to the rival power base his allies had hoped to establish in the Tswapong Hills; another later admitted that they had really wanted their own land and village, and that "the question of [wanting, against Khama's orders, to brew] beer and the church was only an excuse."[23] Trying to avoid such threats, Khama began, in 1896, to court the loyalty of his relatives by sending selected members to govern the districts.²⁴ One son-in-law, for example, who had followed Sekgoma into exile, was rewarded with a district governorship when he returned to Khama's fold.²⁵ The specter of dissolution became real after 1915 in the neighboring and brother state of the Tawana, where political rivalries were destroying centralized rule; most Tawana were moving from the capital to live at their cattle posts.²⁶ Khama was determined that such rampant dynastic tension would not rip apart his own chiefdom.

In the most harmonious times, the district governor simply continued to provide another level of appeal from the local *kgotlas*. He went on conveying messages between these settlements and the capital. In times of conflict, however, his residence in the region would allow him to make detailed reports on acts of disloyalty to the chief. Each governor could command a regiment to build a homestead for him and cultivate a tribute field. Nevertheless, the relocation of governors to the district does not in itself appear to have made Ngwato overrule a heavier burden on subject peoples. On the contrary, at the same time that he made these appointments, Khama stopped demanding tribute. The great chief may well have calculated that the political benefits of renouncing the hunting spoils, iron tools, ochre, and food far outweighed the need to fuel his fortune by participating in the declining Cape wagon trade.

By the same token, the subject peoples no longer needed to be protected from attack after the final defeat of the Ndebele in 1896. Immediately, Khama noted, "[t]here was some grumbling among a few of the people belonging to these tribes [Kalanga, Phaleng, Talaote, Khurutshe] who wished to persuade their people that they ought to be independent nations."²⁷ For Ngwato overrule to be tolerated, therefore, the capital needed to provide new kinds of "protection." This imperative was particularly strong after 1899, when the chief became involved in the protectorate's tax collection, the colonial version of tribute. In this way, the nineteenth century closed with clear signs that the days of weak or sporadic overrule were ending.

The Twentieth Century

Like many of his fellow subimperial rulers, Tshekedi centralized the power of his office and reduced the powers of headmen, including the chiefs of subject peoples who lived in the hinterland.[28] With part of their tax revenues, the Bechuanaland paramount chiefs tried to create bureaucracies responsible solely to themselves and capable of managing the development of their economically stagnant polities. Neither Tshekedi nor his fellow paramounts created new structures for divining popular opinion or for rendering government accountable to the governed. They engineered their "revolution" in political relations strictly from above.

Tshekedi, his tax collectors, and the District Commissioner all embodied the new order of closer government but the governed did not treat them as equally blameworthy. Subject people could accuse the chief of causing oppression and poverty; they beseeched the British administration for liberation.

By now, being governed was becoming an increasingly expensive business. From 1899 to 1938, Bechuanaland Africans had to pay a hut or poll tax to their chiefs who, in turn, handed it over to the protectorate government, keeping 10 percent as a commission for the labor they had delegated to their paid tax collectors and the unpaid headmen who did the actual work of collection.[29] The amount doubled from 10 shillings in cash, grain, or stock in 1899 to £1 in 1907 and remained at that level until 1919 when the system was reformed and the total taxes payable were raised by protectorate fiat to 23 shillings. From 1929, each adult man had to pay in total annually 25 shillings, but the various disasters afflicting the protectorate's economy from 1933 until 1937—drought, cattle disease, closed markets—made tax collection nearly pointless. The rate dropped accordingly to 15 shillings; it rose back to 20 in 1937 but regained the 1932 level only in 1948. Those who failed to pay were often punished by being *"kraaled"* or confined like cattle

Courtesy, McGregor Museum, Duggan-Cronin Collection, Kimberley

Khama III, Tshekedi Khama's father, chief of the Bamangwato, 1872–1873, 1875–1923

Courtesy, McGregor Museum, Duggan-Cronin Collection, Kimbe

Village of Serowe, capital of Ngwato since 1902

Courtesy, Central Archives Depot, Prete

Ngwato cattle post near Serowe

Courtesy, McGregor Museum, Duggan-Cronin Collection, Kimberley

The chief's *kgotla* (men's public forum) in Serowe, the Ngwato capital, 1934

Courtesy, McGregor Museum, Duggan-Cronin Collection, Kimberly

Outpost of Bechuanaland Trading Association, principal trading firm in Ngwato, established in 1888

Courtesy, McGregor Museum, Duggan-Cronin Collection, Kimberly

Ox wagons crossing Shashi River on road to north in northeastern Ngwato, late nineteenth century

Courtesy, McGregor Museum, Duggan-Cronin Collection, Kimberley

Bechuanaland Protectorate Police in early 1900s, Fort Gaberones, later site of capital of independent country of Botswana

Courtesy, McGregor Museum, Duggan-Cronin Collection, Kimberley

Member of Ngwato regiment, wrapped in Union Jack, 1934

Tshekedi Khama (above left) as young man, 1934; (below) at London office in July 1951, two weeks after House of Commons voted not to rescind his order of banishment from Ngwato; (above right) on his return from England to southern Africa in August 1951

Three of Seretse Khama's supporters—including, on the left, a "son of Sekgoma," Peto Sekgoma—awaiting the heir's return from London, 1950

Associated Press Photo

Seretse and his British wife Ruth reunite in Serowe after his return from London, 1950

Associated Press Photo

Tshekedi and Chief Bathoen of Bangwaketse greet British Royal Family at Lobatsi, 1947

in their village and then sent to work in the South African mines.[30]

The lion's share of this revenue went toward paying the costs of administering and policing the protectorate.[31] From 1919, the protectorate chiefs collected an effective 3-to-5-shilling surcharge on the £1 poll tax.[32] It went directly into the Native Fund established that year and was used, after discussion in the Native Advisory Council, at the High Commissioner's discretion for development projects such as schools and boreholes and to fight stock disease.[33] Tribal treasuries replaced the fund in 1938.[34] From them, chiefs received fixed stipends, rather than a commission, and continued to draw funds for social services, principally education. Several chiefs had already established their own treasuries; since 1928, Tshekedi had required his taxpayers to contribute one shilling six pence to a Ngwato tribal fund. There was one additional form of taxation, a source of bitter grievance among the governed—chiefs placed ad hoc levies on their subjects whenever they identified a pressing need such as building a church, financing a borehole, or paying a lawyer.[35]

All the hard work of extracting taxes was directed to a limited number of ends. Both popular and chiefly opinion was growing to consider economic development to be inextricably linked to education, and so the largest sums, apart from those for administration, were spent on the establishment of schools and the payment of teachers. The only other development projects launched in the Ngwato chiefdom during the 1930s were a tribal borehole and dam and a livestock improvement camp. A disgruntled taxpayer in the hinterland might argue that he was paying his taxes to benefit Serowe. Anyone could argue that his tax was vanishing in the following ways: it could finance a livestock improvement center even though Ngwato cattle were embargoed on South African markets;[36] it could pay teachers to prepare students for jobs that did not exist in Bechuanaland; it could pay a lawyer's fees in a protracted case of dynastic rivalry. At the same time, the chief was clearly serving his people less and less as their "milk pail" and "breast." He was now freed, for example, from responsibility for feeding destitutes; formerly, he had watched over them as if they were his children, to use a Tswana metaphor for patronage. Now the money for their food, clothing, transport, and coffins came from the tribal treasury. This sum in 1938—£109—was slightly more than half the amount paid as legal charges—£180—to Tshekedi's Cape Town attorney.[37]

The men who became ethnic politicians must have been jealous of Tshekedi's wealth. While they themselves were paid nothing, Tshekedi drew a handsome salary from the tribal treasury— £1,000 in 1938. He possessed the largest herd of cattle in the protectorate and lived in a fine modern house, one of two in Serowe in 1933 with indoor plumbing. Even the red and white jeep in which he toured his realm provided a flamboyant example of public funds invested for the benefit of the political center. He was growing richer in private wealth by purchasing cattle, machinery, and commodities for himself. Regional chiefs, seeing these spoils of power, yearned to acquire their own; it served their interests, therefore, to encourage an independent sense of ethnic identity among their people. If they could present themselves to the British as Tshekedi's equivalent, albeit on a smaller scale, they might gain control of their tax revenues for purposes of both private profit and public gain.

Following impeccable imperial logic, British administrators turned a deaf ear to the pleas and protests of subject peoples. As a result, the following irony crowned the Pax Britannica: proconsuls of a nation professing liberal democratic values were presiding over the growth of autocratic government and the increased expression of ethnic animosity. The British had indeed achieved a certain kind of peace in the late nineteenth century when they drew boundaries between the northern Tswana chiefdoms and the Boers, the Ndebele, and the Germans, who were encroaching upon them from the east, north, and west. At the same time, these boundaries fenced in the chiefdoms, in effect encouraging political tensions within them to rise. Discontented subject peoples found withdrawal from the jurisdiction of a despised chief increasingly difficult. They were obliged to stay and pay allegiance to him in the form of taxes, labor, and obedience, and when they complained that the chief never consulted them, they gained a sympathetic hearing from no one. The British were protecting the sovereignty of the chiefdoms and the power of the sovereigns.

The economic stagnation of the interwar years did nothing to endear Ngwato or protectorate exactions to subject peoples. Regional government grew more controlling just as the material benefits to be gained from it were waning. In this sense, the legitimacy of Ngwato government was at the mercy of the southern African economy. Ethnic separatism waxed and waned among the governed according to the political and economic benefits from inclusion in a larger polity. When that inclusion enhanced access to power, wealth, or basic resources, subject peoples embraced a wider identity. When they suffered hardship or simply failed to advance, regional particularism blossomed. Conflict ensued when subsistence was threatened. In each of the three regional crises that challenged the twentieth century Ngwato chiefdom, restricted access to land proved to be the decisive spark of litigious disputes heard as far away as London. Material insecurity and ethnic mobilization were intimately linked.

The Birwa Case

In 1921, two years before Khama died, an unprecedented event foretold a new era of troubles for the chieftainship Tshekedi would inherit—a subject people tried to sue their Ngwato overlords. Foreseeing that factional conflict would be vented in relentless litigation, Chief Khama was enraged. "According to my custom," he said, "a subject cannot bring a case against me; it will kill me. [The Birwa chief] has now created a precedent and others will come against me; but I will protect myself."[38] He was rumored to have threatened the British that he would launch a strike similar to a recent "revolution" in Johannesburg if subordinate chiefs and their lawyers were allowed to "persecute" him in this way.[39]

The case began with a forced removal. This act, as damaging to rural people's welfare then as now, stemmed from the peculiar mix of systems of land tenure in the Bechuanaland Protectorate. In 1895, Khama had given a strip of land along the chiefdom's eastern border to the British government, and ten years later the British ceded that strip—the Tuli Block, which ran approximately 8 miles deep along the west bank of the Limpopo River—to the British South Africa Company, which began selling farms there to whites. Over 235 Birwa families lived in the block, and starting in 1910 they were made to live in a northern "reserve" within it, between the Motloutse and Limpopo rivers.[40] Each African man living in the block would have to pay a 10-shilling annual rent to the company as well as a tax to the protectorate government, collected by either a protectorate official or a representative of Khama. The loss of the land annoyed Khama on several counts: the boundaries cut off his people from access to fine pans where they could wash and water their cattle; Ngwato malcontents could escape there from his authority; stolen cattle could easily be run across the Limpopo into the Transvaal to be sold. For these last two reasons, Khama listened sympathetically to the company when it complained in 1920 that the Birwa inhabiting that land were drunken, poaching thieves and should be expelled. As Khama complained to the Resident Commissioner, "Those who went to the Tuli Block . . . went because they can get beer to drink there, as they have nobody in authority to check them. . . . If left to themselves at Tuli Block they will probably steal from the Transvaal or Rhodesia and cause trouble."[41]

The Birwa, led by their chief Malema, countered that they paid rent to the company and tax to the protectorate government and that, therefore, Khama had no right to interfere. They denied that they owed any allegiance at all to the Ngwato chief, who responded by telling them that they must move to Bobonong, another Birwa settlement within Ngwato territory, and be ruled by Khama's son-in-law.[42] They protested that they were not cattle to be "removed at a few days' notice to stand in the Rain. They want time to build Huts for their women and children as they were not going to risk moving in wet weather."[43] The rainy season had begun and many had already plowed.

Khama, unmoved by their plight, sent his son-in-law, Modisaotsile, and a regiment from Serowe to remove the Birwa forcibly. Unspeakable outrages—arson, rape, robbery, torture, slavery, and denial of representation—were said to have been committed by the regiment on the day before Christmas 1920. In the process Malema lost a very large sum of money he had saved. A few months later, Malema and some of his followers who had fled with him to places of refuge in South Africa and Rhodesia returned to the Tuli Block to harvest their crops, but another regiment came from Bobonong to stop them, and Malema was flogged. The Birwa then undertook a step that was to become commonplace in Ngwato politics: they hired a lawyer.[44] Malema engaged the services of Emmanuel Gluckmann, a Johannesburg attorney, in an effort to recover the astonishing sum of £1,640 that he claimed had been stolen from his home during the removal and also to gain for the Birwa the right to live wherever they chose.[45]

Pared down to its central issue, the case concerned two conflicting principles of rights to land. Did people gain access to land by paying allegiance to a ruler or by paying taxes and rent to a landlord? From this pivotal issue sprang a host of related dilemmas that proved to be particularly nettlesome for the British. The truth of the conflicting allegations was hidden in a welter of historical fabrications and ethnic insults. No forum existed for hearing disputes between two chiefs. Should the proconsuls constitute one, and so undermine the great chief and the entire principle of indirect rule? Further, there were no substantive principles to apply in such a case. Clearly, in this gray realm traditional and modern norms were so thoroughly mixed that the machinations of the powerful were starkly revealed without the legitimating gloss of either legality or custom.

Gluckmann was moved to write a pamphlet damning the treatment of him. His version of the litigation not only depicts the acts of violence against the Birwa but also affronts to his own dignity by both Khama and protectorate officials. Khama even told the Birwa, Gluckmann believed, that it was futile to seek the lawyer's help because he was only "an insignificant Jew." Gluckmann suspected that he was made to wait on the veranda of the Resident Magistrate's house while Khama was entertained inside. Clearly, in his own eyes, a man seeking "to extend a helping hand to those dumb, helpless slaves" was unworthy of such treatment.[46]

Gluckmann's account reports the tale as told to him by the Birwa. The Birwa argued that they were not Tswana and had little in common, not even language or custom, with Khama's other subjects. They said they had never recognized Khama's suzerainty; they had paid tax for two years to one of his brothers but only because he described himself as a tax collector for Queen Victoria. They believed that a British officer had confirmed their right of occupation of the Tuli Block land by collecting subsequent rent and tax. When, with support of the protectorate police, Khama's son-in-law invaded their land in December 1920, he had offered the Birwa a single miserable alternative to relocating in Bobonong—the right to leave the protectorate but without their cattle. They were compelled to abandon their plowed fields and to set forth on a six-day forced march to Bobonong. The Ngwato even made them pay cash for their drinking water en route. And once they arrived at their destination, they were compelled to work for others. "They are forced," wrote Gluckmann with feeling, "to work for [the chief's representative] Modisaotsile erecting kraals, building huts, ploughing fields, men, women, and children, without pay, without food, without hope."[47] Gluckmann and the Birwa claimed that Khama, by failing to give reasonable notice of eviction, allowing for peaceful consultation and the reaping of the crops, had committed a breach of Roman-Dutch law.

Khama and the British countered each charge against them. The Birwa, they said, were originally subjects of the Shona and had twice sought refuge with the Ngwato, in the early and late nineteenth century, after attacks by emigrant Swazi and Lobengula's Ndebele army. Only after the Ndebele had been defeated by the Ngwato in 1893 had the Birwa been able to return to their former lands west of the Limpopo. In payment for their liberation, they had agreed to send annual tribute of ivory and lion skins to the capital of the chief who had proved his seniority by freeing them.[48] Between 1903 and 1906 Khama gathered the small scattered settlements of Birwa into larger villages in Motloutse and Bobonong, and their chiefs became mere headmen. The British, in turn, were denying that the Birwa living in the Tuli Block had gained any rights as citizens of the protectorate. True, they had paid rent there, but many had paid no tax. As for the extraordinary sum of cash said to have been stolen from Malema's hut, the amount would need to be verified before it could be believed. Nor could the £40,000 in damages sought by the Birwa suit be justified in light of the fact that the Birwa themselves had, according to custom, burned their own huts as they left. The counterbrief also cited another custom unknown to Gluckmann, that subjects build their chief's home and *kraal* and plow a tribute field for him, and that therefore the labor Modisaotsile requisitioned on their arrival at Bobonong was not at all burdensome.

With so little common ground between the claimants and the dependents, only a long trial could determine where justice lay. But the occasion never arose. Protectorate officials disposed of the case by defining the judicial process in their own interests as they went along. Gluckmann had been paid four hundred head of cattle by the Birwa as a deposit on his one-thousand-head fee, but he was forbidden to market them when the Resident Commissioner ruled that Malema did not have the right to sell cattle for the purpose of hiring a lawyer. Then the Imperial Secretary denied the Birwa the right to legal representation altogether.[49]

Hearings on the case were held, but in Khama's own capital, a place where Malema was unlikely to feel at ease. With the attorney Gluckmann forbidden by the British to be present, the Resident Commissioner threatened to arrest Malema if in his lawyer's absence, he boycotted the enquiry. An investigator, Sir Herbert Sloley, who was an administrator from Basutoland, eventually reported that Modisaotsile had indeed been guilty of maltreating the Birwa; Sloley recommended his removal, but the High Commissioner rejected the recommendation. Sloley rejected all Birwa claims to compensation. It was a highly partisan system of justice. Gluckmann said bitterly that Khama had "to be maintained as if part of the constitution."[50] Because the hearings took place at all, Khama for his part complained, "The Protectorate officials look upon Mr. Gluckmann as their supreme head. . . . I am despised and neglected by the Protectorate administration. . . . The Protectorate is now governed by the laws invented by the Government officials of which no agreement has been signed between the Late Queen Victoria and myself at the time I invited her to protect me."[51] For his pains, Malema was banished from the protectorate, and only in 1944 did he return to live at Mololatau, 25 kilometers southeast of Bobonong, where the rest of his followers had been settled for nearly two decades.

None of the parties involved in this legal sham emerges in a flattering light, not even Malema, the leader of the victims. During the subsequent protracted negotiations for a new place for the Birwa to live, it was learned that not all of Malema's followers had wished to accompany him to refuge among other Birwa in Southern Rhodesia or the Transvaal and that some Birwa disputed his right to pledge their cattle to hire a lawyer. Two years later, at a large meeting in Palapye, the former rebels (except for Malema, who had fled to the Transvaal) swore loyalty to Khama's son and successor. They were officially reintegrated into the fold.[52] Whether this capitulation represented a long-standing or a recent split within the Birwa ruling family or a shrewd assessment of the relative disadvantage of life among white settlers, is not known.[53] What is clear is that both parties were struggling, one to maintain, the other to aggrandize its own wealth and power. The struggle between them took place in this form because a new suzerain had introduced itself over both political levels. Malema had mistakenly gambled in his law suit on the sincerity of imperial rhetoric and on the responsiveness of imperial institutions. He had failed to recognize that British interests in a low-cost administration would prevent their responding sympathetically to an appeal for justice.

Ethnic epithets and claims had a history, but they had never before had an audience.[54] Khama explained to the British the rightful subservience of the Birwa in the following terms: "The fathers of these men carried ivory for me before I freed them," and "The MaBirwa were my grandfather's [Kgari's] people, and are still my people."[55] Malema used ethnicity to deny his allegiance and subordination to Khama. The BaNgwato swore at him, in response, for having had the audacity to challenge Khama's rule. They shouted at him, during the Serowe inquiry, for failing to salute Khama with sufficient deference and for failing to take off his hat when he spoke. They continually interrupted his giving of evidence, and even denied him the use of a stool.

Ethnicity was a tool for making and for denying political claims. It was not itself an indication that a group was part of an inflexible hierarchy. Birwa ethnic separatism did not develop after this incident. Malema's people were indeed acutely distressed by their sacrifice of a harvest and by their forced removal, but they recovered and no further crisis ensued.[56] Nor did all Birwa rebel. Some even grew to be considered as Ngwato. Their disunity suggests that ties of loyalty to a patron and his faction remained a more powerful determinant of public behavior than the idea of being Birwa itself.

The Khurutshe Case

Tshekedi suffered his own first subimperial crisis in 1927, the year after he assumed the regency, in the curious case of the Khurutshe. What he saw as this subject people's simple and punishable insubordination turned up in the South African and British press as a report of denial of freedom of worship. A small group of the Tswana-speaking Khurutshe living in the northeast corner of the chiefdom had been trying to worship in the Church of England against the chief's decree that the London Missionary Society should monopolize worship among the Ngwato and their subjects. Because the Anglican church was involved, the sound of this protest reverberated all the way from its point of origin in the northeast corner of the chiefdom to Lambeth Palace. As in most causes célèbres, the matter was far more complicated than enthusiasts, defending either Ngwato chiefly supremacy or the separation of church and state, imagined it to be.

The historical origins of the two groups are not revealing. Both the Khurutshe and the Ngwato claimed to be senior. The Khurutshe were, in fact, the progenitors of the Kwena and the Ngwato; both had hived off from the Khurutshe in the eighteenth century. But the Ngwato asserted their seniority through an entirely different definition of rank. They argued that because the Ndebele had subjugated the Khurutshe, the Khurutshe's weakness and lack of valor had made them junior; they had, in fact, paid tribute to the Ndebele from 1840 until 1864, when they fled to the Ngwato and began to pay tribute to that chiefdom instead. The Khurutshe admitted that they had found refuge in Ngwato lands but they planned to stay there no longer than necessary and to return to Selepeng, their ancestral home. After the British South Africa Company defeated the Ndebele in 1893, the Khurutshe tried to go home, but by then Selepeng was hardly a haven. To gain the right to live there, Chief Rauwe of the Khurutshe was required to sign a contract with the Tati Company, a gold mining concern, agreeing that his people would pay a tax to the company on each of their huts and also to provide labor for the struggling mines, to trade only in company stores, and to refrain from hunting game. The area of land on which they were to live was not only smaller than the tract that they had previously occupied in Ngwato territory, but was now the home of four other chiefs and their followers as well,[57] and the Khurutshe, therefore, could not maintain the typical Tswana pattern of dispersed settlement. With space too scarce for a nuclear village with separate plowing fields and cattle posts, they had to adopt the Kalanga system of concentrating these activities in single homesteads within scattered hamlets. A crisis of local political authority ensued.[58] Chief Rauwe's local authority had been broken by his inability to ensure that his people would have large and well-watered pastures. He could no longer serve as the protectorate government's liaison with both Kalanga and Khurutshe groups in the northeast.[59]

Rival Christian sects provided new fora for articulating these local grievances. In 1904, Chief Rauwe converted to the Church of England, splitting away from his paternal cousin and rival who remained a member of the London Missionary Society. He had many practical reasons for a change of allegiance. Patterns of inheritance ensured that endemic factional conflict would be focused between agnates, and conversion would give institutional backing to a rival faction. Further, Rauwe's relationship to both Khama and the London Missionary Society had become complicated by marital turmoil. Rauwe maintained two concubines, one of them Khama's daughter Baboni, and the other an Anglican. The London Missionary Society would recognize neither concubine as his wife. Choosing the second woman as his wife, Rauwe converted to the Church of England, in part, no doubt, to gain a measure of freedom from the London Missionary Society directives and from pressures exerted within his polity by its converts.[60]

In that same year the Tati Company evicted the Khurutshe from Selepeng. Rauwe's appeal to the protectorate government against the eviction failed, and the company set aside a mandatory reserve for all Tati District Africans. Rauwe and his rival were compelled to live there for five years with their followers in cramped quarters. In 1913, Rauwe's faction, complaining about lack of land and the high prices charged by company stores, sought permission to move back to Ngwato territory and to establish a village to be called Tonota. Khama made Rauwe sign a written agreement that he and his followers would not drink liquor and would not adhere to the Anglican church. Rauwe's followers appear to have obeyed this dictum until 1922, when the London Missionary Society faction, with Khama's blessing, moved to Tonota from Tati in revolt against high grazing fees. Factional politics were set alight once again. The dissension between the two factions was sufficiently strident to evoke from a local poet an image of their two leaders (missionary society adherent Molefe and Ramosenyi, Rauwe's successor from 1918) as fighting dogs whom Chief Khama (the "rhinoceros") would have to separate.[61]

> The rhinoceros objects to angry men being neighbors,
> to Molefe being the neighbor of Ramosenyi.
> Hail to you, ender of fights,
> separator of the twin dogs!
> Pull apart your dogs, they are fighting,
> the bull dogs are clawing each other's backs,
> for they see that behind you there is meat.

The smaller missionary society faction was free to worship locally, and the Anglicans were permitted to attend services only in Francistown and against the Ngwato chief's wishes, because Francistown was outside his control. The Anglican's protests aroused no sympathy in either Sekgoma or his successor, Tshekedi; both refused to allow an Anglican church to be built in the reserve. When the Anglican Bishop of Kimberley raised the issue again in 1927, Tshekedi enquired sarcastically whether the government intended "that I should rule these people through the Bishop." In office barely a year, he feared that the newspapers would exploit the story. "[T]he whole affair," Tshekedi said, "is not a religious movement, but an attempt to obtain independence and undermining of my authority." He decreed that the recalcitrant Anglicans must move to the capital at Serowe,[62] where he could keep them under close watch and tighter control.

The Khurutshe refused to move, and in a *kgotla* meeting at Serowe Tshekedi's men sought to convince the acting Resident Commissioner that the Khurutshe insubordination was intolerable. Only one Khurutshe was permitted to speak in his group's defense. Tshekedi and his allies maintained that in joining a denomination other than the chief's own, the Khurutshe had not exercised freedom of religion, an alien concept suitable only for "civilized nations," but had rejected the chieftainship and had, therefore, broken the law. "We take religion and the Chief to be the same thing." Only disaster could possibly result if the British opted to support the Khurutshe position. Shrewd speakers hinted darkly of an Ethiopian, or black nationalist church, revival. If the British allowed the insubordination of the Khurutshe to go unpunished, they would destroy the chieftainship and "scatter" the Ngwato.[63]

The visiting British official, in his reply to the irate chiefly faction, promised that the British would allow no new religion to be established without the consent of the appropriate authorities. As an Englishman, he felt obliged to insist repeatedly, nevertheless, that "[y]ou cannot chain a man's mind." "Most natives know you cannot force people in the matter of religion," he said, adding a marvelously contradictory message, "There is only one Church and if anyone is disobeying the Chief's order, the Government will support the Chief as long as you do not compel the people to believe in a religion they do not believe in."[64] The meeting ended with neither party having relinquished their stated values, but the British had in fact capitulated to Tshekedi's faction.

Three months later a regiment arrived to force the Anglicans to move to Serowe. Complaints about damages to huts inevitably arose; one Khurutshe went over Tshekedi's head to the Resident Magistrate, undoubtedly compounding his estrangement from the chief. He claimed £29 in compensation.[65] British officials, though they were clearly chagrined at having to transgress the principle of freedom of worship, did not hesitate to back Tshekedi's authority. One wrote in 1927, "I am anxious that Tshekedi should feel that he will be supported by the Government in the lawful exercise of his authority as Chief and while I could not approve of any steps which would partake of the nature of religious compulsion I entirely agree that the natives in question should be warned that any future disobedience of a lawful order of the Chief will be severely punished."[66] The British had passed the matter back into the chief's hands. Proper procedures should be followed. The chief as well as the government and the Bishop of the diocese should be consulted by the Khurutshe Anglicans before building a church or establishing another religion. The result was to affirm power at the center. The chief's authority was upheld.

One predictable moral emerges from this tale. Strong-arm tactics never won any devotion to Tshekedi or any loyalty to the Ngwato state. On the contrary, the Anglican faction among the Khurutshe failed to fulfill even one of the responsibilities of Ngwato citizenship. For two years they refused to build huts in Serowe, living in borrowed housing and spending as much time as possible at their cattle posts in the north. They performed no regimental labor; they never paid their respects to Tshekedi in the *kgotla* or attended meetings there[67] until 1931 when, presenting themselves as a body, they asked to be allowed to return to their homes. Three years later, Tshekedi did let them go to Tonota.[68] The power of ordinary people to evade the directives of the Ngwato state was intact.

References to rank litter the language of this dispute. In accusations demonstrating the flexibility of the concept of seniority, peoples of inferior standing were charged with trying to "arrogate supremacy" by asserting independence from the Ngwato. Although each Ngwato myth of origin admits that the Khurutshe were senior because they had spawned the Ngwato in antiquity, each myth asserts that the Khurutshe were demonstrably inferior to the Ngwato because they had been subjugated by the Ndebele. One agitated Ngwato swore to the British, "we are afraid because the Government places servants above us to lead us. The Bahurutshe were originally the servants of the Matebele and came to Khama for salvation,"[69] and thus were forever servants. With history pitted against religion in a contest to win the ear of the British, history—or the Ngwato version of it—won because it was on the side of the chief.

The story of Ngwato-Khurutshe relations reveals in microcosm a phenomenon common throughout southern Africa, that when land loss undermined local chieftainships and created social turmoil, it gave rise to new forms of political expression and new ways of resisting established government. Religious sects had provided to subject people a basis for new claims of rights and even for independence. While individual conversion cannot, of course, be explained solely by political motivation, the church did attract converts, in part, because it offered new political skills and a new way of interpreting experience that were, in some respects, better suited to the emerging social order. Missionaries and others who ignored the political logic of conversion pridefully blinded themselves to the fact that people in alien societies often used them as pawns. New religious organizations bristled with threats to the established order, particularly in societies like that of the Tswana, where there was virtually no formal political office apart from the chieftainship. Because religious sects were sanctioned by the imperial overlords, they provided a new core around which challengers to the chief could rally. Thus active dissidents could create a furor out of all proportion to their numbers. In this case only a dozen people had succeeded in embroiling the highest levels of British administrators by invoking the powerful theme of freedom of worship. Simply by refusing to obey the chief, they revealed the weakness of his coercive force.

The Mswazi Case

In the Birwa and Khurutshe cases, separatist sentiments had been successfully thwarted and contained. The Mswazi case, on the other hand, showed clear signs of ascending nationalist separatism. The Mswazi were a Kalanga clan, numbering in 1930 about 600 taxpayers. They rebelled against Ngwato overrule in a crescendo of ethnic tension. In the end the Mswazi both ran and were driven from the chiefdom.

The Kalanga, speakers of a Shona dialect, had no corporate identity and were therefore unlikely candidates for ethnic chauvinism. The rebellion fueled the growth of Kalanga identity as separate from and embattled by the Ngwato. Tshekedi feared that the rebellion would spread throughout the entire northeast, the Kalanga region of his realm, "eventually destroy(ing) the Bamangwato tribe."

The people whom Tshekedi accused of wanting "to be a tribe apart" had a diverse ethnic heritage. Mswazi, the founding headman who gave his name to the Kalanga hamlet, was descended from the Sotho-speaking Pedi chiefdom in the eastern Transvaal. One version of the "clan's" past describes them as descended from a migrant band of Pedi who had assimilated Kalanga language and culture and from a motley group of refugees from the Ndebele.[70] During the last quarter of the nineteenth century, the Mswazis moved from place to place in Kalanga country, seeking to avoid becoming victims of regional rivalries. Ethnically diverse, like other peoples who had endured the *mfecane*, they were tied to no particular piece of ground.

Each side in the Mswazi dispute indulged in freewheeling and self-serving historical reconstruction to justify its own claim to independence and suzerainty. Together they produced, as one dazed American journalist put it, "claims and counterclaims, diametrically opposed in fact and implication ... a maze of quasi-legal and official verbiage."[71] Because the Kalanga region constituted the border between the territories of Lobengula, the last great Ndebele chief, and Khama, it had been the object of a long-standing tug-of-war. Each ruler staked claims to land with reference to strategically advanced cattle posts or tributary relations. Some Kalanga, for example, denied that they had ever tendered their submission to Khama and claimed that they had been involuntarily incorporated into the Ngwato chiefdom when boundaries were drawn in 1899. The Mswazis, in particular, had been living in Ndebele territory near the Rhodesian border town of Plumtree and, so the history went, they had been welcomed to the Ngwato side of the border by a local chief who was related to them and who had been granted leave to settle by Khama's father.[72] Before that they had moved back and forth seeking refuge from civil unrest in both chiefdoms.

This historical interpretation was vigorously contradicted by the Ngwato, who saw the Kalanga as cowards and vagabonds. Sheltered by the Ngwato when they fled from the Ndebele, they had returned north to Ndebele land during the civil war between Khama and his father. In the last Ndebele war with the British South Africa Company, they had refused to leave the Ndebele, convinced that no one would ever conquer them. Only in 1900 did they ask Khama for permission to cross into his territory.[73]

Given the malleability of oral history and the frequency with which alliances were struck and broken, it is pointless to try to construct a uniform image of Ngwato-Kalanga relations. Neither the Ngwato nor the Kalanga version is utterly convincing. One clear political metaphor for subordination did emerge from the tangled web of alliances: the Kalanga were taunted as cowards because they had been unable to throw off Ndebele domination. History proved their inferiority.[74] As one praise poet sang,

> The brindled cow [Tshekedi] has been kicking,
> the speckled one with a slanting horn;
> that horn once poked travellers,
> it ripped the stomachs of the Mhafshas [Mswazis];
> the Kalaka presently deceived themselves,
> likening themselves to Khama's son.[75]

When they acted as if they were Khama's sons by taking independent action, they were forgetting their low rank.

The chieftainship remained the dominant popular metaphor for discussing political rights. The Mswazis and the Ngwato referred only occasionally in their public discourse to the two grievances—taxation and competition over land—that were driving them toward violent confrontation; the language of rank and authority tended to crowd out the material roots of the crisis. The roots of the crisis lay deeper.

Mswazi's hamlet, called by his own name, had been boxed in by the Tati Concession on the east and by the cattle posts of high-ranking Ngwato on the west, probably because Khama had advanced segments of his royal herds as a strategy to claim former Ndebele lands for his own chiefdom. The Ngwato claims took precedence; the Kalanga were compelled to squeeze up against one another so that the rich Ngwato could have ample space. Sarwa herders of the Ngwato attacked and destroyed at least two Kalanga cattle posts,[76] and Kalanga cattle that strayed from this congestion into the Tati Concession were confiscated.

It was hard for the crowded land to support the growing cattle and human populations. The old concentrated pattern of Kalanga settlement—residence, fields, and pasture in one location—no longer satisfied anyone; "what we can now graze in a village is a cat," one bitter Mswazi complained at a fruitless public hearing.[77] With only brief fertile periods on the high veld's granite sands, the Mswazis needed to rest their plowing lands after every ten to fifteen years of use; and because the European plow had extended the amount of land that could be cultivated, they wanted more of it, in order to grow cash crops, than ever before. During a wet year cattle were kept near the fields, but during a drought they had to be moved to outlying wells and river beds. At such times, the Kalanga needed far more land than they appeared to be using when the rains were good.

As in the Khurutshe case, cramped quarters charged political life with tension. With Kalanga headmen responsible for regulating land use, they could lose adherents if their ability to regulate use was blocked. Those whose fortunes were declining would, by tradition, switch their loyalties to a royal brother. And because Mswazi had been elevated to the chieftainship of his village by Khama, and some of his relatives could claim greater seniority, one brother and a cousin tried to use the turmoil to unseat him.

Along with, and even because of, these looming crises, the Mswazis did experience one boon—the proximity of the Tati Concession markets had encouraged them to produce crops for sale. They reaped fair crops when elsewhere in Ngwato lands no one harvested. They also experimented successfully with new cash crops like tobacco. Commercialization of production and land shortage had occurred far earlier here than in the other Ngwato-dominated areas, leading the British to call the Kalanga one of the most progressive groups in the protectorate. Hints of their commercial attitudes toward cattle—different from those of the more saving Ngwato—may be glimpsed in acerbic Kalanga responses to Ngwato harangues: "An ox is not like a bicycle. You cannot ride it away and then pump it up before you sell it. . . . It must grow fat."[78]

Those without land were obliged to become labor migrants, with young men the principal victims of the land shortage. They, especially the teachers and shop assistants among them, were the main supporters of Mswazi. By the late forties, no fewer than one-third of the hamlet's taxpayers were working outside the district: "he went over the border on account of hunger,"[79] was how their absence was often described. On the Rand, many were employed by building contractors. Grouped in similar occupations and often belonging to mutual aid societies, many found that their sense of Kalanga identity was enhanced rather than diluted by living away from home.

To fill the coffers of his new tribal treasury, Tshekedi intensified his efforts to collect all back taxes and use them to develop and defend the chiefdom.[80] Headmen were made liable for part of the arrears owed by their ward members. Ardent tax collection and fiscal centralization served the interests of bureaucratic efficiency but alienated local political elites. In the depression of the early thirties, the payment of taxes was increasingly difficult and provoking. The Mswazis were earning cash and therefore had to pay taxes, but they resented being taxed for no visible benefit. They felt that their tax monies were being spent to develop the capital at Serowe. In 1929, for example, the Mswazis charged that "We were told that if we could pay Hut Tax for 25/- [shillings] we could get our school free yet now we have to pay for our Teachers. And our schools are not being given qualified Teachers at all all the qualified Teachers remain at Serowe [sic]."[81] Tshekedi also explicitly discriminated against the Mswazis by vetoing missionary plans to open a hospital in Bokalaka, the Kalanga region surrounding Mswazi's hamlet.[82] With only meager funds and few opportunities for economic development, the Mswazis were frustrated by the lack of return on their taxes, and their frustration was heightened by a land shortage that was driving them to seek alternative employment. The crisis escalated as the conditions of Mswazi life deteriorated.

The growth of Mswazi resistance was matched by Tshekedi's determination to crush it. In his protests to high protectorate officials, John Mswazi, headman of the hamlet and successor to the founder, was breaking a rule dear to the hearts of Tshekedi and other bureaucrats that seniors be addressed through their subordinates.[83] The case obsessed Tshekedi. The repeated flouting of this simple procedural rule endangered his chieftainship and called attention to the chief's newly subordinate and dependent role. It advertised the end of his monopoly of political life.

By the time the small Kalanga clan and their Ngwato overlords came to blows, tensions between them had been steadily escalating for more than two decades. The following narrative traces the spasmodic development of their public conflict from its mild beginning in 1926 to its violent end in 1947. The first overt confrontation occurred when the Mswazis found excessive the Ngwato demand that they pay both a hut tax and, effectively, a labor tax by working to erect a fence at the Rhodesian border. When the Mswazis deserted the fence site in 1926, ostensibly to pay their hut tax, the chief's representative slapped on a six-cattle fine for "disobedience."[84]

The Mswazis' acts of passive resistance grew increasingly provocative, and the Ngwato struck back more and more harshly. In 1929 Mswazi traveled to Mafeking to complain directly to the Resident Commissioner against an additional tax Tshekedi had levied without explanation or consultation. For his impertinence, Mswazi was tried, and publicly derided, in the Serowe *kgotla*: "We do not want clever people upsetting our chieftainship. They want progress and yet indulge in inprogressive [sic] habits [like polygamy]. . . . They do not know how to pay tribute. . . . When they were with the Matebele, the Matebele used to take even their children. . . . We do not agree that our peace and chieftainship should be upset by cowards."[85] When Mswazi continued to address complaints directly to colonial administrators and critics such as the Ballingers, who devoted their careers to expressing African interests in South Africa, the British agreed to Tshekedi's proposal that Mswazi be replaced by a Ngwato headman named Rasebolai Kgamane, one of Tshekedi's most senior relatives; Mswazi was to be shipped to Serowe.[86]

John Mswazi's compulsory absence failed to cow his village. The cattle levy remained unpaid and letters from the Mswazis continued to bypass the capital and land on the desks of exasperated protectorate officials.[87] By 1932 both Mswazi and Tshekedi preferred that the clan leave the Ngwato chiefdom entirely and perhaps forever. The British did not agree.[88] Fearful of encouraging the massive secession of malcontents, the British refused to find another place for them to live, and they allowed Mswazi to return home. Deeply angered that his nemesis would continue to plague him, Tshekedi warned that the ox levy, now two years overdue, would still have to be paid; "we overlooked many of their transgressions but now that they are not leaving our country and the Government has failed we will set a law for them and judge them for ourselves."[89] He accompanied a regiment to Bokalaka to extract the beasts by force. Despite this setback, the Mswazis had cause to celebrate three months later when Mswazi returned to the village from exile, triumphantly seated on a white horse.[90] With their leader restored, his followers lapsed into a less contentious spirit until the middle of the Second World War.[91]

During that deceptively quiet decade, the land crisis worsened. Neither Tshekedi nor the British bothered to understand the nature of Mswazi's and all other Kalanga farming. More plentiful, earlier rainfall in the north dictated earlier plowing than in the south, but the Ngwato chief gave belated permission for northern plowing to begin. The Kalanga needed land for fallow, but Tshekedi cut into their system of clientship by decreeing that only headmen could allocate land. He fined people who borrowed land and confiscated their grain. With this cavalier act, he was in effect filling the coffers of the tribal treasury with the wealth created by rich and poor Kalanga who had exchanged land for labor.[92]

Because his people were becoming impoverished under Ngwato rule, John Mswazi sought asylum for them in 1943 in the unlikely haven of the white settler colony in Southern Rhodesia. The Southern Rhodesian government would not grant asylum. Mswazi returned to Bokalaka and shortly afterward Tshekedi moved there for the month of July and refused to allocate any additional land to the Mswazi village. Tshekedi calculated that Mswazi had committed ten acts of disobedience, in addition to seeking refuge in Southern Rhodesia. He saw that John Mswazi was sent to prison for disobeying all ten chiefly orders. Passive gestures of noncompliance continued, such as failing to attend meetings, including the one at which Tshekedi was to reallocate land, and failing to pay tributary labor or fines; slights the Mswazis aimed at the chief's local representative insulted the chief himself. The Mswazis threatened, "we might one day break something which belongs to the Bamangwato people which is very slippery and fragile, like a glass."[93] Tshekedi, understanding himself to be that glass, sought British tacit support to move the village and to depose John Mswazi as soon as he was released from his eighteen-month stay in prison. In the meantime, Tshekedi forbade the Mswazis to plow. The British agreed to depose Mswazi but were reluctant to move the village "during the war, when garbled accounts of the action taken by Government were likely to have an upsetting effect on men" in the army.[94]

In 1945, John Mswazi was out of prison. His supporters greeted him with jubilation and, for the first time, responded with violence and spontaneous bitterness toward both imperial and subimperial officials who had come to deport the chief from the Kalanga area. The crowd pummeled and hurled stones at one white member of the Bechuanaland police, as well as at Tshekedi's local representative and one local loyalist.[95]

This brief defiant act provoked a massive display of imperial might that confirmed how dependent imperial relationships were on the appearance of might and the panoply of power. The Resident Commissioner, A. D. Forsyth Thompson, prepared to ask Southern Rhodesia for the loan of several armored cars and for a supply of tear gas bombs. He arranged for Tshekedi to call up a regiment of 150 of his men armed with rifles, sticks, spears and axes. He had one Union Defence Force and two Royal Air Force planes fly overhead. Plans were made to surround the hamlet after dark and to give the Mswazis an hour to surrender. If they failed to do so, "the cordon around the village was to be maintained, the water supplies captured and the people starved into submission."[96] The 35 core members of Mswazi's supporters were seized and trucked to Serowe, where they were declared "banished" and their possessions were sold.

Despite the intimidating and impoverishing display of imperial and subimperial might, the Mswazis adamantly reaffirmed that they were British rather than Ngwato subjects. They continued to pay their taxes directly to the protectorate government. They were, in consequence, inviting the full weight of retribution from the Ngwato. In October 1947, 600 armed Ngwato men, led by Oteng Mphoeng, surrounded Mswazi's village, ostensibly to protect the Ngwato tax collector and to remove 150 more "ringleaders" and their families, and denied the Mswazis access to any of the wells where they were accustomed to water their cattle.[97] Threatened with starvation and fearing annihilation, half the clan, about 1,400 people, crossed the border illegally into Southern Rhodesia. Tshekedi placed an armed cordon at the border and allowed only those who submitted to his authority to return.

When the Mswazis learned of Rhodesian stock limitations and high taxes, some opted for submission to Ngwato authority by returning and paying their taxes. Their decision was often fraught with latent household tension and many families split in half. Possessing only their portable property, some of the impoverished exiles who opted to stay in Rhodesia suffered a further setback when they received a fraction of the value of their stock, forfeited to the Ngwato when they crossed the border. Tshekedi had sold their confiscated cattle at public auction and paid the expenses of the occupying forces with half the proceeds.[98]

Shortly after this debacle, Tshekedi escorted Sir Evelyn Baring, the British High Commissioner, on a triumphant tour of his domain. Flushed with victory, he may have communicated to his guest a certain disdain toward the peoples of his own hinterland. Baring himself, taking liberties with Kipling as well as with the peoples themselves, likened them to "lesser breeds without the law." Racing over the rough veld behind Tshekedi's red and white jeep, the proconsul, a veteran of four years of imperial service in India, observed with apparent approval that his host governed it "faintly like an Indian state."[99] On the eve of its ultimate crisis, the Ngwato chiefdom was being successfully transformed, it seemed, into a modern state.

At first sight, the protracted dispute appeared to offer evidence of long-standing and bitter ethnic tension. During the many *kgotla* meetings, all of which failed to resolve the dispute, the Ngwato denigrated the language, the customs, and the heritage of the Kalanga, the language group to which the Mswazis belonged. They were taught lessons of rank. When they complained that the chief's representative tried cases without consulting them, one royal man called them impertinent for questioning seniors. The Ngwato politely reminded the British that the "lesser should obey the great." In the *kgotla,* they rudely taught the Mswazis the same lesson by deriding their leader: was Mswazi a cow or a person, a fly or a cat? Charging that their leader had refused to disinter a corpse for investigation by a European medical officer, they even insinuated that Mswazis engaged in witchcraft.

The ethnic prejudice apparently permeating this crisis was in fact largely produced by it. The rebellion did not spread to other Kalanga villages. Mswazi's, with its peculiar burden of land shortage and internecine conflict, was the only one to resist Ngwato overrule. Its residents had begun their resistance by objecting to the terms, rather than to the fact, of their inclusion in the Ngwato chiefdom. Was it not the right of all Ngwato to have cattle posts? "We find," some Mswazis complained, "that only when we are required to do something we are regarded as Ngwato [sic]."[100] One Kalanga soldier wrote to the High Commissioner from the Italian front, "Our men are now returning from the army, what were they fighting for? Were they fighting for freedom of mankind or were they fighting for the freedom of the Bamangwato and [the] slavery of their own people?"[101] From this bondage had come poverty and the desire for independence. To protect themselves, they set about affirming and even creating a sense of solidarity. Derided in the Serowe *kgotla* for being unprogressive polygamists, witch doctors and poor cattlemen, they asserted their right to speak in Ikalanga, their mother tongue. They beseeched the British for "white missionaries of our own, having missionary stations in our land who will learn our language and help us to make books in our language like other tribes."[102] They asked that the British appoint a commission of historians and anthropologists to find the "cause" of the conflict in "culture, tradition, customs."[103] When they or their neighbors succeeded in establishing a school or church independently of Serowe, both the British and the chief saw it as a place where a "sense of independent nationalism" was being fostered, and they had it destroyed.[104] The destruction may have undercut the organization and expression of separatist sentiment. It certainly worsened the prospects of landless people who were trying to invest in alternative employment. In this way, the cycle of deprivation and separatism deepened.

Like the Birwa and Khurutshe before them, the Mswazis had banked on an imperial alliance that never materialized. From the beginning of the affair, officials at the highest and lowest levels of protectorate government candidly hoped to gain Tshekedi's "full confidence by helping him to maintain his authority." As a result, they spurned the lesser plaintiffs as "sullen and obstinate," as "Communistic.... and semi-educated."[105] They marshaled both customary—that is traditional—and received—that is British—law.[106] They made liberal though sloppy use of Isaac Schapera's *Handbook of Tswana Law and Custom* to justify their partisan actions; when the book describes the chief's former power to banish rebels and to put them to death, it refers more to dynastic rivals than to subject peoples who wanted to secede. Protectorate officials also trained their arsenal of codified law against the Mswazis. They engaged in complicated casuistry to give Tshekedi's acts—such as his forced removal of tax defaulters and impounding of fugitives' stock—the imprimatur of the King's law.[107]

"Traditional" ethnic tension grew with the modern innovations of wage labor, freehold land, and bureaucratic government. It grew not because subject peoples were necessarily opposed to these innovations but because modernity was bringing declining standards of living to some areas of the periphery. The chief perversely met shortages of land with closer, more controlling, and more expensive government. Although he continued to demand collective responsibility and to punish whole communities, he was failing to guarantee collective security. British overrule protected him from being accountable for his people's security of land tenure even while he was becoming a territorial monarch. Like the South African government in the 1960s, he was able to launch his own unilateral betterment schemes and, like the South African government, he rode roughshod over popular opposition.

"Lesser Breeds without the Law" 173

Those who suffered most from these new extremities used imported institutions to press the British for communal rights. They called upon religious freedom, the king's law, and history to win a sympathetic hearing. In a new and creative way, people in the hinterland were trying to solve the old problem of protecting themselves from government. Formerly, they had tended to move quietly away rather than obey the chief's directives. Now they were claiming independence on the basis of ethnic difference.

Regional separatism occurred in areas where the market was disrupting inherited patterns of patronage. All three case studies discussed here took place on fringes of privately owned land. Sustained resistance occurred in the one area where people were experiencing multiple hardships. There, land shortage impaired the chief's ability to ensure his people's subsistence. Labor migration decimated the labor force of households. And the Ngwato chief was determined to crush opposition to his taxes and levies before it spread to other regions.

The chief defended his punitive actions by codifying relationships formerly noted for their flexibility and distance. Backed by the British, he had no need to co-opt the political elite of his hinterland by consulting them prior to imposing new demands. He banished his disobedient subjects, destroyed or confiscated their property, removed them to the capital at Serowe. In effect, he was asserting that property rights depended on his assessment of their political loyalty. Yet another irony of the Pax Britannica stems from this principle. The chief was amassing a fortune he would claim as his inalienable property at the same time as he was removing the property of his disloyal subjects and enforcing their collective responsibilities. His private fortune was growing as the new bureaucracy began to take over his own responsibilities for the welfare of the Ngwato. In this sense, the ideology of patriarchy was cloaking the transformation of inherited relations of dominance and subordination.

The "Indian state" that the proconsul saw flash by the windows of his jeep in 1948 existed more in his mind's eye than on the fringes of the Kalahari. It is true that the chief was, in effect, trying to create his own southern African version of a progressive monarchy, and that the "lesser breeds" were resisting control as they had always done. The twentieth century had brought them new organizational weapons to use in their struggle, while the burgeoning state had a new protector whose might could be called upon to repulse those challenges to its authority. Sanctioned by newly minted tradition but still enfeebled by its newness and poverty, a new political order was being born. Yet another category was being added to the spectrum of enemies who would soon bring down Tshekedi's regency and the chieftainship itself.

Chapter Five

"Things Fall Apart"
The Decline of the Ngwato Chieftainship, 1948-1956

Kgosi thutubudu e oleloa matlakala. (A chief is like an ashheap on which is gathered all the refuse.)
Tswana proverb

The Ngwato chieftainship fell in 1949. A succession dispute, a common event in Tswana history, precipitated the fall. This particular dispute had an unprecedented ending. Both the office and its occupant lost their powers. The chieftainship never recovered its monopoly of the power to organize Ngwato society, and the most senior member of the royal family never again ruled. Observers have found the cause of this upheaval in various quarters: in the machinations of the British government, or whites generally, or dynastic rivals, or in Tshekedi's autocratic habits, and even in the idea of "seniority."[1] Tshekedi, in fact, lost power because several disparate sources of opposition to his rule—women, young men, subject peoples, dynastic rivals—coalesced after the Second World War.

Tshekedi's office fell victim first to British imperial politics and then to the growth of the nation-state, which could better manage the relations of private property. The fall of the chief snapped the tension between the collective and individualistic impulses within Tswana society. With the chief gone, people enjoyed greater freedom to "scatter"—to live and work independently of their family groups and wards. Anarchy was not loosed upon the Ngwato world when the chief fell; rather, old restraints on individual enterprise were discarded, and a new definition of political legitimacy was being born.

The Economic Context

Why were the people of the Ngwato chiefdom becoming politically articulate and active at this particular moment? Two dramatic developments had occurred earlier in the forties: an unprecedented proportion of Ngwato men had left the reserve during the war years; by 1946 they had brought or sent back to the chiefdom an unprecedented amount of cash. Even though these two developments were of limited duration, they affected contemporary expectations of material prosperity.

The large-scale exodus of labor that began in 1941 represented a dramatic change in the habits of the Ngwato. Only one decade earlier, it had been, in the words of one District Commissioner, "almost impossible to get a native to go to the Gold Mines."[2] The rate of migration varied from region to region within the chiefdom, but only in areas like Bokalaka, which suffered from a land shortage, had it been substantial. When the war began, Tshekedi saw a splendid opportunity to win British support for his crusade against incorporation in the Union. After calling, in June 1941, a *letsholo* or compulsory meeting of all the men in the chiefdom, he energetically recruited soldiers to serve with imperial forces in the Middle East. By suspending Native Recruiting Corporation recruitment in 1942 and by pressuring tax evaders, he mustered more than 5,000 soldiers for King George VI. They constituted half of the entire protectorate army, the African Auxiliary Pioneer Corps. These efforts stimulated an unknown number of young men to avoid military service by fleeing secretly to employment in the Union; the result was a massive exodus of able-bodied men: by 1943, nearly 60 percent of the Ngwato chiefdom's taxpayers were away from home.[3]

The absence of men threw the burden of plowing and tending

cattle on women and children. In 1944 a District Commissioner remarked, "Although it has not been uncommon for some years to see women ploughing, the number of children engaged in this occupation was very noticeable this last year—in many cases children with insufficient strength were handling the plough while others equally small were doing their best to drive the oxen."[4] Without drawing any specific connection, he also noticed an increase in female "insanity" during the war years.[5] Clearly not all women and children suffered equally. Those women who received remittances from their absent men could purchase the shortfall in their own diminished subsistence production. Family groups with access to herders, whether Sarwa, family, or hired, could protect their herds from neglect and sell cattle on the recently opened and booming Johannesburg market; not until the war ended were the stultifying cattle quota restrictions reintroduced. Most female household heads who received no remittances relied on beer brewing to survive, and yet Tshekedi, like his half-brother and father, had prohibited the sale of beer; these women most acutely needed a voice in the *kgotla*.

Pioneer Corps recruits brought and sent unprecedented amounts of cash into the chiefdom. While a mine laborer had since 1933 been remitting annually about £9 of his pay, amounting to an annual total of £16,000 to £20,000 remitted by all recruited miners, the soldiers were sending home thousands of pounds each single month. The commissioner distributed £66,875 to their families during their first thirteen months in service. Much of the cash was garnered by Serowe traders, some reaping suspiciously high profits.[6] The boom reached its peak when the soldiers returned and in 1946 collected their savings—of sums up to £40—and began spending it on consumer goods and on restocking their herds.

One District Commissioner blustered in 1946 that the ex-soldiers acted as if they expected to find employment locally at army rates of pay.[7] The ex-soldiers blustered back that the government had not responded to their applications for financial aid from the Bechuanaland Soldiers Benefit Fund.[8] Not only had no jobs been created for veterans within the chiefdom, but the chief was making *new* demands for unpaid labor. In 1947 Tshekedi ordered 2,000 men to Bokalaka, where their regiments were to move to discipline the Mswazis. The following year a regiment was called out to construct a secondary school, the "Tuskegee of South Africa," as Tshekedi envisioned it, at a place called Moeng in the remote Tswapong Hills. The young men on the site were required to provide their own rations and to work continuously for a year with no breaks and little leisure. In addition to the regimental labor, Tshekedi asked each Ngwato family between 1946 and 1948 to contribute one ox for a total of £100,000 to pay the initial costs of constructing Moeng College. When another cattle levy had to be imposed to finance the repairs caused by the poor workmanship of the first building contractor, people did begin to grumble. Some men today admit that they disliked the work because they were not paid, yet I have met no one who is willing to declare that the regimental labor obligation was so onerous that it sparked a rebellion. After all, people say, the school was potentially for the benefit of everyone. The most privileged young men, later among the vanguard of anti-Tshekedi sentiment, did not have to perform regimental labor in any case. Those men with access to cash could buy their freedom from regimental labor obligations, while "the unemployed" had to work. In short, the regiments did not provide catalysts of popular resentment. Rather, the rejection of Tshekedi's rule must be seen as a consequence of concurrent demands for labor and property upon a recently and briefly enriched people.

In 1948, a foot-and-mouth epidemic struck. It prevented anyone from selling his cattle. The tribal treasury went nearly bankrupt. In 1942 a severe drought set in. With little respite over the next decade, the drought dried up surface waters, causing the death of many cattle and a negligible harvest.[9] This convergence of disasters was not new in Tswana history but no other period of drought, disease, and levies had followed upon such widespread prosperity based on cash. The massive inflow of cash had raised popular expectations of attainable affluence but by 1947 the amount of cash coming into the economy had dwindled nearly to prewar levels. The fall of Tshekedi must be seen within the context of the boom and bust economy of the postwar years. Only then does the particular constellation of his enemies become intelligible.

The Marriage

Throughout Tshekedi's long career, he had looked toward the time when he would transfer the chieftainship to his nephew Seretse; he attended so carefully to the details of Seretse's interests that he shopped personally in Johannesburg for Seretse's bridles, saying that only the best were suitable for "the [next] chief."[10] In 1944, when Seretse was twenty-three, Tshekedi and some elders thought that he was old enough to assume office and to begin to learn the ways of the *kgotla* that his Western education at Lovedale, Tigerkloof, and Fort Hare had not taught him. Seretse asked for a postponement while he studied to become a barrister in Great Britain. Throughout his three-year absence, his uncle refused to make decisions that would "mortgage the future in so far as the future Chief is concerned" because he would shortly be transferring power to him.[11]

In September 1948, Seretse announced in a letter to his uncle that he would be returning from Britain in the company of his twenty-two-year-old bride. "I realize that this matter will not please you," he wrote, "because the tribe will not like it as the person I am marrying is a white woman."[12]

Seretse judged his uncle correctly. Upon his return he would learn how much popular opposition he had aroused. Even before leaving Britain, he had begun to appreciate the extent of his uncle's displeasure. Tshekedi had immediately contacted the Resident Commissioner in Bechuanaland and three days later Sir Evelyn Baring, the High Commissioner. Baring cabled the Commonwealth Relations Office for advice and learned that, at this stage of the affair, British policy was laissez-faire. Officials in

London felt that since they had no legal grounds for objecting to the marriage, they should adopt a public position of strictest neutrality and leave Seretse to consult the tribe. Through his contacts in Britain, Tshekedi tried to prevent the wedding. Despite the blocking efforts of the Bishop of London and members of the London Missionary Society, Seretse Khama and Ruth Williams were married on 29 September 1948.

Tshekedi primed his lawyer, Douglas Buchanan of Cape Town, to begin a long legal battle in defense of the principle that no woman could become the wife of the chief unless she had been accepted by "the tribe." Buchanan argued that Seretse was well aware of the customary procedure because he would not have been the heir apparent if the tribe had accepted the marriage of his elder half-brother's mother. True to his legal training and Tshekedi's directives, Buchanan listed a formal series of steps by which a legitimate chiefly marriage was established,

Once the chief-to-be has made his choice, he seeks the approval of a senior royal uncle who in turn approaches the ruling chief, or points out another uncle who should approach the chief. If the ruling chief agrees, the royal leaders of the tribe are consulted individually. Ultimately, a private official meeting is held at which the decision is taken. If favourable, the proposal is announced in a public *kgotla* meeting. At any stage of this procedure, if serious objection is raised, the matter can be dropped.[13]

In this description and in likening Tswana custom to the rules governing the lives of the British royal family, Buchanan was revealing a legalistic logic that failed to take account of the political machinations that actually determined Tswana succession. Buchanan ignored, in short, that dynastic clashes in the precolonial Ngwato chiefdom had never been resolved by an external arbiter of justice or by reference to an abstract set of legal codes. They were ended by the victory of the stronger over the weaker faction. The questions to be resolved here are whose faction was stronger—Seretse's or Tshekedi's—and why.

After Seretse's return to Bechuanaland in October 1948, three public meetings were held among the Ngwato to discuss his marriage. They were preceded by one restricted to his senior relatives. Only one of the fifteen men in attendance reportedly approved of the marriage. The first public meeting began two days later and ran for four days in the *kgotla* at the heart of Serowe. Between two and three thousand people from all parts of the chiefdom attended this November *kgotla,* but they could hardly be called representative of all Ngwato. In a highly significant move, Tshekedi had denied access to younger regiments in order to ensure that only men over forty years of age were present; he felt that the young were growing too insubordinate. Women were in any event prohibited from attending *kgotla* meetings. As Seretse was aware, but powerless to prevent, these two restrictions skewed the expression of popular opinion against him.

For four days the older men sternly lectured Seretse on Ngwato history and the imperatives of custom. Only seven people spoke in favor of his marriage, while seventy-eight opposed it. The sole issue that divided the majority was whether Seretse should be allowed to return to Britain where he had left his bride and interrupted his legal studies. Some speakers favored asking the British government to annul the marriage. Others were content to assert the authority of tradition. As one senior member of the royal family intoned on behalf of his relatives, "We have the power to control you, we made Tshekedi chief, we have not given you the power as yet and therefore you cannot order us to follow your wishes."[14]

At this stage of the crisis, the loudest and most numerous voices raised against Seretse's marriage, though not against Seretse himself, belonged to royalty. Royalty was asserting its right to be consulted before any act by the heir could be considered lawful. This principle was one of many pushed forward during the *kgotlas*. Most statements asserted the vitality of other traditions which, if they had ever existed, had already fallen into disuse: for example, that Seretse's bride should have been chosen by Tshekedi, not by Seretse; also, that it showed disrespect to the Chief's *kgotla* to speak there in favor of the marriage; or that Seretse had no right to reply to a chief in the *kgotla* because he was not yet a chief himself. As Tshekedi closed the meeting, he threatened to leave Ngwato for a senior chiefdom elsewhere if the majority turned against him.

Seretse's second and farewell public *kgotla,* on 28 and 29 December, from which younger men were once again excluded, ostensibly upheld the traditionalist viewpoint. But an undercurrent of dissent had become apparent. Many speakers contrived to address the *kgotla* in such ambiguous terms that they could not easily be counted as pro- or anti-Seretse. One man asked, "When does the tribe begin to fear and respect the chief's son?" and was answered by a voice in the audience, "[In 1944] when he was given a regimental name." Some speakers candidly told Tshekedi that they had assumed a position in the *kgotla* they did not dare to express outside it: "We know the chief's ability and so we do not speak freely expressing the whole truth. Always outside the meeting we all say we want that woman but when we are here in your presence we say something different." Even the principle of the supremacy of royalty had begun to be mildly challenged; Seretse had, after all, one speaker said, asked the whole tribe, including commoners, and not just his royal uncles whether he should return to England, a tactic that led Tshekedi to dismiss the emerging support for Seretse as "insignificant people of no standing in the Tribe, not capable of ever assisting the Chief."[15]

Two competing paradigms of argument emerged on the issue of rank. One suggested that the debate properly belonged in the hands of the older notables, and of royalty in particular, because "they have ruled with past chiefs," the other that the debate belonged to the whole tribe because they would bear the costs of any disturbance. Seretse noted that people were "afraid of speaking because they fear to lose their property and employment." One commoner wearily revealed his practical reason for refusing to oppose the marriage: "we dislike to be asked to pay a levy in money or in kind to defray any court expenses."[16] The people who were willing to state publicly that they had been moved by such material considerations were still in the minority.

Only 31 spoke in favor of the marriage, while 115 opposed it. A few days later, Seretse left this legal wrangle for England where, ironically, he sat for his bar exams.

In the meantime Tshekedi tried to extract from imperial representatives a legal confirmation of the verdict of the November and December *kgotlas*. Because the protectorate administration continued to swear that it possessed no legal power to exclude Ruth Khama from the territory, Tshekedi and his lawyer approached the High Commissioner. Besides asking for Ruth's exclusion, they asserted that Seretse was not competent ever to be chief and should not even be permitted to reside in the reserve as a private individual. Tshekedi himself was insinuating the idea that the British would later adopt for their own purposes: Seretse was morally unfit to be chief. They then committed the tactical error that ended Tshekedi's regency: they asked for yet another *kgotla*, which they asserted would prove that all Ngwato opinion was opposed to Seretse.[17]

When Tshekedi referred to "all Ngwato opinion," he was probably deferring to the democratic sensibilities of the British. In fact, except for his daily tally of the pro and con speakers at the preceding *kgotlas*, he had not compromised his view that the sole legitimate decision maker in the chiefdom, acting as the judicious assessor of tribal opinion, was the chief himself.

During the crisis, the "sons of Sekgoma [I]," the descendants of Khama's brothers, had been trying to assert the dwindling powers and privileges of their rank. Tshekedi had tolerated their rhetorical contributions in the *kgotla* as long as they were opposed to the marriage. But Ngwato factions were being forged during secret nighttime meetings. Tshekedi tried to learn their membership and their sentiments by sending spies and by calling his own night meetings to discover by subtraction who was missing. During the two-day December *kgotla* he had attempted to intimidate the burgeoning opposition by announcing the names of both royalty and commoners he knew to be meeting secretly. That the intimidation failed became apparent during the third and final *kgotla*. On 20 June 1949, after Seretse's return from writing his exams in London, more than 3,500 men gathered once again, mainly from Serowe but with scatterings from all corners of the chiefdom. At the six-day hearing, many men wore their World War Two uniforms. Defections into Seretse's camp now split the once united front of royalty. Serogola Seretse—Seretse's cousin and, until shortly before, the chief's deputy—spoke, winning considerable support for his statement: "The talk is no longer about the wife but about the chieftainship. Sekgoma's son, not Khama's, is the chief. Seretse is the chief. I say, let the woman come and their child shall succeed."[18] Fearful that he would appear to be abandoned by the traditionalists, Tshekedi asked the "sons of Sekgoma" who opposed the marriage to come to his side. Nine senior headmen came forward to signify their support for the regent.

Seretse, eager to tally his popular support, now invited his leading supporters to the dais and addressed the assemblage. Calling all to sit close, he first asked, "All those *not* in favor of me and my wife stand up." Forty people rose. Then he invited those favoring him and his wife to stand. The mass of the assembly rose to its feet, cheering him with the traditional blessing, the Tswana word for rain, "Pula! Pula! Pula!" An official protectorate observer described the moment as "a stirring spectacle, a magnificent expression of public sentiment."[19] For perhaps the first time in Ngwato history, the people had voted directly, without reference to ward headmen or to any other seniors. Tshekedi cried out, "If this white woman comes, I go. My nephew has killed us! I warn you, my nephew, son of Sekgoma, they are not speaking truly. They are using you as a tool!"[20] Tshekedi did not say who was "using" Seretse, but "they" were, undoubtedly, those other "sons of Sekgoma" or descendents of Sekgoma I who were seeking to regain their ancestors' powers as chief makers and councillors.

Tshekedi now announced his departure from the chiefdom to Rametsana in the northeast corner of Kweneng near the Ngwato border; "he emphasized that he was going out a free man, free to return when he liked, and that he would often be seen in Serowe."[21] True to his ideal of deference to rank, Tshekedi had asked for refuge at Rametsana among the Kwena because they were senior to the Ngwato.

Popular allegiance had shifted massively between November 1948 and June 1949. The secrecy that necessarily surrounds the building of factions has obscured the strategic details of the realignments—who was allied to whom and for what reasons. Nevertheless, an examination of how the problem was defined at different times can help explain the apparent shifts in popular opinion. Tshekedi had defined the crisis as Seretse's marriage to a white woman and her resulting status as wife of the heir to a chieftainship—*mohumagadi*, mother of the tribe. Both the "sons of Sekgoma" and the first *kgotla* had rejected her in this role and refused to consider Seretse's marriage as legitimate. It is clear that Seretse was not, as a corollary, deemed unfit to rule as chief. An interpretation that he was morally unfit was imposed on the first two public *kgotlas* by Tshekedi himself when he was reporting to Sir Evelyn Baring in April 1949. But the Ngwato, in the meantime, became aware that disapproval of the marriage might cost them the sole heir, that is, the only son of the previous chief, Khama's son, Sekgoma II. By the third public *kgotla* in June many people feared that Tshekedi would be able to use a vote of disapproval to keep the chieftainship for himself; indeed, some Ngwato had become convinced that Tshekedi had, to ensure that he could remain chief, used witchcraft to persuade Seretse to marry an Englishwoman.[22] As Serogola, the influential royal cousin, stressed, "It was suspected that Tshekedi had ambitions."[23] Certainly no other Ngwato but Tshekedi ever suggested to the British that Seretse's marriage to a white woman had made him incompetent to be chief.

At first, Ruth Khama's race probably signified two fearsome prospects to the Ngwato: the vague threat of being incorporated in the Union, because some may have feared that the Union might invade to protect white integrity, and a more general threat to the maintenance of Ngwato integrity as traditionalists defined it—"To marry a white woman is to finish our tribalism." Tshekedi spelled out this logic to a newspaper reporter clearly and passionately the week after the final *kgotla*:

> The thing that cuts deep into my heart is that this tribe of ours is heading for disintegration. . . . My work in the past twenty two years, the plans I have for the tribe's future welfare, all now go overboard because of a white woman 6000 miles away who has never seen Africa in her life. . . . A chieftainness who could not speak the language would be completely stumped. The coming of a white woman can lead only to chaos and disintegration.[24]

Perhaps in deference to the British observers present at all the *kgotla* meetings, lesser Ngwato raised the issue of race only occasionally. A few people offered insulting jibes, saying that Seretse's children would be mules. More pointed out that his marriage would end the royal family, perhaps resulting in leadership by a white chief.[25] Others alluded to the denigrating treatment Africans had suffered at the hands of "coloreds" and whites: "I cannot accept a woman who will probably send dogs after me when I attempt to go to her home." One Ngwato quietly reminded his fellows not to pursue this objection too ardently: "By saying we object to colour, we are objecting to the Protectorate. Our protectors are of a different colour, we cannot disregard them; they are here."[26]

The fear of economic and political retaliation by South Africa shaped the contradictory behavior of the British after the final *kgotla*. Protectorate officials had been present at each of the three public meetings. At times they had warned about the possible consequences of Seretse's marriage. One official had reminded the Ngwato that the protectorate was still economically dependent on the Union; Bechuanaland would suffer if South Africa, choosing to punish it for tolerating the interracial marriage, closed labor markets and refused to send supplies of maize in a drought year. Nevertheless, British policy was not to interfere; overt imperial meddling, it was feared, might drive the Afrikaner government, in power in Pretoria since May 1948, toward secession from the Commonwealth. When Sir Evelyn Baring met Seretse on 5 July, he gave him the distinct impression that he would be installed in the chieftainship by the end of the month. At the same time, Baring rejected Tshekedi's insistence that a judicial enquiry be held into Ruth Khama's status.[27] Less than a week later, the official British position on Seretse's chieftainship was completely reversed. Early in July, Baring decided to avoid giving official recognition to Seretse as chief; by the end of the month his recommendation had won over the entire British cabinet. In effect adopting Tshekedi's request for an enquiry into Seretse's suitability, Baring was hoping to postpone and perhaps avoid a confrontation with the Union.

Baring's about-face had derived from his consultation with Douglas Forsyth, since 1941 secretary and effective head of South Africa's Department of External Affairs. Forsyth's analysis had in turn originated in a discussion with the recently elected and "desperately worried" Prime Minister, D. F. Malan. They all reasoned, in Baring's words,

if we recognize Seretse the extremists will override the more moderate Nationalists. They believe that Seretse's recognition would enable them to exploit colour feeling without exasperating English-speaking South Africans.... They would thus fight the battle for a secessionist republic with the ideal war-cry and at the ideal time.[28]

Eight months later, after Malan had publicly condemned the marriage and begun to demand the transfer of the High Commission Territories, Jan Smuts ventured the same analysis. Replying in March 1950 to Winston Churchill's request for his views, he wrote that recognition of Seretse as chief would "be looked upon as a capitulation, which might seriously damage British authority, and indeed all government authority in South Africa." He went on to repeat the analysis that had led Baring to conceal the true logic of his actions: "public opinion here would harden behind Malan's claim for the annexation of the protectorates to the Union, and in case this claim were refused, the extreme course of declaring South Africa a republic would at once become a live issue."[29] When it appeared that Seretse's marriage would have dire consequences for imperial politics, the British eagerly snapped up Tshekedi's suggestion that Seretse be denied the chieftainship on grounds of incompetence and abandoned their weak initial commitment to let the tribe decide.

Even the objectives of the commission of enquiry, presided over by Sir Walter Harragin, High Court judge of the territories, were skewed by the perceived need to exclude Seretse. The first object of the enquiry was to determine whether the June *kgotlas* had been properly convened and assembled, and whether they had been conducted according to custom; the second was to learn "whether Seretse Khama was a fit and proper person to discharge the functions of chief."[30] These terms of reference were defined shortly after both the South African and Southern Rhodesian governments began to express open hostility toward the Ngwato heir.[31]

The hearings were held in two places because relations between the regent, the heir, and their followers were growing increasingly strained. Tshekedi chose to give his evidence in Lobatse, the seat of the High Court, 250 miles to the south because, he said, he feared for his life in Serowe. No more than one hundred people listened to the testimony from the public gallery of an ordinary courtroom. With a marked air of suspicion, he presented verbose oral and written evidence that Seretse was unfit for the chieftainship. In Serowe, Seretse presented his own evidence before three thousand people jammed around a marquee. Looking directly at Harragin and the other two commissioners, Seretse replied to the charges, "I claim the chieftainship because it is due to me and the tribe wants me. My morals are as good as any chief or better and though I have not received any training in native administration, I will have the advice of headmen and uncles of great experience." Comparing his assessment of his own moral and educational strengths with Tshekedi's opportunism, he said, "All his undertakings or decisions against his own interests and ambitions have been made with qualifications."[32]

Most of Tshekedi's charges accused Seretse of transgressions against "native law and custom": people did not vote in the *kgotla*; only the chief could put questions to them there; Seretse had improperly shifted the issue from the marriage to the chieftainship and so had "stampeded the tribe into an improper decision."[33] Tshekedi blamed the British for blocking him from using force to suppress the "rebellion" before it had taken root. He would have had the weight of customary law behind him, he added, because "there is no such thing as a decision given by a majority of the persons present. . . . the chief's power of decision at a *kgotla* presided over by him is *absolute*. . . . the *kgotla* is the chief acting with the advice of the people present."[34] Tshekedi was still presenting his voice as the sole source of legitimacy in the chiefdom.

People commonly believed that Tshekedi was selfishly trying to wrest the chieftainship from Seretse, a popular impression the British government stoked by treating Tshekedi as the plaintiff "for the sake of convenience and clarity." Many Ngwato believed that the British favored Tshekedi and were planning to split the northern and southern protectorate between South Africa and the future Central African Federation. In an attempt to quell this perception of his motives, Tshekedi renounced the chieftainship for himself and for his descendants, but he failed miserably in his efforts partly because he steadfastly depicted Seretse as unfit for the chieftainship because of his irresponsible marriage; "The moment the people lose their respect for a king he is obviously shorn of his value and he ceases to exist."[35] And yet even Tshekedi could not deny that Seretse had won substantial popular acclaim. Tshekedi's reputation for deviousness was confirmed in the popular view by his effort to submit a draft scheme for the government of the Ngwato Reserve *by* the Kwena chiefdom, in which he had been given refuge and from which he hoped to retain control of his people.

In December 1949, Harragin ruled that the *kgotla* was properly convened and conducted, but that Seretse was not fit to be chief: that recognition of Seretse would cause disruption in Ngwato; that he was a prohibited immigrant in South Africa; and "a friendly and cooperative Union of South Africa and

Southern Rhodesia is essential to the well-being of the Tribe and indeed the whole of the Bechuanaland Protectorate."[36] In these decisions, Harragin was responding to the imperatives of imperial politics. He did not disguise the logic of his ruling in the report he gave to the British government, and so the report was suppressed.[37]

Local power had passed from Tshekedi to become firmly lodged in the hands of the British government. The British did not know what to do with it. Evelyn Baring provided the direction for most of the government's subsequent actions until his transfer to Kenya in July 1951. Although he pressed the Commonwealth Secretary to exclude Seretse forever from the protectorate and the chieftainship, he managed to win only a five-year period of exclusion. The Labour government was clearly mystified by the "tribal" politics and fearful of being accused by liberal voters of collusion with South Africa; the five-year exclusion represents the government's compromise with Baring's advice. Indeed, their quandary was so great that Prime Minister Clement Attlee even wrote directly to the District Commissioner in Serowe for his views. Attlee worried,

we are invited to go contrary to the desires of the great majority of the Bamangwato tribe, solely because of the attitude of the governments of the Union of South Africa and Southern Rhodesia. It is as if we had been obliged to agree to Edward VIII's abdication so as not to annoy the Irish Free State and the United States of America.[38]

Baring and the Commonwealth Relations Office eventually concluded that Seretse and his wife Ruth should be called to London for consultations. Basing their strategy on Baring's assessment of the couple as opportunists, the British resolved to offer Seretse a £1,100 annual income in exchange for a promise never to enter the protectorate. They planned to exile him for five years if he refused. Seretse repeatedly rejected the bribe, explaining that the tribe would feel that he had betrayed them. The British government promptly made public the news of his five-year term of exile even before he himself learned of it. People at home in the protectorate would not have been surprised by the British subterfuge; the Ngwato who assembled in the Serowe *kgotla* in February 1950 had already expressed doubts about the willingness of the British government to consult genuinely with Seretse and had recommended that neither Seretse nor Ruth Khama should respond to the invitation to London.

Patrick Gordon Walker, the Labour Secretary for Commonwealth Relations, announced in Parliament on 8 March that the chieftainship was suspended until "the disappearance of the present tendencies to disruption which threaten the unity and well-being of the tribe." The next month he revealed his logic in his diary.

> All along I was convinced that he could not be recognized. I had been impressed by Baring's dictum that we could only hold the High Commission Territories from the Union so long as white opinion there was divided and cool (as it now is): if it became inflamed and united we would be helpless.... We would certainly lose the High Commission Territories to the Union. This would not directly affect our interests, but it would subject two million Africans to oppression. It would probably drive the Union out of the Commonwealth and inestimably weaken us in any war with Russia.[39]

Shortly afterward the White Paper appeared, replacing the suppressed Harragin report. This official version of the crisis contained a number of untruths and half-truths, all calculated to obscure the emphatic influence of South African pressure on British policy. It ignored Baring's initial willingness to accept the verdict of the third *kgotla* and his subsequent consultation with representatives of the Union government. It camouflaged the act Churchill was to call "a very disreputable transaction"—Seretse's invitation to London for "consultation" after his exile had been decided. It denied that South Africa and the issue of miscegenation had in any way influenced British policy: "His Majesty's Government are fully aware of the very strong feelings that are aroused on the subject of the merits or demerits of mixed marriages, but that is not the issue which is here raised.... [N]o representations on this matter have been received from the Government of the Union of South Africa or Southern Rhodesia."[40]

The White Paper announced the suspension of the *kgotla* and the beginning of direct rule. The voice of the people was to be cultivated following a brief interim period of direct rule by the District Commissioner. His duties would then be transferred to "a small council of leading and suitable persons as soon as they are prepared to come forward and serve in such capacity."[41] To the authors of the White Paper, the council solution undoubtedly seemed the most just and efficient means of ridding the chiefdom of its "tendency" to suffer from royal feuds. They argued that the democratic development of the chiefdom would be inhibited by the presence of Seretse and of Tshekedi. They were correct. And yet they failed to perceive the corollary: no government could function that excluded Seretse. The lesson became immediately apparent. When Baring, shortly afterward, traveled to Serowe to address the Ngwato, the Ngwato boycotted the *kgotla*. The wife of the local labor recruiter wryly observed that Baring had arrived at the Serowe *kgotla* "all dressed up in his plumes and feathers, ready to attend the *kgotla,* and they tried hard to find a few natives for him to talk to, but no one would go."[42] Two months later the Ngwato prevented the District Commissioner from speaking by shouting him down. The banishment of Seretse precipitated a period of violence and civil disobedience that was to last three years.

The banishment of both leaders in March 1950 caused a lacuna in political authority that the British tried to fill by appointing as Native Authority the most senior member of royalty available, Keaboka Kgamane. Keaboka was already Tshekedi's enemy; he had been jailed by the chief for a year and a half on charges of spreading the rumor among Tswana soldiers that Hitler had bombed half of England. The British also began to urge the creation of representative councils. Many Ngwato responded by resisting the directives of all central authority. Nor were their motives always partisan. Large numbers of people now began to leave Serowe to live year round at their cattle posts and fields and manage their agricultural production without being drawn into disputes. Throughout the chiefdom, people exploited the absence of a strong central power by failing to pay their taxes. Some tax evaders deliberately chose to cripple the Ngwato treasury by contributing instead to a fund for Seretse's lawyers. Bo-Seretse, as supporters of Seretse were called, traveled to regional *kgotlas* urging Ngwato to boycott foot-and-mouth inspections of cattle and meetings called by the District Commissioner. As a consequence of this pattern of resistance the British proved powerless to impose the councils in the face of pervasive social and political disorder.

Occasionally, tensions between the two factions erupted into violence, usually precipitated by a "Rametsana," or follower of Tshekedi, who was attempting to remove his property—cattle, furniture, Sarwa—from the chiefdom. If, for example, the division of an inheritance had not been accepted by all family members, an attempt to leave the chiefdom with all or part of it could cause a furor. The first public riot in Serowe occurred in April 1950 for precisely this reason, when a mob prevented one of Tshekedi's most prominent supporters from removing sixty-four cattle of his disputed inheritance. They drove away the cattle, dismantled his cart, and manhandled police who tried to stop them. Their victim baldly summarized their motives: "They do not like us because of our belongings that we would like to get from them."[43] Other Tshekedi partisans, particularly those in positions of authority, such as schoolteachers or seniors who lingered in the reserve, were physically assaulted by people who feared that they would use their influence to insinuate Tshekedi back into power, whereupon Tshekedi would banish all his opponents, something he had been noted for doing since his accession.

The second riot occurred in July 1951, when three hundred young men of the Malekantwa regiment, headed by a senior royal man, Lenyeletse Seretse, tried to evict a group of Rametsanas who returned to Serowe for their belongings. Besides collecting their cattle, they were filling two 3-ton trucks with their furniture and female servants. The mob manhandled and threw stones at them, in effect obeying Keaboka's command that they be ejected. The young men had grievances of their own, however, as Lenyeletse revealed when he blamed "white men" and "old men" for "delay[ing] them too long." Young men commonly felt that Tshekedi was allied to these two barriers to their material progress and independence.[44]

The attackers defended their acts with extraordinary definitions of the connection between property and citizenship rights. "Anyone who leaves the country must leave his cattle behind," one Seretse partisan explained, "Cattle are communal property and I as a Mongwato have a claim against them."[45] This explanation represents yet another attempt to win advantages in an alien legal system by inventing a Ngwato customary law. Such casuistry was an attempt to conceal that the Bo-Seretse had in effect adopted one of Tshekedi's favorite means of quelling political opposition: banishment with the forfeiture of property rights. And so the victims were left to cry, impotent against the mob, "The property is mine. Tshekedi allocated it to me. He distributed it. He gave me permission [to leave Serowe with it]."[46]

Given the ferocity with which many Ngwato expressed their opposition to Tshekedi's return, the British hardly needed to send an investigative commission to divine popular opinion. They knew how unpopular Tshekedi had become. But although in February 1951 Secretary of State for Commonwealth Relations Patrick Gordon Walker had personally addressed the Serowe *kgotla* as part of a new strategy "to make it clear that Tshekedi is out," as well as "to allow an anti-Ruth feeling to develop,"[47] he sent three men—H. L. Bullock, W. M. Macmillan, and D. L. Lipson—in July 1951 to report on "the attitude of the tribe to Tshekedi's return to the Bamangwato Reserve as a private individual."[48] For a year Tshekedi had been trying to gain the right to enter the reserve, ostensibly to oversee his vast herds of cattle. He had been unable, he said, to leave his property in the care of a reliable representative and it was being ruined by neglect. Some Bo-Seretse did not trust Tshekedi's motives, and others were using his absence to acquire some of his property for themselves.

Gordon Walker had asked his three delegates, so incongruous a trio that one *Life* magazine photographer likened them to the Marx Brothers, to hold a *kgotla* to be attended by both factions. But whenever Tshekedi's followers tried to join a public hearing convened for the observers, they were chased away and sometimes required police protection. The mob feared that their testimony would allow Tshekedi to return, to seize the chieftainship, and to discipline viciously those who opposed him. Only one village allowed the Rametsanas, Tshekedi's followers, to stay.[49] The three observers concluded gratuitously that because "emotions now run dangerously high throughout the tribe," Tshekedi should not be permitted to return to the Ngwato Reserve in any capacity.

His Majesty's government, led by the Conservative Party since October 1951, fostered popular Ngwato suspicion of its partisanship to Tshekedi by announcing, on the same day the three observers reported their contrary conclusions, that Tshekedi could return to Ngwato if he shunned tribal politics. It simultaneously offered Seretse a job in Jamaica with the Colonial Service, a curious offer to a man who had been deemed morally unfit to be chief. By March 1952, the Commonwealth Relations Office was soiling the last vestiges of its reputation among the Ngwato for impartiality by denying that Seretse could ever be chief and by allowing Tshekedi to reenter the reserve. This novel attempt to be decisive after years of playing for time brought the crisis of authority closer to its climax.

Only one act remained before the plummet to violence. A six-man delegation of senior royal Bo-Seretse placed yet another cattle levy on the Ngwato to pay for travel to London in April 1952.[50] There they presented to Lord Salisbury, the new Commonwealth Relations Secretary, their people's refusal to elect or cooperate with an appointed chief. When Salisbury steadfastly rejected Seretse as chief, the delegation asked that Seretse be allowed to assist the tribe in another capacity: "as a result of such a scheme," they proposed, "a more democratic form of government might be brought about and the trust and faith in the British government might be restored."[51] Salisbury deflected this plea with the familiar, but now desperately inadequate, bureaucratic advice that it should go through the proper channels and be presented first to the Resident Commissioner. In May, the Bo-Seretse received a definitive rejection. An order-in-council was issued denying Seretse, Tshekedi, and their children the possibility of holding any position of responsibility in the tribe. The statutory order empowered the High Commissioner to designate a chief, and it forbade any petition on behalf of Seretse to reach the High Court. Thus, in May 1952, the full weight of imperial law was finally thrown against the steadily eroding political order in the Ngwato Reserve.

The result was rioting. When the delegation of rebuffed royal headmen returned to Serowe, its leader, Keaboka Kgamane, resigned, reportedly because he sensed the welling of popular dissatisfaction with his failure to ensure Seretse's return. On 26 May 1952 the District Commissioner, P. G. Batho, tried to address the *kgotla* at which the delegation was formally to announce its failure. He was shouted down and, when he tried to leave, a menacing crowd surrounded his car. Batho retaliated by completely closing the *kgotla,* and by stationing a police guard there. Unrest simmered throughout the weekend, with illicit meetings met by arrests. On Sunday, 1 June, the police moved to disperse the massive crowds that had gathered defiantly to listen to pro-Seretse speakers. At least one member of the mob shouted for the Europeans to come to the front so they would not harm fellow Africans. They turned on the police and three Sotho policemen were killed. The District Commissioner was stoned. He survived by driving through the mob.

After the melee, the Bo-Seretse closed ranks to protect the identities of the people who had actually committed the murders. Although the High Court subsequently conducted two trials— one for public violence and one for murder—all witnesses denied that the accused or anyone else was involved.⁵² With the closing of the *kgotla,* resentment of British authority had risen to such a pitch that, in a sense, the fifteen hundred people in the crowd were equally responsible for the violence.

Anti-European sentiments had often been expressed even before the riot. One eighty-year-old man was said to have threatened, "These Europeans seem to think this country belongs to them, today they will all die."⁵³ Antagonism toward the British overlords was caused in part, of course, by the suspicion that they were backing Tshekedi, but the mistrust was compounded by diffuse fears that the government would take over the land and enforce a compulsory de-stocking policy. By suspending the *kgotla,* the British were also risking every Ngwato's livelihood. Cattle sale permits would no longer be issued to help prevent the sale of stolen stock. Disputes over cattle and other property would fester unresolved. The absence of the indigenous judicial authority of the *kgotla* could not help but encourage illicit activities, particularly at the expense of the propertied members of Ngwato society. The number of related cases brought to the District Commissioner leapt upward: he judged seven times as many "crimes against the social economy" in 1952 as he had in 1951, twice as many "offences against property"; cases of public violence rose from zero to thirty-eight.⁵⁴

Between May 1952 and July 1953, no African tribunals functioned. This hiatus in indigenous political authority helped to undermine the principle of collective authority that Tshekedi and his predecessors had so ardently upheld. From a distance, Tshekedi urged, "Law and order throughout the reserve cannot be restored unless the principle of responsibility of the headmen [for the behavior of the residents of their villages] is strictly applied."⁵⁵ Tshekedi was referring explicitly to the illegal ousting of his supporters from positions of authority and employment in the reserve.⁵⁶ His complaint reveals the extent to which the system of local government by headmen had become dependent on a strong chieftainship. When the office of the chief became weak, mob rule could result; a faction within a village might try to punish an alleged offender without receiving any reprimand or sanction from above. As late as 1955, ward *kgotlas* still had not reopened, because headmen were said to be opposed to the appointment—on 13 May 1953—of Rasebolai Kgamane—another senior royal man and partisan of Tshekedi—as "Native Authority." When he tried his first case against a Bo-Seretse in 1953, mob violence was, according to one story, averted only by seating Rasebolai between two civil servants.[57] Tshekedi blamed this lawlessness on his own absence, but other forces were also at work.

The Factions

Compared with Seretse's motley array of partisans, the men who accompanied Tshekedi into exile at Rametsana were a coherent group dedicated to serving the regent and his vision of the chieftainship. Among the best-educated men of middle age in the chiefdom, they had held positions of high responsibility in Tshekedi's administration. They were also among the richest, bringing twenty-five to thirty thousand head of cattle with them into exile. They proudly referred to one another as "the cream of the crop."

In June 1949, forty-three of these men signed a declaration that they would accept the Kwena chief's invitation to settle in the lion-ridden wilds of Rametsana rather than compromise their principles and allegiance by remaining in Serowe. Five were chief's representatives to the districts of Ngwato, twenty-one were headmen, three were subheadmen, and all of the remaining fourteen had served the tribal administration in skilled capacities like secretary and treasurer. With them went lesser tribesmen, many of them "children" of Tshekedi or his administrators. These dependents had too little material liberty to take stands on political principles. "I want to be where [Tshekedi] is because of his cattle," one herder explained, "Tshekedi and Seretse are all my chiefs."[58] The Bo-Rametsana were united in their commitment to one ideal—the service of Tshekedi. As one notable explained, "It was not a question of loving power or position, which we all had. It was a question of moving off with a man we could not do without."[59]

Despite the fervor of their support for the heir, the Bo-Seretse, for their part, came from such diverse backgrounds that their unity could only be ephemeral. During the weekend prior to the police action, speakers addressing the multitude had revealed tensions growing among the Bo-Seretse. One man expressed his resentment of female intrusion into public life by swearing that the women had started the disturbance by forcing their way into the *kgotla*. Some speakers asserted that they had no will apart from that of the royal headmen, "Our masters [royal headmen] spoke and what they said was just as good as having been said by ourselves." Others clearly resented having no independent political voice; one man suggested that the Commissioner speak to the genuine leaders of the people "because we have already driven away the Royal headmen."[60] The fragile alliance of Young Turks with arch-conservative royalty ensured that no new principles of government would be espoused. Seniority remained the dominant metaphor for legitimacy, even while groups—young men and women—that had never before possessed political voices were making themselves heard in public for the first time. Seretse was thus the ideal candidate for both "traditional" and "modern" reasons.

Tshekedi blamed the debacle on the self-aggrandizing machinations of the "sons of Sekgoma," and to a certain extent, he was correct. The royal "uncles," angry at their exclusion from power, had energetically organized anti-Tshekedi sentiment at the secret night meetings. Later, during the absence of the regent and heir, they ran the administration and directed the Bo-Seretse lobby. Some called them "men afraid of losing the sweets of office."[61] Their public role was so visible that some observers have mistakenly supposed that royalty were Tshekedi's only committed opponents. The idiom of seniority tended to dominate public debate and to swamp the new voices protesting

Tshekedi's management of the chiefdom. The regent himself did not credit his people with the right to take political stands independently of their seniors.

The young men were criticizing Tshekedi for reasons contrary to those expressed by the older royalty. In calling Tshekedi's rule harsh and autocratic, educated young men, in particular, were rejecting his definition of their collective responsibilities.[62] They protested, for example, the punishment of an entire ward when one of its members brewed beer. Many younger men, especially those who had not yet inherited cattle, resented the levies Tshekedi imposed and invested in development schemes that yielded few opportunities for local employment. Whenever the tribal administration expanded, the new jobs went to devoted servants of the chief, leading to the popular accusation that Tshekedi's followers "chased Seretse away in order to get employment."[63] Tshekedi had also tried to control the ways in which returned migrants spent their money. A young man who wanted to establish a transport business, for example, could be told what his route should be or even be denied permission to buy a vehicle. Some speakers at the *kgotlas* hinted that resentment at these bureaucratic and economic restrictions had poisoned relations not only between the chief and young men but between fathers and sons generally. Older men warned the young that they would bring ruin to the tribe by demanding the right to influence public life independently of ward headmen. Men who had avoided military service by laboring in South African cities could well have been radicalized by witnessing the growth of the African National Congress as a mass movement.

At the same time, women were breaking their ancient political exclusion. Although they were rarely organized into articulate and self-conscious pressure groups, they were prominent in the massive demonstrations in Seretse's favor. They banded together independently of men, circulating petitions and asking for audiences with imperial authorities.[64] In fact, as a group they were known to be more bitter than men in their denunciation of Tshekedi.[65] From time to time they vented their ferocity with force—assaulting policemen, surrounding the District Commissioner's car, and threatening Tshekedi. During the June riot, they had led the mob into the officially closed Serowe *kgotla,* crying, "The *kgotla* belongs to us!"

Tshekedi had requisitioned female tributary labor on "warlands" while the men who drove their ox-drawn plows were gone, and female grievances had grown during the war years as their labors waxed and their support waned. The women of Mahalapye, a railway siding, were particularly vociferous against Tshekedi because he had harshly opposed both prostitution and beer brewing, the only means apart from domestic service in South Africa by which a woman alone could survive. Labor migration had made women increasingly vulnerable to abandonment and poverty, and so it is not surprising that they should have vented their resentment toward the leader under whom they had suffered new hardships. Beer brewing was a female occupation and the principal means by which poorer women could gain access to the wages of migrant laborers. Especially after the massive migration of men in the early forties had diminished the agricultural production of some households, most women needed money to purchase subsistence. Some wealthy women also split from their husbands over the issue of Seretse's succession, possibly because of their own ties to the ruling family, but also because of a clear desire to gain a public voice. They too believed that Seretse would open to them the *kgotla* meetings from which women had always been excluded.[66]

Also, the resentment of subject peoples against Ngwato domination found a convenient focus in Tshekedi. Bokalaka, where Tshekedi had recently crushed the Mswazis' attempt to secede, was particularly fertile ground for pro-Seretse sentiment. At least one Kalanga headman opposed allowing Tshekedi and his followers to plow in Ngwato territory, noting that the Mswazis had been forbidden to do so. The people of Madinare published a petition denying him permission to plow in their region: "Just as he is determined to make it impossible for them to have their Chief, they will do all in their power to foil his intentions."[67]

Even residents of an area as remote as the Botletle River could express relief at having no overlord appointed by Serowe: "We are now all chiefs of the river."[68] The crisis in central authority allowed regional peoples with no commitment to either party to refuse to obey any external directive and especially not to pay their taxes. They expressed simple joy at liberation from Serowe's domination and refused for years to perform such acts of obeisance as building a home for their appointed governor; "some years ago," one Kalanga headman explained, "people could be ordered around like Bushmen but today they [have] become clever and knew what their rights were."[69]

In addition to these readily identifiable categories of people estranged from Tshekedi's rule, other, more ambivalent reactions were voiced by clients who were simple herders in the hinterland. We can hear their voices and imagine their unspoken logic in the following case because they were employed by either Seretse or Tshekedi while the two were quarreling over Khama's inheritance. In 1950, Tshekedi launched a three-year battle to control the royal cattle posts at Nata, "my family ranching area."[70] In justifying his claims, he was revealing the commercial logic that would affect political behavior even in the hinterland.

While he defended the indissolubility of political allegiance and property, Tshekedi was busily rendering communal property private, especially in his own house. "I inherited," he said, "all Khama's cattle and thus inherited the area in which they were run."[71] Tshekedi argued that Khama had passed on to him private rights to land. At Chadibe, south of the Tswapong Hills, a perennial spring had attracted Khama to establish a "private field." Tshekedi inherited the garden and irrigated about 250 fruit trees. Over the course of time, he had hired five European farm managers and had paid some laborers, though much of the labor was free. He exempted the local men from regimental labor because they assisted him in fencing, as well as in plowing with their own oxen and in reaping. The proceeds from the sale of the crops in Serowe went into Tshekedi's own pocket because, he said, no funds from the tribal treasury had been spent on the field. Tshekedi further argued that Khama had owned two Tuli Block farms as his personal property because he had not discussed their purchase in the *kgotla*. By the same token, Tshekedi now owned herds of cattle descended from unclaimed strays. In appropriating these cattle, he had indulged in a liberal interpretation of customary law, as stated by Schapera, which cautioned that "he should use them on behalf of the tribe."[72] Even Tshekedi's claim to Nata may be seen to represent a departure from "custom" he had previously defended. He continued to claim that ranching area after he had left the Ngwato reserve and had sworn allegiance to the Kwena chief. Thus, a man who had once destroyed the property of political exiles was now arguing that political and property rights were divisible. Tshekedi had, in short, been manipulating two different legal and labor systems to enhance his wealth and power, and, in consequence, since his accession in 1926, he had been collecting an array of enemies who resented his success.

The process of rendering public property private and developing it for the market was beginning to affect the lives and therefore the political behavior of ordinary people. First, modern water points, called boreholes, were costly to bore, at £200, and to operate, at £1,000 per year, and their unrestricted use could hurt a modernizing rancher financially as well as erode the land around them; eroded land, in turn, produced stunted calves and eventually a degenerate herd. A rancher also needed capital to construct dipping tanks if he were to rid his cattle of ticks. A "progressive" rancher needed to "breed up" his herds, and he could do so only if inferior beasts were prevented from breeding with them. Tshekedi, for such reasons, tried to limit the number of beasts grazing and people plowing at his water points.[73] In the absence of fencing, this strategy meant restricting his clients from enjoying their formerly limitless use of his breeding stock, which was now sometimes imported and therefore costly.

For the time being, the political voices of clients expressed a mixture of sentiments and views of the world; it was too early in the process of profound social change for new political idioms to have eclipsed the old. A man could still explain why he obeyed the ex-regent in the following inherited terms: "I could not refuse to leave as I am inferior to Tshekedi and must obey him. I always obey my seniors. I think Tshekedi would have hurt me if I had refused to obey him. I do not know how."[74] And yet, other overseers and herders were deciding to change their affiliation to Seretse. Further, some Sarwa were complaining that Tshekedi was wrongly appropriating the offspring of their cows, alleging that his bulls had sired them.[75] Such a mixture of idioms and beliefs reflected that the patriarchy was truly in its twilight years.

The Fall

Throughout his regency, Tshekedi had been foremost among the chiefs who were trying to establish economic independence from the Union, but during the depressed thirties, his resources had been scarce. He had marshaled those resources—regimental labor, tribal taxes, and paltry grants-in-aid—to sink boreholes, to build dams and hospitals, and to improve roads. But he knew the limitations of these piecemeal projects; for example, after he set up tribal granaries so that people would not have to buy their grain back from traders at higher prices, the grain had to be sent to South Africa for milling. Therefore, he drew up expensive schemes for educational and economic development; he was to advocate them after the war. A railway should be built to Walvis Bay, he said; it would allow Bechuanaland's produce to be carried to Britain—coal, canned and frozen beef, vegetables grown in the Makarikari Pan. "These activities," he wrote, "will more than absorb the whole population and provide ample work and opportunity for all Bechuanaland youth in their own country and make us economically independent of the Union, whose only benefit to our people is an opportunity to work in the mines on a 'cheap labour' basis."[76] Agricultural experimentation would take place on the communal lands that had grown food for the imperial war effort. A borehole-drilling scheme would enlarge the Ngwato pastures and a northern abattoir would be established, enabling Tswana to send their beef to markets in Northern Rhodesia and the Congo. Europeans would be prohibited from opening new stores in the Ngwato chiefdom so that the Ngwato could break the trading monopoly enjoyed by a couple of dozen white families.

The grandeur of these schemes was evoked in part by the postwar promise of increased Colonial Development and Welfare funds. Even before the money became available, Tshekedi had moved ahead and begun the schemes the chiefdom could afford: he hired a white agricultural adviser, and he established a tribal garage and machine shop. In the breadth and creativity of his vision, Tshekedi was virtually unique among his people.

The Ngwato themselves had not been consulted when these plans were devised; Tshekedi simply assumed that his subjects would contribute their labor and wealth obediently. Yet this assumption had been challenged by popular unrest during his regency. Tshekedi had formulated no scheme by which he could divine the mood of his people. He assumed, for example, that they would acquiesce to his plan for cooperative stores, rather than demand the liberty to set up their own independent shops. He further assumed that people would willingly continue to pay a war levy even after the war had ended, and that they would in addition begin, in 1948, to pay the protectorate's graduated tax on cattle. He volunteered regimental labor to sink a chain of northern boreholes—"the tribe will do the work"—in December 1948, at precisely the same time as he was losing his coercive powers.[77]

The enforced absence of both Seretse and Tshekedi from Serowe canceled most communal activities in the chiefdom. The previously unthinkable was happening: strangers settled in wards without asking permission; independent churches were introduced to break the monopoly of the London Missionary Society; tribal lands were no longer plowed; regiments failed to perform public works; people unilaterally decided to move their cattle to new grazing areas; they refused to pay taxes. The British never managed to establish their much-heralded popular councils.

Tshekedi's development plans became idle hopes. When he withdrew to Rametsana, he effectively halted the economic development of the chiefdom. The elaborate schemes he had been devising since the depression remained paper visions. Many grand plans simply vanished because their originator, commonly seen to be "a visionary, with a fanatic grip upon his cause,"[78] was no longer in a position to urge them on the far less creative protectorate administration and on his people. Storage silos for tribal grain to be consumed during drought years were not filled after 1949. The construction of the agricultural and academic secondary school at Moeng became plagued by quarrels. The fund to establish a tribal cooperative store was compelled to pay off its subscribers and dissolve.

Early in the crisis Tshekedi had foreseen its consequences for the chieftainship. He had announced to Harragin in 1949 that he was "very doubtful whether the chieftainship of the Bamangwato people will ever be revived"; his sincerity may be somewhat suspect, as he was at the time urging the federation of Ngwato and the Kweneng.[79] In 1951, he told a British audience he would "never be a chief again." He went on to suggest that chiefs had a progressive role to fulfill in guiding political development until "an appreciable number" of their people were "sufficiently enlightened to grasp the principles of elected councils"; if they were denied this role, he warned, a radical minority might demand "'the abolition of some institutions which are still held in sacred respect by the masses.'"[80] He explained later that he made this plea not because he wished to meddle in politics but "because as a substantial cattle owner it was very much in his interests and in the interests of other property owners that there should be good and stable forms of Government in the Territory."[81] Clearly, the chieftainship was no longer providing good and stable government. Tshekedi, as well as Seretse, was growing to believe that patriarchal institution to be outmoded.

In 1956 Tshekedi and Seretse both renounced any claims to the chieftainship for themselves or their children. The Conservative government in Britain was favorably disposed to their announcement for a number of reasons: the Labour party had announced that it would allow Seretse to return to the protectorate as soon as it regained office; for five years, people had been demanding Seretse's return and rejecting local councils—in part because they feared that the councils would bring restrictions on stock and land. The protectorate government was eager to conclude a mining agreement with the Anglo-American Corporation, but the "tribe" would not negotiate in the absence of the two Khamas. These concurrent pressures encouraged the British government to release Seretse from exile. But Seretse's return in 1956 had the predictable effect of splintering his faction. As soon as he made clear his support for the tribal council and for a democratically elected national government, his conservative relatives turned their backs on him and even began to plot his overthrow in a new, but quite impotent, series of secret night meetings. Their reverence for "seniority" clearly reflected their hopes for the revived power and influence of royalty, but the last days of "seniority" were passing.

For his own part, Tshekedi fell for reasons that were both conservative and progressive. People opposed him because he was a less generous patron than his ancestors had been; he had bound too few members of Ngwato society to himself by gifts and privileges. Consequently his faction was too small to preserve his regency. Also, people could quite sincerely oppose him because he was only the junior claimant to the chieftainship. Yet at the same time that Tshekedi gained opponents for these "traditionalist" reasons, he acquired others who resented the conservative nature of his rule. People who yearned to own property chafed under his ability to veto their use of it, under his imposition of heavy fines, and under his failure to create an economic climate in which their modern wealth could prosper.

Tshekedi's enemies had grown in kind and in number. The first overt opposition to his rule had come from his relatives, many of whom argued that they no longer received the preferential treatment they had been raised to expect. They were joined in time by less exalted ranks of Ngwato society: poor women who brewed beer; subject peoples who believed that he was excluding them from the material benefits of his new administration; young men who wanted to spend their earnings free from his supervision. The political order broke down when these diverse aggrieved parties coalesced in 1949. They were bound together less by ideology than by the fact that each in its own way had been rendered insecure by the contraction of indigenous networks of patronage. The growth of the desire to invest, which many of them shared, was cutting across traditional access to plenty. People were now investing in things more than in people.

This was a stage in the development of capitalist property and labor relations, rather than a complete rupture with the past. The process of excluding people from private property was still in its early phases during the second quarter of this century. Land remained communal, although capital investment in private water points had already begun the process of exclusion. Unpaid labor continued to be claimed by chief, headmen, and masters as a customary right. Nor is the reason for the slow development of capitalist relations hard to find. The region's great marketplace in the Rand bought only two commodities—cattle and labor—from the Ngwato Reserve. It paid little for either one, and its demand fluctuated in response to politics and disease. The inconstancy of South African markets kept the impetus to commercialize agricultural and pastoral production quite weak. In the context of this general estrangement from the modern riches of the Rand, Tshekedi's valiant efforts to create an economically independent modern state were doomed. When he imposed levies to support his development projects, he not only engaged in a nearly futile exercise to introduce cash relations in an area where there was so little cash, but when the returns on these projects proved to be meager, he also fueled popular opposition to his rule. Both Tshekedi and the chieftainship were falling victim to the relative poverty within South Africa's periphery.

The second quarter of this century also constitutes a stage in the political development of the region. The chief was trying to transform his polity into a "tribal" state. In the 1960s a nation-state would be constructed on these foundations. This state and not the chiefdom would be able to garner the riches offered by other countries in the form of international aid. This state and not the chiefdom would create a bureaucracy capable of employing the newly educated Tswana youth. This state and not the chiefdom would make formal laws, and back them with coercive force, to regulate capitalist property and wage relations. The chieftainship fell not simply because the incumbent had earned opprobrium as an autocrat among the majority of his people, but also because its institutions were outmoded.

The political language spoken by the actors in this story tends to obscure the facts of social change. The ideology celebrating the chieftainship masks transformations occurring in Ngwato society from the late nineteenth century on. Decisions in the *kgotla* continued to be described as the result of agreement of "tribal" opinion, and yet the chief was busily creating rules to legitimize and enforce his new powers. While he invested his wealth in private property, he continued to be addressed, and beseeched, as the "milk-pail" of his people. He also remained a "lion" in popular praises despite his inability to influence events in the foreign places where his younger male subjects worked. The social processes at work recast chiefly powers and gradually diminished the *kgotla*'s role as the forum where people negotiated and advertised the relationships that shaped their lives. Customary political ideology endured, even as capitalist property and labor relations undermined the legitimacy of the old patriarchal order.

Conclusion

Kgosi ke kgosi ka morafe. (A chief is chief by the people.)
Tswana proverb

Today, a stroll through Serowe reveals the destruction of much of what Tshekedi Khama fought for. Many homesteads lie vacant, their thatch shabby, their yards overgrown with weeds; mud walls are crumbling. The village's highly itinerant population shuttles between cities, fields, cattle posts, and Botswana's as well as South Africa's mines. They no longer need wait for the chief to approve their right to depart. Many wards now have no resident headman. Bottle stores have been introduced against Tshekedi's and Khama's prohibition of the sale of liquor; now one of the most profitable forms of local investment, such stores and their gleaming mounds of litter can be found in every section of the village.

The chief today is, in fact, an acting chief, an appointee, since the hereditary ruler, Seretse Khama's son Ian, is serving at the head of the armed forces. A house of chiefs sits in the Botswana parliament, but the chiefs do little more than preside over the councils and affairs of local government. Only old men discuss political authority in terms of seniority; in the days before independence when there were no "politics," they say wistfully, "everyone knew his position."[1] Those days are gone.

When I asked one old man, a paragon of the old order and Tshekedi's right-hand man, what the regent would have thought of the state of the village and chiefdom today, he replied, "His heart would have been broken."[2] This assessment is probably correct even though Tshekedi—part patriarch, part capitalist rancher—had acknowledged a few years before his death in 1959 that the chieftainship was outmoded. Perhaps he foresaw that a new capital, Gaborone, would become the political and economic center of a mineral-rich nation. He might have agreed with those today who decry that rapidly growing city as a parasite on the pastoral economy, leeching resources for its own development that should have gone into rural areas. As these national investment and migratory patterns signify, the small society and its values have been superseded by the nation-state.

Botswana is frequently lauded as virtually unique in Africa because it enjoys a free press and multiparty parliamentary democracy. "An oasis of tolerance and nonviolence amid civil strife and political chaos," one journalist writes, voicing the enthusiasm of many. Botswana's vice president, Peter Mmusi, explains why: "We haven't learned democracy from America or England. It is inborn"; Botswana's modern democracy, he argues, "grew from a system developed by our forefathers."[3] Mmusi was clearly referring to the uninhibited debate ideally occurring in the *kgotla*. The ideological face of the old order—its reverence for rank and collective responsibility—did slip easily from the public discourse of Botswana politics. The patriarchal chieftainship faded readily there.

The ease of Botswana's transition is stunningly apparent when it is compared with South Africa's Bantustans. They have a different tale to tell. There apartheid policy helped ensure that the patriarchy did not fade or die within them. The Bantu Administration Act ossified and perverted the patriarchy when the structures of Bantustans first began to be erected in 1951. That act perpetuated and elaborated the tradition of bureaucratically controlled chieftainships begun in the early 1900s. The cost has been the popular legitimacy of many incumbents. Some residents of the Bantustans swear that even the police and jailers fail to believe in the legitimacy of their work or in the states themselves. And yet, in some respects, seniority survives. Competitors for public office in the homelands today often frame their claims in terms of genealogical seniority,⁴ and people sometimes use that same concept to reject the claims of Bantustan leaders.

One principal reason why some rural folk, including at one time the people of Ngwato, have clung to "tradition" is their fear of losing their land and social security. They gilded the chieftainship with myths and memories of a time when chiefs ruled fairly and "were loved and popular with the people, for the true unaffected love they evinced to their people and unimpeachable honesty with which they served them." This particular reflection comes from the anticolonial organization Lekhotla la Bafo. Founded in Basutoland after the First World War, it explicitly sought to revive the office from the inefficient and corrupt languor into which it had fallen since the days of Moshoeshoe. For the members of Lekhotla la Bafo and for many other rural peoples, the chief was a bulwark against land loss—"if we no longer have our chiefs then our country will be gone"—and a symbol around whom resistance could be organized.⁵ William Beinart has stressed that rural folk in Pondoland, at least until 1950, did not necessarily want to be incorporated into a common South Africa: "Chieftaincy provided the kind of institution, and set of symbols, behind which rural people could unite at a local level and stake claims to land and communal rights."⁶ Traditional gender relations have been similarly praised, even by women, because they evoke a social order and time when women enjoyed greater security from abandonment and poverty. Jean Comaroff has repeated wistful remarks made by southern Tswana women as they look back to an idealized time when "men were men" and supported them. Comaroff sees the rituals of the Zion Christian Church as recreating the patriarchal social order because in that sect "females are clearly subordinated to the collective control of males."⁷ Perhaps the subordinate status of women in rural southern African society today can be called an ideological, and for poorer women a practical, residue of the precolonial patriarchal order.

The growth of capitalist property and labor relations undermined, albeit in a slow and tortuous way, the legitimacy of the old patriarchal order in the Ngwato chiefdom. Because it was located on the periphery of an industrial revolution, Ngwato experienced profound political and ideological changes at different tempi: wage labor and private property relations grew at different rates, markets for labor developed faster than markets for local products, some social strata adopted capitalist relations far earlier than others, inherited political language was used to explain a social order even as it was being transformed. As a result, popular ideas tended to reflect an ambiguous mixture of new and received strategies for survival and advancement. And yet, the old patriarchal order was undermined more effectively in Bechuanaland than in other parts of southern Africa. There are several reasons for this relative ease. Some were conjunctural; only Ngwato, after all, had its new and uneasy coalition of chiefly enemies forged and ignited by a royal romance that invited imperial intervention. But there were other, deeper factors setting Ngwato in particular and the Tswana in general apart from chiefdoms elsewhere in southern Africa.

Tswana chiefs did not devote much energy to erecting structures that obliged people to respect the chieftainship and its values. For all his political acumen, Tshekedi relied, rather, on exhortations and fines. The Tswana chiefdoms did not sequester their young men in age regiments for years at a time, as the Swazi ruler tried to do. Their national rituals were never elaborated to serve as a focal point of national identity, as the Swazi *incwala* ritual was made to do after 1921. The Tswana chiefs did not tighten regional government to the extent the Sotho did by placing sons to rule subordinate chiefdoms.

Further, the power relations in Tswana politics were not entrenched by colonial or regional overlords, as they were, for example, in Swaziland. From 1950, the British promulgated laws explicitly aiming to enhance the power of the Swazi monarch, giving him virtually the sole power to legislate, restoring his criminal jurisdiction, and granting him independent authority over tax revenues. The logic was similar to that stated more bluntly by the Tomlinson Commission in 1955 when it suggested how to develop genuinely independent Bantustans: "to give the force of law to traditional tribal institutions and customs and to develop higher, purely Bantu, authorities on lines analogous to these institutions and customs."[8] In contrast, in the Bechuanaland Protectorate, the British waged protracted reformist battles in the 1930s.

Neither the Tswana elite nor commoners expressed their class interests in a patriarchal program as many other southern Africans did. The Swazi aristocracy, for example, as Hugh Macmillan has recently argued, contrived "traditionalism" as a strategy to advance their own petit bourgeois interests; it was the means by which "an emergent rural elite . . . established itself in exclusive political control over an increasingly complex society."[9] Shula Marks has made a similar point about the service Inkatha provided to the Zulu petit bourgeoisie from the time of its founding in 1928; the Zulu royal family and the Natal *kholwa*, or Christian Africans, allied to create Inkatha "as a deliberate attempt to reduce the tensions which had arisen within Zulu society as a result of the growth of internal social stratification."[10] Neither did groups of Tswana commoners argue coherently for the retention of patriarchal custom as, for example, the members of Lekhotla la Bafo had done. Common people exerted their conservative bias, as always, in such isolated acts as continuing to exhort the chief to create rain.

Why did virtually no one in the Bechuanaland Protectorate seize on "tradition" and succeed in imposing it on the Tswana? Based on the material presented in the preceding chapters, I would argue that the means by which the rich sought to remain dominant were shifting, almost imperceptibly, during the late colonial period to codified law and private property, that is, to the language and practices of liberal democracy. The nature of the pastoral economy in Bechuanaland played a major role in this shift in elite values. Cattle were the first local product to be commercialized. As the market encouraged cattle ownership to become more individualized, ranchers found that it served their interests to stress less the collective values of the old patriarchal order. Further, those members of the elite who were using part of their cattle wealth to educate their children in mission schools believed more in "progressive" than in "traditional" principles; they shared this belief with the Christian-educated elite of rural South Africa. Unlike the "progressives" and "loyalists" of the South African reserves, they were not subject to restrictive segregationist land policies that drove them either toward collaboration, however ambiguous, or toward "traditionalism" as a form of resistance.[11]

In short, the liberty that people have enjoyed to acquire wealth apart from the chieftainship has had a profound effect on their allegiance to that office and its values. Where alternative sources of patronage have not sprung up in rural areas, the chieftainship has remained vital. Conversely, the development of alternative, that is, independent sources of wealth has spelled ruin for the chieftainship-based patriarchy and its values. During the period examined in this book, cash wages were too low to allow alternative patrons to evolve, and the protectorate government itself was chronically impoverished. Only after independence, and especially after the 1960s, when Botswana's mineral riches—including reputedly the greatest diamond strike of the century—began to be exploited, did the independent state start reaping revenues that allowed it to respond to popular pleas for water, jobs, and welfare.[12] Labor migration modified the precolonial social order. Not until independence was that order transformed, hence the twilight nature of those years. In the Ngwato case, this transformation occurred only after the shrinking patronage and increased exactions of the chief had already alienated a large and diverse part of the population from his rule and, less articulately, from the order he represented. In this sense, Tshekedi Khama facilitated, as a capitalist rancher, the fading of the order that he defended as a patriarch. In contrast, because of the patterns of South African financial support, the Bantustan bureaucracies serve as virtually the sole local sources of wealth and patronage in those impoverished societies. The Mercedes-driving habits of their luxuriously housed politicians are by now legendary.¹³ "Warlords," with whom the South African state colludes or to whom it has abandoned township government, now control urban enclaves in a similarly patriarchal fashion.

In Ngwato, the political consequences of southern Africa's industrial revolution burst into public display in 1949 when four thousand men leapt to their feet in the *kgotla* and voted their regent out of power. Their act reflected the twilight of the patriarchal era. As the work of survival had been changing in southern Africa over the past century, so had local patterns of political support. After the Second World War, fewer and fewer people believed that patriarchal institutions and values served their interests. The chieftainship and rank had once signified a continuous process of hierarchical exchanges; they were becoming more and more the means by which inherited privilege was justified. In the postwar era not even the elite would need this defense. Their privilege was becoming protected more by law and less by the imperatives of patronage and the rhetorical shield of rank. On the periphery of South Africa's industrial revolution, a patriarchal political system was being transformed from above and below. At the same moment, apartheid policy to the south was seeking to withdraw that system from the flux of history.

Notes

Abbreviations Used in the Notes

The British Administration
D.C.: District Commissioner (after 1934)
D.C.S.: District Commissioner, Serowe
H.C.: High Commissioner for South Africa and the High Commission Territories
R.C.: Resident Commissioner
R.M.: Resident Magistrate (before 1934)
R.M.S.: Resident Magistrate, Serowe
S.: Secretariat

Other
A.A.C.: African Advisory Council
BNA: Botswana National Archives, Gaborone
BTA: Bamangwato Tribal Archives
CO: Colonial Office
DO: Dominions Office
L.M.S.: London Missionary Society
N.A.C.: Native Advisory Council
PRO: Public Record Office, Kew

Introduction

1. William Burchell, *Travels in the Interior of South Africa*, 2 vols. (London, 1822–1824; reprint, Cape Town: C. Struik, 1967), vol. 2, pp. 358, 362.
2. H. H. Gerth and C. W. Mills, eds., *From Max Weber: Essays in Sociology* (New York: Oxford University Press, 1958), pp. 225, 239. Tshekedi Khama was formally installed as Ngwato regent in January 1926, though he had begun to exercise chiefly functions in December 1925; he stopped functioning as regent in 1949 and formally gave up the regency in 1950.
3. G. E. Nettelton, diary entry for 25 March 1930, Nettelton Papers, University of Cape Town Library.
4. Deputation to the Secretary of State for Dominion Affairs by Tshekedi Khama, Acting Chief of the Bamangwato Tribe in the Bechuanaland Protectorate, 27 March 1930, p. 7, Ballinger Papers, A3.1.3, William Cullen Africana Library, University of the Witwatersrand.
5. Tshekedi Khama, "The Judicial System of the Bamanwato [sic] Nation in relation to the New Native Tribunals Proclamation of 1934 Promul-

gated in January 1935," n.d., BTA box 12, file R-51, Botswana National Archives.
6. The nephew, Seretse Khama, was the son of Khama's oldest son and successor, Sekgoma II, who ruled briefly from 1923 to 1925. Seretse Khama became the first president of the independent state of Botswana, holding office from 1966 until his death in 1980.
7. John Mackenzie, *Austral Africa*, 2 vols. (London: Sampson Low, 1887), vol. 1, 22. The origin and meaning of the word *Tswana* have been much debated. One theory attributes it to a Xhosa corruption, later adopted by whites and the Tswana themselves. See D. M. Ramoshoana, "The Origin of Secwana," *Bantu Studies* 3 (1927): 197–98.
8. One notorious example of this meddling is the appointment of Botha Sicgau as chief of Eastern Pondoland in 1939 and as the man to introduce rehabilitation there in 1953, despite the greater popularity of his half-brother Nelson Sicgau. Govan Mbeki, *The Peasants Revolt* (London: International Defense and Aid, 1984), pp. 118–34.
9. Tshekedi Khama to Patrick Duncan, 4 March 1955, Tshekedi Khama Papers, Private Collection, Pilikwe, Botswana.
10. For the former perspective, see Judy Kimble, " 'Clinging to Chiefs': Some Contradictions of Colonial Rule in Basutoland, c. 1890–1930," in *Contradictions of Accumulation in Africa*, ed. Henry Bernstein and Bonnie K. Campbell (Beverly Hills: Sage, 1985), p. 31.

1. "A Shape with Lion Body and the Head of a Man"

1. Isaac Schapera, *A Handbook of Tswana Law and Custom* (London, 1955; reprint, London: Frank Cass, 1984).
2. William Burchell, *Travels in the Interior of South Africa*, 2 vols. (London, 1822–1824; reprint, Cape Town: C. Struik, 1974), vol. 2, 359.
3. The population of one southern Tswana town, Litakun, was estimated as early as 1812 to be 5,000, and it covered almost 2 square miles; a century later the population of Serowe, the Ngwato capital, was 25,000. By the 1940s, there were over 300 wards in Ngwato and 113 of them, numbering 200 to 400 people each, were located in Serowe. Burchell, *Travels*, vol. 2, p. 514; Isaac Schapera, *The Ethnic Composition of Tswana Tribes* (London: London School of Economics, 1952), p. 65.
4. Jean Comaroff, *Body of Power, Spirit of Resistance, the Culture and History of a South African People* (Chicago: University of Chicago Press, 1985), chapter four.
5. R.C., *Bechuanaland Protectorate Annual Report 1888* (London, 1889).
6. Madalon T. Hinchey, ed., *Proceedings of the Symposium on Drought in Botswana* (Hanover, N.H.: Clark University Press in association with the Botswana Society, 1979).
7. Schapera, *Handbook*, 67–68, 248–50.
8. Adam Kuper, *Wives for Cattle. Bridewealth and Marriage in Southern Africa* (London: Routledge & Kegan Paul, 1982), p. 164.
9. James R. Denbow and Edwin N. Wilmsen, "Advent and Course of Pastoralism in the Kalahari," *Science*, 19 December 1986, pp. 1509–15.

10. The competitors tended to be agnates. They usually found allies among their linked sisters, whose marriage cattle paid their own bridewealth, and their mothers' brothers. While the language of seniority was applied exclusively to men, women were the primary means by which men could change their rank. As well as using endogamous marriage strategies, men shifted their support from one patron or political faction to another to manipulate their social standing. At the same time they expressed unambiguous support for a ranked social universe. The result of this contradiction was a highly individualistic culture. Comaroff, *Body of Power*, pp. 49–54; John Comaroff and Simon Roberts, *Rules and Processes, The Cultural Logic of Dispute in an African Context* (Chicago: University of Chicago Press, 1981), chap. 2.
11. Gary Okihiro, "Hunters, Herders, Cultivators and Traders: Interaction and Change in the Kgalagadi, Nineteenth Century" (Ph.D. diss., University of California, Los Angeles, 1976), p. 87.
12. Thomas Tlou, *A History of Ngamiland 1750 to 1906, the Formation of an African State* (Gaborone: Macmillan, 1985), pp. 42 and 47.
13. S. M. Molema, *Montshiwa 1815–96, Barolong Chief and Patriot* (Cape Town: C. Struik, 1966), pp. 31, 34.
14. John Mackenzie, *Ten Years North of the Orange River, A Story of Everyday Life and Work among the South African Tribes from 1859–1869* (Edinburgh, 1871; reprint ed., London: Frank Cass, 1971), pp. 410–11.
15. In 1835, for example, two factions clashed over the chieftainship: one followed Sekgoma I, the eldest son of Chief Kgari, who had died that year, though Sekgoma's mother was a junior wife; the other followed Macheng, who was the de jure son of Kgari, and the biological son of a Ngwato regent who had "raised seed" with Kgari's widow, a senior wife. It is said that Sekgoma grudgingly deferred to Macheng's seniority and actually stepped down from the chieftainship in his favor. The same deference was apparent in 1873 when Khama III abdicated in favor of his father, Sekgoma I, whom he had ousted from power the previous year, and went into exile. In both cases, the graceful gesture was followed by the junior marshaling arms to wrest back his office from the senior. These events suggest that the incumbents deferred to custom when their factional support was weak.
16. Burchell, *Travels*, vol. 2, pp. 347–48.
17. Ibid.
18. Ibid.
19. Ibid., p. 386.
20. Ibid., p. 431.
21. Basil Sansom, "Traditional Rulers and Their Realms," in *The Bantu-Speaking Peoples of Southern Africa*, ed. W. D. Hammond-Tooke (London: Routledge & Kegan Paul, 1974), p. 255.
22. O. F. Resheng, former Serowe land allocator, interview with author, Serowe, 1981. The chief chose first, preferably black clay or red loam soil near a dependable water supply, and then the ward headmen were made overseers of blocks of arable land. Their requests were handled by a land allocator to whom the chief had given jurisdiction over a specific region. The less exalted members of Tswana society received their land through

the hierarchical chain ordering all aspects of public life: the headmen divided the blocks among the heads of each cluster of agnatically related families within their wards; these seniors in turn divided their lands among the heads of their constituent households; and a married son received land from his father.

23. See, for example, the case of Kgamane's vacillating adherence to Christianity in chaps. 21–23 of Mackenzie's *Ten Years North of the Orange River*, and Anthony Dachs, *Khama of Botswana* (London: Heinemann, 1971).
24. The decision to follow a patron into exile was not motivated solely by factional allegiance. In the absence of property law, secession conveniently served to divide cattle ownership among competing family members, that is, a son might thereby acquire his inheritance early.
25. Mackenzie, *Ten Years*, p. 129.
26. John Mackenzie, "Native Races of South Africa and Their Polity," *British Africa*, vol. 2 of The British Empire Series (London: Kegan Paul, Trench, Trubner, 1899), p. 181.
27. John Comaroff, "Rules and Rulers: Political Processes in a Tswana Chiefdom," *Man* 13 (1978): 1–20.
28. Elizabeth Lees Price, *Journals Written in Bechuanaland, Southern Africa, 1854–83*, ed. Una Long Gill (London: E. Arnold, 1956), p. 166.
29. Isaac Schapera, *Praise Poems of Tswana Chiefs* (Oxford: Clarendon, 1965), p. 238.
30. Robert H. Bates, *Essays on the Political Economy of Rural Africa* (Berkeley: University of California Press, 1983), p. 42.
31. Schapera, *Praise Poems*, pp. 239, 245 (emphasis added).
32. Burchell, *Travels*, vol. 2, p. 450.
33. Isaac Schapera, *Married Life in an African Tribe* (London: Faber, 1940), p. 305.
34. Misfortune, especially illness, afflicted those who quarreled with older living relatives. This curse, called *kgaba*, emanated from the spirits of the recently dead who had prayed to their great ancestor for help in punishing an errant junior. Isaac Schapera, "Oral Sorcery among the Natives of Bechuanaland," *Essays Presented to C. G. Seligman*, ed. E. E. Evans-Pritchard, R. Firth, B. Malinowski, I. Schapera (London: Routledge, 1934), p. 302.
35. See, for example, Kevin Shillington, *The Colonisation of the Southern Tswana 1870–1900* (Johannesburg: Ravan, 1985), pp. 15–16.
36. Because cattle milling in *kraals* obliterated the precise location of graves, the malign were deterred from digging up human remains to use as medicine. Tshekedi Khama denied that any chief in Ngwato territory had ever had his grave tampered with in this way. Tshekedi's annotations to Schapera's *Handbook*, p. 59, photocopy in African Collection (uncatalogued), Manuscripts and Archives, Sterling Memorial Library, Yale University.
37. Mackenzie, *Ten Years*, p. 383; Isaac Schapera, *Rainmaking Rites of the Tswana Tribes* (Leiden: Afrika-Studiecentrum, 1971).
38. Mackenzie, *Ten Years*, p. 384.
39. Schapera, *Rainmaking Rites*, p. 27.

40. Mackenzie, *Ten Years,* p. 383.
41. Schapera, "Oral Sorcery," pp. 302–03.
42. Comaroff, *Body of Power,* p. 114.
43. Ibid., p. 67.
44. Max Gluckman, "The Kingdom of the Zulu of South Africa," in *African Political Systems,* ed. Meyer Fortes and E. E. Evans-Pritchard (London: Oxford University Press, 1940), p. 31.
45. Tlou, *History of Ngamiland,* p. 33.
46. Comaroff, *Body of Power,* p. 57.
47. Julian Cobbing, "The Mfecane as Alibi: Thoughts on Dithakong and Mbolombo" (unpublished seminar paper, University of the Witwatersrand, 1987).
48. Okihiro, "Hunters, Herders," pp. 86–87, 27–28.
49. Mackenzie, Ten Years, p. 359.
50. The *mfecane* only partly explains the expansion of the Ngwato chiefdom's population and its rise as a regional power. Not all of the incorporated foreigners were refugees from the havoc. It is quite impossible even to estimate the proportion of those refugees: there is no record of their numbers; they were incorporated into wards with other foreign family groups; and their reasons for agreeing to pay tribute may never have been recorded.
51. Mokgalo Selepeng, interview with author, Gaborone, 1981.
52. J. G. Sandham, "Trade among the Tswana in the Nineteenth Century" (M.A. essay, University of London, School of Oriental and African Studies, 1969).
53. "Tribes beyond the Frontier," *South African Commercial Advertiser,* 6 January 1823; J. Read, New Lattakoo, to the Governor, 22 February 1818, Cape Town Archives, CC/co. 90. I am grateful to Margaret Kinsman for these and other references on the subject.
54. Fanuel Nangati, "Early Capitalist Penetration: The Impact of Precolonial Trade in Kweneng (1840–1876)" (Paper presented to the Symposium on Settlement in Botswana, Gaborone, 1980).
55. Peter Warwick, *Black People and the South African War 1899–1902* (Johannesburg: Ravan, 1983), p. 47.
56. Emery Roe, "Development of Livestock, Agriculture and Water Supplies in Botswana before Independence: A Short History and Policy Analysis" (Ithaca, N.Y.: Cornell University, Rural Development Committee, 1980), pp. 38–39.
57. Q. N. Parsons, "Khama III, the Bamangwato and the British, with Special Reference to 1895–1923" (Ph.D. diss., Edinburgh University, 1973).
58. Mackenzie, *Ten Years,* pp. 130–31; David Livingstone, 1849, quoted in Sandham, "Trade among the Tswana," p. 22.
59. The reference is to the followers of Mogolopolo who originally lived at Lephephe. Schapera, *Ethnic Composition,* p. 72.
60. John Comaroff and Jean Comaroff, "Christianity and Colonialism in South Africa: The Tswana Case," *American Ethnologist* 13, no. 1 (February 1986): 1–22.
61. *Parliamentary Papers,* "Further Correspondence Respecting the Affairs of South Africa 1878–9," C. 2220, LII of 1878–79, pp. 42, 45–47.

62. Khama to Sir Henry Barkly (trans. J. D. Hepburn), 22 August 1876, *Parliamentary Papers,* C. 1748, pp. 251–52, quoted in Parsons, "Khama III," p. 44.
63. Captain R. R. Patterson, a British agent in Shoshong on a fact-finding tour, to Sir Theophilus Shepstone, governor of the Transvaal, *Parliamentary Papers,* C. 2220, LII of 1878–79, pp. 235–39.
64. Khama (per Rev. J. D. Hepburn) to Lewanika, chief of the Barotse, 17 July 1889, Rev. François Coillard Papers, folio I, 1., Royal Commonwealth Society, London.
65. Letter of Khama, Seretse, Kebailele, Sephekolo and forty-seven others, Serowe, to King Edward VII, 14 April 1910 (Union of South Africa, *Bechuanaland Protectorate Confidential Reports,* no. 353, Pretoria Archives) quoted in Kathleen Mullagin, "Alfred Jennings: The Political Activities of the London Missionary Society in Bechuanaland, 1900–1935" (Ph.D. diss., St. John's University, New York, 1974), pp. 106–107.
66. This perspective is exemplified by the work of Bessie Head, *Serowe, Village of the Rain Wind* (London: Heinemann, 1981); Mary Benson, *Tshekedi Khama* (London: Faber, 1960); Harold Robertson, "From Protectorate to Republic: The Political History of Botswana, 1926–66" (Ph.D. diss., Dalhousie University, 1979).
67. Sir Hercules Robinson, 1885, in *Blue Book,* C. 4588, p. 106.
68. *Bechuanaland Protectorate Annual Report* 1888, London, 1889.
69. Lobengula to Khama, 10 March 1887, *Parliamentary Papers,* C. 5237, LIX of 1887, quoted in Parsons, "Khama III," p. 72.
70. Tswana chiefs to the Colonial Office, *Parliamentary Papers,* C. 7962, 1896, quoted in Isaac Schapera, *Ethnic Composition,* p. 14.
71. Copy of a letter from R. Wardlaw Thompson, L.M.S., London, to J. Mackenzie, n.d. (1895), BTA, box 12, file R-21, BNA. Original copies of the two maps (1885 and 1899) may be found in the Cape Archives Depot, where they are numbered M1/3349 and M3/457, respectively. A third map of poor quality, dated 1878, reflects Khama's original claims to land up to Victoria Falls, near to Maun and then in a straight line south to the Kweneng. Khama withdrew these grand claims in favor of allowing the northern portion, north of the Makgadikgadi Pan, to be proclaimed the property of the British Crown (M1/2543, Cape Archives).
72. For most of the colonial period, the protectorate administration had the following shape: until 1924, the Colonial Office, then the Dominions Office, and later the Commonwealth Relations Office ran its affairs, appointing the R.C. who controlled departmental officials and D.C.'s from his office in Mafeking. The R.C.'s correspondence went through the H.C. to London. The H.C., moving between the two capitals of Pretoria and Cape Town because he was also, until 1928, the Governor-General of South Africa, had supreme local authority.
73. In 1896 the chiefs lost the ability to manage their foreign affairs independently of the British. In 1919, the British allowed all *kgotla* cases to be appealed. They established a curious court to hear them; it was composed of the D.C. and the chief himself.
74. In 1899 a hut tax of 10 shillings was imposed on all initiated Tswana men. In 1907 the amount was doubled to £1. Although collectors could

be sensitive to cases and periods of poverty, they were obliged to press for eventual payment. The *kgotla* often sentenced habitual defaulters, as well as debtors, to a contract of mine labor, and a portion of their pay would be attached.

75. In 1909 the South Africa Act had prepared the way for the establishment of the Union of South Africa the following year. It was commonly assumed that the three High Commission Territories would eventually be incorporated, after their citizens had given their consent. As Lord Selborne explained to the Bechuanaland chiefs at Mafeking in March 1910, "in the natural course of things [the transfer] would take place some day." Lord Hailey, *Native Administration in the British African Territories,* part 5, *The High Commission Territories: Basutoland, the Bechuanaland Protectorate, and Swaziland* (London: H.M.S.O., 1953), p. 207.
76. Captain Patterson in C. 2220, LII of 1878–79, p. 236.
77. Serathi Magama, interview with author, Lerala, Botswana, February 1980.
78. Isaac Schapera, *Tribal Legislation among the Tswana of the Bechuanaland Protectorate, A Study in the Mechanism of Cultural Change* (London: London School of Economics, 1943).
79. Reverend Alfred Jennings to F. H. Hawkins, 3 September 1912, as quoted in Kathleen Mullagin, "Alfred Jennings: The Political Activities of the London Missionary Society in Bechuanaland, 1900–35" (Ph.D. diss., St. John's University, New York, 1974), p. 120.
80. *Times of London,* 21 October 1893, p. 8b.
81. W. C. Willoughby, L.M.S. missionary, to London Missionary Society, London, 4 and 12 October 1896, quoted in Parsons, "Khama III," p. 160.
82. Khama to Chief Isang, 1 May 1921, quoted in Isaac Schapera, *Tribal Innovators: Tswana Chiefs and Social Change, 1795–1940* (London: Athlone, 1970), p. 185.
83. Schapera, *Rainmaking Rites,* p. 43.
84. A. G. Leonard, *How We Made Rhodesia* (London: K. Paul, Trench, Trubner, 1896), p. 16.
85. From *From Max Weber: Essays in Sociology,* ed. H. H. Gerth and C. W. Mills (New York: Oxford University Press, 1958), p. 217.
86. Schapera, "The Political Organization of the Ngwato of the Bechuanaland Protectorate," in *African Political Systems,* ed. M. Fortes and E. E. Evans-Pritchard (London: Oxford University Press, 1940), pp. 78–79.
87. Between 1909 and 1912, lung sickness caused a quarantine to be imposed on cattle for export, and from 1911 to 1924 the herds were stunted by recurrent drought and locust plagues.
88. Michael Hubbard, "Desperate Games: Bongola Smith, the Imperial Cold Storage Company and Bechuanaland's Beef, 1931" (Paper presented to the History Departmental Seminar, University College, Botswana, March 1981), p. 5. The South African government was also trying to force the transfer of the High Commission Territories. In October 1924 Prime Minister J. B. M. Hertzog suggested to the H.C. that the weight restrictions could be avoided if the British government agreed to the transfer. C. Colclough and S. McCarthy, *The Political Economy of Botswana: A*

Study of Growth and Distribution (Oxford: Oxford University Press, 1980), p. 258, n. 11.
89. In 1924 an 800-pound minimum weight was set for the importation to South Africa of live oxen, and in 1926 it was raised to over 1,000 pounds. The result was a dramatic drop in exports of Bechuanaland's cattle—from over 23,000 in 1925–26 to under 8,000 the following year.
90. The R.C. as quoted in S. Ettinger, "South Africa's Weight Restrictions on Cattle Exports from Bechuanaland, 1924–41," *Botswana Notes and Records* 4 (1972): 25.
91. J. Chapman, *Travels in the Interior of South Africa, 1849–63: Hunting and Trading Journeys from Natal to Walvis Bay and Visits to Lake Ngami and Victoria Falls,* ed. Edward C. Tabler, 2 vols. (Cape Town: A. A. Balkema, 1971), vol. 1, p. 151. The reference is to 1854.
92. Eugene Casalis, *The Basutos or Twenty-Three Years in South Africa* (London: J. Nisbet, 1861), pp. 155–56.
93. *Report of the Commission on the Griqualand Labour Question,* included in Cape of Good Hope, Government Notice No. 102, 1876, p. 65. The compulsion proposed was forced labor on public works by all unemployed men who lingered more than five days at depots en route to Kimberley.
94. *The West Griqualand Government Gazette,* 20 October 1877, p. 138. "Report on Labour Generally during the Year 1876," enclosed in W. Coleman to Colonial Secretary, 8 April 1878, folio 11, GLW 118 (947). I am grateful to William Worger for giving me these and the preceding reference.
95. Khama to Major W. Owen Lanyon, Kimberley, 15 March 1877, in C. 2220, LII of 1878–79, p. 79.
96. F. W. Panzera, Assistant Commissioner, B.P., quoting a letter to the Transvaal Labour Commission, which he had written 6 July 1903 but which he did not want published in the press. Transvaal, *Report of the Transvaal Labour Commission,* Johannesburg, 1903, p. 226.
97. R.C. (Ralph Williams) to Khama, 21 May 1903, BTA, box 11, file R-K1, BNA.
98. H. S. Walker and J. H. N. Hobday, "Report on the Cattle Industry of the Bechuanaland Protectorate with Recommendations for Improving Its Organization and Assisting Its Future Development," Mafeking, October 1939, V. 1/5/1, BNA.

2. "Full of Passionate Intensity"

1. Tshekedi stressed in his notes on Isaac Schapera's *A Handbook of Tswana Law and Custom* (London, 1938), that *regency* was an English concept for which there was no Setswana equivalent; "whoever takes up the duties of chieftainship is a chief until someone else takes up according to the right of succession." In addition to resisting the suggestion that a regent had less than the full powers of the chieftainship, he put question marks in the margin next to Schapera's remarks that a regent's delay in vacating his office had occasioned his assassination. Tshekedi's notes on

Schapera's *Handbook*, pp. 61, 62, photocopy in Manuscripts and Archives, Yale University Library.
2. Commission of Enquiry held at Serowe 15 November–1 December 1937 [Raditladi Enquiry], fo. 222, African Collection (uncatalogued), Manuscripts and Archives, Sterling Memorial Library, Yale University. (Hereafter, African Collection.)
3. Gabolebye D. Marobela, interview with author, Gaborone, 1980.
4. Adrien Jousse and H. M. Palphramand, memorandum, 25 March 1937, BTA box 18, BNA. The same point was made by H. S. Walker and J. H. N. Hobday in their "Report on the Cattle Industry of the Bechuanaland Protectorate with Recommendations for Improving Its Organization and Assisting Its Future Development," Mafeking, October 1939, V. 1/5/1, BNA.
5. The scarcity of labor recruiters was due partly to the chief's desire and power to limit their numbers. In the early 1930s there were only four labor recruiters in the Ngwato chiefdom. The Serowe Chamber of Commerce brought up the issue of labor recruitment twice in its minutes between 1902 and 1931 (in 1902 and 1926) and then only in regard to the recruitment of northerners. Minutes of the Serowe Chamber of Commerce, which were in 1980 in the private possession of Mrs. Minnie Shaw, Palapye.
6. Tshekedi to Attorneys Kieser and McLaren, Mafeking, 19 May 1934, BTA box 13, file R1-C2, BNA. See also, Michael Hubbard, "Desperate Games: Bongola Smith, the Imperial Cold Storage Company and Bechuanaland's Beef, 1931" (Paper presented to History Departmental Seminar, University College, Botswana, March 1981).
7. Marobela, interview, 1980. In 1931 Margaret Hodgson learned that European farmers buying African milk to make cheese had lower prices and a wider profit margin than those using their own milk. Margaret Hodgson, diary entry, 30 June 1931, Ballinger Papers, A2.3, University of Cape Town Library.
8. S. J. Ettinger, "South Africa's Weight Restrictions on Cattle Exports from Bechuanaland, 1924–41," *Botswana Notes and Records* 4 (1972).
9. *Parliamentary Papers*, "Financial and Economic Position of the Bechuanaland Protectorate: Report of the Commission Appointed by the Secretary of State for Dominion Affairs, March, 1933" (Pim Report), Cmd. 4368, X of 1932/33, pp. 43–44.
10. Christopher Colclough and S. McCarthy, *The Political Economy of Botswana: A Study of Growth and Distribution* (Oxford: Oxford University Press, 1980). The authors argue that taxation made the distribution of cattle among the Tswana more unequal.
11. Sol T. Plaatje, *Sechuana Proverbs with Literal Translations of the European Equivalents* (London: K. Paul, Trench, Trubner, 1916), p. 71.
12. Isaac Schapera, *A Handbook of Tswana Law and Custom* (London, 1955; reprint, London: Frank Cass, 1984), p. 56.
13. Michael Crowder, *The Flogging of Phinehas McIntosh, A Tale of Colonial Folly and Injustice, Bechuanaland, 1933* (New Haven: Yale University Press, 1988), p. 24; Ronald Hyam, "The Political Consequences of Se-

retse Khama: Britain, the Bangwato and South Africa, 1948–1952," *Historical Journal* 29, no. 4 (1986): 924.
14. John L. Comaroff, "Rules and Rulers: Political Processes in a Tswana Chiefdom," *Man* 13 (1978): 1–20.
15. Michael Crowder, "The Succession Crisis over the Illness and Death of Kgosi Sekgoma II of the Bangwato, 1925: Western versus Traditional Medicine" (unpublished paper, n.d., given to me by the author).
16. Sekgoma accused his father of grooming Ratshosa for the chieftainship even though Khama had explicitly threatened to bequeath his "kingdom" to his two favorite brothers. J. M. Chirenje, *A History of Northern Botswana, 1850–1910* (Rutherford, N.J.: Fairleigh Dickinson University Press, 1977), p. 42.
17. Crowder, "Succession Crisis," p. 3.
18. L. D. Raditladi, "The Destiny of Seretse Khama, Royal Head of the Bamangwato People," chap. 1 (unpublished ms. in the possession of Zachariah Matumo, Gaborone, n.d.).
19. Tshekedi Khama's testimony to Raditladi Enquiry, 10 May 1937, fo. 208, African Collection.
20. At one time, the Ngwato had no formal investiture ceremony for a new chief. They claimed that they had adopted the leopard-skin ceremony in accordance with the wishes of the administration. Schapera, *Handbook,* p. 60.
21. "Temporary Ruler of the Bamangwato," *Cape Times,* 21 January 1926, Rev. Ernest Baker Papers, MSB.39, South African Library, Cape Town.
22. R.C.,(Jules Ellenberger) to H.C., (Lord Athlone), telegram, 20 January 1926, DO 9/1/ D. 1398, PRO.
23. Mathoame, quoted in the Minutes of Meeting at Resident Magistrate's Office, Serowe, 19 December 1925, [R.M., Tshekedi, Gorewang Kgamane (third in line in succession), the council, and headmen in attendance], DCS 4/1, BNA.
24. In 1924, Mphoeng and several of his relatives had complained to the R.C. that the Ratshosas were usurping the headmen's functions and inhibiting educational progress. The petitioners also warned that the power of witch doctors was growing. Three years earlier, Mphoeng said, Simon Ratshosa had threatened to banish him. The Ratshosas had also provoked the royal petition by supporting the Kalanga of Mmadinare, who claimed that they were excessively flogged and fined by their appointed chief, Phethu Mphoeng. Petition to R.C., 21 January 1924, by Phethu Mphoeng, Nwako Nkobele, Lekgoba Sekgoma, Oteng Mphoeng, Lebang and Disang Raditladi, BTA 16, R1-P1, BNA.
25. This narrative is based on R.C. (Jules Ellenberger) to H.C. (Lord Athlone), 21 April 1926, DO 9/1 D. 5347, PRO; Chief Tshekedi Khama v. Simon Ratshosa and Another, *South African Law Journal* 49 (1932): 246–55; Julian Mockford, *Khama, King of the Bamangwato* (London: Jonathan Cape, 1931).
26. Petition of S. and O. Ratshosa to His Excellency, the Governor General, 4 December 1930, William Ballinger Papers A3.1.22, William Cullen Africana Library, University of the Witwatersrand.
27. Tshekedi traveled to London primarily to negotiate a new mining conces-

sion and a new mining law that would govern the activities of the British South Africa Company in his chiefdom. He particularly feared that South Africa would demand the incorporation of Bechuanaland once mining development took place. See Michael Crowder, "Resistance and Accommodation to the Penetration of the Capitalist Economy in South Africa: Tshekedi Khama and Mining in Botswana, 1929–59" (Paper for discussion at the University of London, Institute of Commonwealth Studies Decolonisation Seminar, 10 October 1985).

28. The quotation is taken from an interview held between Tshekedi and Lord Passfield, the Secretary of State for Dominion Affairs on 1 April 1930. Ballinger Papers, A3.1.3, p. 12, Witwatersrand.

29. In the late twenties, however, the Dominions Office had accepted the recommendation of the R.C., Jules Ellenberger, that it was inadvisable to curb the chiefs' judicial powers: "the Natives are aware that they have the right to appeal to the European courts from the Judgement of a Chief. . . . [I]t is a matter of small importance how extensive the powers of a Chief may be in theory so long as they are not, in practice, exercised to the detriment of his subjects." Sir Bede Clifford, Imperial Secretary, Cape Town, to A. C. C. P. Parkinson, D.O., 5 October 1927, DO 9/7/D 10247, PRO. Passfield denied that the Native Administration and Native Tribunal proclamations were spawned by the Ratshosa case, though that case had explicitly highlighted "the absence of statutory authority for the exercise of jurisdiction by the Courts of the Chiefs." Notes of the 1 April 1930 meeting between Passfield and Tshekedi in the Dominions Office, p. 7, Ballinger Papers, Witwatersrand.

30. Tshekedi to R.M.S., 21 March 1932, BTA, box 13, file R1-B1, BNA. Baboni and her sister MmaKhama had been banished after the 1926 shooting. Both women complained at the time that they had received no share of Khama's estate.

31. Gasetshwarwe was illegitimate in the sense that Khama had not given his consent to his parents' marriage. His mother was the sister of Sekgoma II's barren wife but as she had not been formally invited to bear his children in her sister's stead, she was considered simply to be his concubine. The fierce royal pride of Gasetshwarwe may be glimpsed in the following tirade, which he delivered to the R.M., "Tshekedi is my servant. He is not good enough for me to dispute the chieftainship with . . . I am the son of Sekgoma. I am chief. . . . I will go to my death roaring as a lion as I am the son of a lion—the son of Sekgoma." Gasetshwarwe to R.M.S., 19 December 1932, BTA, box 14, file R1-G1, BNA.

32. Oitsile Mosweu, referring to the sons and allies of Ratshosa, speaking at the *kgotla* enquiry into Baboni's claims, 20 July 1932, BTA, box 13, file R1-B1, BNA.

33. R.C. (Lt. Col. C. Rey) to H.C., 2 February 1932, S. 78/1, BNA.

34. R.M.S. (A. Cuzen), to R.C., 7 April 1926, DO 9/1/D. 5347, PRO.

35. J. Ratshosa, evidence to the Tagart Commission, 1 August 1931, S. 204/8, BNA.

36. S. Ratshosa, Bechuana Law Committee, 5 August 1932, BTA 17, P1-R4,

BNA. See also Q. N. Parsons, "Shots for a Black Republic? Simon Ratshosa and Botswana Nationalism," *African Affairs* 73 (1974): 449–58.
37. G. E. Nettelton, D.C.S., described Monamo, the subordinate regimental leader, in this way, 13 December 1930, DCS 15/10, BNA.
38. He was, by his own admission, a "distant relative of Khama." Moanaphuti Segolodi, evidence to the Tagart Commission, 23 July 1931, fo. 56, S. 204/8, BNA. Perhaps more important, he was the brother-in-law of Disang Raditladi.
39. Moanaphuti Segolodi to William Ballinger, 8 September 1930, Ballinger Papers, A3.1.16, Witwatersrand.
40. Moanaphuti Segolodi on "Slavery," 9 September 1930, BTA, box 16, file R1-P1, BNA.
41. Kesebonye Sephekolo, Segwesabone Tshukudu, Kerontshitswe Tshukudu, P. G. Tiro, Moanaphuti Segolodi, Makgasana Molefi, Morake Ranaka, Osupile Kebonang to R.C., 19 October 1930, DCS 15/7, BNA. Curiously, Moanaphuti originally opposed Tshekedi not because he was taking a principled stand for civil rights but because he believed that he had been defamed by the regent. Moanaphuti Segolodi to Tshekedi Khama, 6 July 1930, [in Setswana] Ballinger Papers, A3.1, Witwatersrand.
42. In fact, the 1924 petition had not mentioned regiments, *letsholo*, or flogging.
43. Moanaphuti Segolodi, evidence to Raditladi Enquiry, 1937, fo. 5, African Collection.
44. Gaditshwane Motsholakgetse, evidence to Raditladi Enquiry, 1937, fo. 9, African Collection.
45. Moanaphuti Segolodi to William Ballinger, 8 September 1930, Ballinger Papers, A3.1.16, Witwatersrand.
46. Kesebonye Sephekolo, Segwesabone Tshukudu, Kerontshitswe Tshukudu, P. G. Tiro, Moanaphuti Segolodi, Makgasane Molefi, Osupile Kebonang, Morake Ranaka, G. Motsholakgetse to R.C., 28 November 1930, DCS 15/7, BNA. A handwritten note by Tshekedi in this file alleges that four Raditladis (Disang, Lebang, Kelethokile, Oonetse Disang) were associated with the petition although they did not sign it.
47. Tshekedi Khama to R.C. (Charles Rey), 27 May 1931, and Rey to Tshekedi, 2 June 1931, BTA, box 21, BNA; R.C. (Rey) to H.C., 30 September 1931, S. 158/9, BNA.
48. Tshekedi to the Economic Committee, 1 December 1932, BTA, box 21, BNA.
49. Charles Rey, *Monarch of All I Survey, Bechuanaland Diaries, 1929–37*, ed. Neil Parsons and Michael Crowder (Gaborone: Botswana Society, 1988), p. 83 (entry for 28 August 1931).
50. G. E. Nettelton, D.C.S., *Annual Report for 1930*, 14 January 1931, DCS 12/21, BNA. The three British visitors wrote about their visit: William Ballinger and Margaret Hodgson, *Britain in South Africa*, no. 2, *The Bechuanaland Protectorate* (Alice, South Africa: Lovedale, 1932); Leonard Barnes, *The New Boer War* (London: Hogarth, 1932).
51. Rey, *Monarch*, p. 77 (entry for 15 June 1931).
52. Petition of Ngwato headmen to H.C., 30 July 1931, DCS 15/9, BNA.

Clements Kadalie was a pioneer African trade unionist in South Africa who had founded the Industrial and Commercial Workers Union of South Africa and built it in the 1920s into the first modern mass movement of black people in South Africa.
53. Rey, *Monarch*, p. 81 (entry for 21 July 1931).
54. The phrase "inherited grievances" was used by Chief Isang of the Kgatla during the enquiry to describe the following characteristics of the petitioners: Kesebonye, Segwesabone, Kerontshitswe, and Osupile had been in exile with Sekgoma II and had just returned; Kesebonye was a grandson of Tshukudu, Sekgoma I's old enemy, his sister had married a Ratshosa, and the Ratshosas had kept their guns at his place; P. Tiro had been in exile in Rhodesia during Khama's time; Makgasane, a supporter of Sekgoma II, had spent fifteen years in exile in Rhodesia with his father; Dingalo Nthebolang was a cousin of the Ratshosas and was married to a daughter of Disang Raditladi, another rival of Tshekedi.
55. Evidence of Othusitse at the enquiry into the petition against regimental labor, Serowe, 13 December 1930, DCS 15/10, BNA. The word *lerotse* (pumpkin) is used to describe a disinherited chief who has retained ritual precedence.
56. K. T. Motsete to William Ballinger, 10 September 1930, Ballinger Papers, A3.1.18, Witwatersrand.
57. Motsete was a cofounder and leader of the Bechuanaland People's Party in 1960.
58. Motsete to Ballinger, 10 September 1930.
59. Kesebonye Sephekolo, speaking at the regimental labor enquiry, 13 December 1930, DCS 15/10, BNA. In 1933, Kesebonye was sentenced to ten years in hard labor for conspiring to overthrow Tshekedi and replace him with Gasetshwarwe, who was at the same time sentenced to seven years in hard labor. D.C.S., *Annual Report for 1933*, S. 360/15, BNA.
60. Pelaelo Tiro, speaking at the regimental labor enquiry, 13 December 1930, DCS 15/10, BNA.
61. Ten years later the problem persisted: Tshekedi called out three Khurutshe regiments, for example, in 1940 to work on the railway line, but only thirty people showed up and they argued over the 1-shilling daily wages. Tshekedi to D.C., 22 June 1940, BTA, box 14, file R1-F1, BNA.
62. The speaker was, in the words of the R.M., a "raw native." G. E. Nettelton, *Report on the Regimental Labour Enquiry*, 13 December 1930, DCS 15/10, BNA.
63. Ibid.
64. Barnes, *The New Boer War*, p. 178. See also Hodgson and Ballinger, *Bechuanaland Protectorate*, p. 55.
65. Gaditshwane Motsholakgetse, speaking at the regimental labor enquiry, 13 December 1930, DCS 15/10, BNA.
66. Tshekedi to R.M.S., 10 March 1931 and 27 April 1931, BTA 21, BNA. Tshekedi swore that he was sensitive to the heavy demands of regimental labor: he tried to ensure that no village was required to do hard labor for two successive years; if men were away for five months, especially during a drought, he knew that their homesteads would suffer.
67. Simon Ratshosa, "How the Basarwa Became Slaves and Why the Chief's

Word is Law," n.d. (1926), S. 43/7, BNA. Ratshosa's efforts clearly spawned awareness of the Sarwa problem even among South African Communists. See "The Fallacy of 'Africa for the Africans,'" *South African Worker*, 30 July 1926. This article was brought to my attention by Eileen Flanagan.

68. Acting Resident Commissioner (Col. R. M. Daniel) to H.C., 7 August 1926, S. 43/7, BNA.
69. Janet Hermans, "Official Policy towards the Bushmen of Botswana: A Review, Part I," *Botswana Notes and Records* 9 (1977): 62–63.
70. The protectorate administration was fearful of contriving a confrontation with the Union of South Africa by repudiating its Masters and Servants legislation. The L.M.S. was embarrassed in 1934 by the allegation that one of its missionaries owned slaves. The charge was initially made by William Ballinger and then was printed in a London newspaper, the *News Chronicle* (5 November 1934), before being retracted by Ballinger. The missionary, Reverend A. E. Jennings, defended himself by saying that he paid his Sarwa herders in cattle and milk. A. J. Haile, memorandum, December 1934, L.M.S. Papers, Africa Odds, Box 1, School of Oriental and African Studies, London.
71. E. S. B. Tagart, *Report on the Conditions Existing among the Masarwa in the Bamangwato Reserve of the Bechuanaland Protectorate and Certain Other Matters Appertaining to the Natives Living Therein*, October 1931 (Pretoria: Government Printer, 1933). Rey suggested that Ballinger sit on the commission of enquiry but he was opposed by the H.C., who distrusted Ballinger's allegedly self-advertising tendencies. Rey also suggested D. D. T. Jabavu, whom Tshekedi had recommended. Suzanne Miers and Michael Crowder, "The Politics of Slavery in Bechuanaland: Power Struggles and the Plight of the Basarwa of the Bamangwato Reserve, 1926–40," in *The End of Slavery in Africa*, ed. Suzanne Miers and Richard Roberts (Madison: University of Wisconsin Press, 1988), pp. 172–200. Rey noted that Tagart was sent out to investigate Sarwa slavery as a result of Rey's own request for an enquiry. Rey, *Monarch*, pp. 67, 80 (entries for 30 April and 13–19 July 1931).
72. Deputation to the Secretary of State for Dominion Affairs by Tshekedi Khama, 27 March 1930, p. 10, Ballinger Papers, A3.1.3, Witwatersrand.
73. Tagart, *Report*, pp. 6–7.
74. Tshekedi to R.M., 18 January 1934, BTA, box 15, file R1-M1, BNA.
75. Transcript of discussion with the R.C. (1930?), BTA, box 14, BNA.
76. Marobela, interview, 1980.
77. During the regimental labor enquiry, 13 December 1930, Kesebonye's servants revealed that he had fined his Kgalagadi *malata* for disobeying his command to plow his lands, and that he also told his servants to build huts and yards, collect grass, and make rafters, bricks and corn bins for his own use.
78. Special Court Case Records, no. 8, 1931, BNA; Rajaba Monageng, interview with author, Serowe, 1980. Further examples of hostility between masters and servants may be found in witchcraft allegations or in the apparently spontaneous decision of a regiment to return a traveling Sarwa to his master. Rey noted that because there was a technical flaw in the

evidence, the High Court could not convict Rajaba of murder, and so the maximum sentence was fifteen years and a flogging. Rey, *Monarch*, p. 66 (entry for 30 April 1931).
79. Oitsile Mosweu, evidence to the R.M., 17 November 1928, S. 43/7, BNA.
80. R.M., Francistown, to Government Secretary, 12 November 1928, S. 43/7, BNA.
81. In the jail register, located in 1981 in the D.C.'s storeroom, Serowe, thirty-two of the seventy-six people in jail from April to December 1929 are recorded as having been Sarwa convicted of stock theft. The R.M., G. E. Nettelton, noted that on release, many of these former stock thieves obtained wage employment. 21 December 1929, S. 47/1, BNA.
82. Alfred Yorke Page Wood, evidence to Tagart Commission, 22 July 1931, S. 204/8, BNA. According to J. W. Joyce, Kalanga, while not owning Sarwa, did employ many, paying them one cow for three years service. "Report on the MaSarwa of the Bechuanaland Protectorate," 28 December 1936, BTA, box 15, file R1-M1, BNA.
83. J. W. Joyce, "Report on the Masarwa in the Ngwato Reserve, Bechuanaland Protectorate," League of Nations, Advisory Committee of Experts on Slavery, Geneva, 1938 [*League of Nations Publications*, 6. B. (Slavery) C 112, M 98, Annex 6], p. 65.
84. S. S. Dornan, "The Tati Bushmen (Masarwas) and Their Language," *Journal of the Royal Anthropological Institute* 47 (1917): 44.
85. Setlalethoto (interpreter and orderly for Tagart), evidence to the Tagart Commission, 9 August 1931, folio 83, S. 204/8, BNA.
86. Tshekedi Khama, evidence to the Tagart Commission, 20 July 1931, S. 204/8, folio 23, BNA.
87. Ibid., folio 28.
88. For a book-length discussion of the incident, see Crowder's *The Flogging of Phinehas McIntosh*.
89. One of the enduring questions from the case is whether McIntosh was actually flogged or whether he was manhandled as he moved unexpectedly toward the chief. Crowder, *The Flogging*, p. 209.
90. Decision by the Acting H.C. announced at Serowe, 14 September 1933, BTA, box 20, BNA.
91. Admiral E. R. G. R. Mountevans, *Adventurous Life* (London: Hutchinson, 1946), p. 196.
92. Article in *Die Vaderland*, 13 September 1933, quoted in Crowder, *The Flogging*, p. 64.
93. The speaker, Tsogang Sebina, was addressing a *kgotla* meeting called in June 1938 to discuss transfer. Fourteen hundred Ngwato attended. Other speakers added the following criticisms of South Africa: Africans were shot at like guinea fowls there; South African laws restricted their ability to grow corn and to sell firewood; Africans could not own land in the Union. Several speakers explicitly blamed the Union for their restricted markets. Record of *kgotla* meeting, 14 June 1938, BTA 15, R1-L1, BNA. Z. K. Matthews wrote to Tshekedi at about the same time warning him that the protectorates would be the price of South Africa backing Britain in a European war. After the war, he predicted, South Africa would

emerge as a colonial power with the three protectorates as the nucleus of her colonies. Z. K. Matthews to Tshekedi, 3 June 1938, BTA, box 15, file R1-L1, BNA.

94. Raditladi later ran the Francistown African Employees Union and founded the Bamangwato National Congress in 1952 and the Bechuanaland Protectorate Federal Party in 1958. He also wrote poetry, drama, and a novel in Setswana and translated *Macbeth*.
95. V. Ellenberger, D.C.S., recommendations, Raditladi Enquiry, fo. 195, African Collection.
96. Tshekedi Khama, speech at Raditladi Enquiry, 10 May 1937, fo. 217, African Collection.
97. Disang Raditladi, testimony in Raditladi Enquiry, fo. 158, African Collection.
98. The purpose behind cattle-sale permits was to curb the sale of stolen beasts; most Tswana owned too few to bother branding them.
99. Disang Raditladi, testimony in Raditladi Enquiry, fo. 163, African Collection.
100. Rey, *Monarch*, p. 136 (entry for 26 June 1933).
101. G. E. Nettelton, *Annual Report of the District Commissioner, Serowe*, 6 January 1936, DCS 21/9, BNA.
102. R.M.S. to Assistant R.C., Mafeking, 3 April 1934, DCS 19/1, BNA.
103. Tshekedi to D.C.S., 24 April 1940, DCS 29/6, BNA.
104. Botswana allege that taxes are far more easily evaded in independent Botswana than they were in the Ngwato chiefdom during Tshekedi's regency. *Kgotla* case records concerning property reveal that people took great care to preserve their receipts in order to avoid being fined as defaulters.
105. Tshekedi, "Further Memorandum as to the Economic Position—Natives' Hardships—Distribution of the Cattle Quota," 28 August 1935, BTA 12, R-U1, BNA. Three years later, Tshekedi would correspond with Sir John Harris of the Aborigines Protection Society in London on the subject of establishing a northern abattoir. Harris explicitly hoped that the development of a ranching industry would be "one means of safeguarding Bechuanaland against transfer." J. H. Harris to Tshekedi, 10 November 1938, BTA, box 12, file R-U1, BNA.
106. Emery Roe, "Development of Livestock, Agriculture and Water Supplies in Botswana Before Independence: A Short History and Policy Analysis (Ithaca, N.Y.: Cornell University, Rural Development Committee, 1980), pp. 29–32.
107. Roe, in "Development," p. 40, argues that migration continued at its higher rate through the 1940s in part because the cost of cattle was rising relative to the earnings from migrant labor; the cost of setting up or improving a small herd was lengthening the period of time a man needed to spend in the mines.

3. The Defense of Patriarchy in the *Kgotla*

1. Isaac Schapera, *A Handbook of Tswana Law and Custom* (London: Oxford University Press for the International African Institute, 1938).
2. Xeroxed copy of Schapera's *Handbook* annotated by Tshekedi Khama, African Collection [unprocessed additions], Manuscripts and Archives, Sterling Memorial Library, Yale University.
3. Ibid., p. 126. Schapera later put this desire down to Tshekedi's "prudish" nature and to his dislike of the anthropologist's preoccupation with reconstructing the past rather than "recognizing that the Tswana were Christians, modern people who had been to school." Quoted in Jean Comaroff and John L. Comaroff, "On the Founding Fathers, Fieldwork and Functionalism: A Conversation with Isaac Schapera," *American Ethnologist* 15, no. 3 (1988): 561, 563.
4. Martin Chanock, *Law, Custom, and Social Order, the Colonial Experience in Malawi and Zambia* (Cambridge, England: Cambridge University Press, 1985).
5. Simon Roberts, "The Tswana Polity and 'Tswana Law and Custom' Revisited," *Journal of Southern African Studies* 12, no. 1 (1985): 76. This concept is developed more fully in Roberts' *Rules and Processes: The Cultural Logic of Dispute in an African Context*, coauthored with John L. Comaroff (Chicago: University of Chicago Press, 1981).
6. John Mackenzie, reply to questionnaire, 29 November 1881, *Report of the Government Commission on Native Laws and Customs* (Cape Town, 1883), appendix C (vol. 2, part 2), p. 231. Fifty years earlier, William Burchell noted that he had never witnessed or heard of any capital or corporal punishment during his stay among the Tlhaping to the south. William Burchell, *Travels in the Interior of South Africa*, 2 vols. (London, 1824; reprint, Cape Town: C. Struik, 1967), vol. 2, p. 544.
7. Phethu Mphoeng quoted in the transcript of the Commission of Enquiry held at Serowe, 15 November–1 December 1937 [Raditladi Enquiry], p. 48, African Collection (uncatalogued). Manuscripts and Archives, Sterling Memorial Library, Yale University. (Hereafter, African Collection.)
8. Tshekedi's marginal comments stress that common, not royal, headmen are "senior" in divisional courts; that is, even though the royal headman announces the decision, the common headman is the most "influential." Annotated copy of Schapera's *Handbook*, p. 102.
9. Both observations were by John Mackenzie. The first is from his reply to questionnaire, 29 November 1881, p. 246. The second is from his *Ten Years North of the Orange River, A Story of Everyday Life and Work among the South African Tribes from 1859–1869* (Edinburgh, 1871; reprint, London: Frank Cass, 1971), p. 133. It is noteworthy that in the far more remote Tawana chiefdom, even by the 1930s, few cases reached the chief's court from the courts of his district representatives. E. H. Ashton, "Notes on the Political and Judicial Organization of the Tawana," *Bantu Studies* 11 (1937): 67–83.
10. Schapera, *Handbook*, p. 52.

11. Jean Comaroff, *Body of Power, Spirit of Resistance* (Chicago: University of Chicago Press, 1985), p. 101.
12. Ibid., p. 100.
13. J. D. Hepburn, *Twenty Years in Khama's Country*, ed. C. Lyall (London: Hodder and Stoughton, 1895); John C. Harris, *Khama, The Great African Chief* (London: Livingstone, 1922); Louise Knight-Bruce, *The Story of an African Chief: Being the Life of Khama* (London: K. Paul, Trench, Trubner, 1893); E. Lloyd, *Three Great African Chiefs: Khame, Sebele, Bathoeng* (London: T. Fisher Unwin, 1895). The argument that Khama's ardently puritanical habits were responsible for his legal innovations is also advanced by Isaac Schapera in *Tribal Innovators: Tswana Chiefs and Social Change, 1795-1940* (London: Athlone, 1970).
14. Schapera, *Handbook*, p. 145.
15. This scene was observed by J. Howard Pim in Palapye in 1890. Pim to his father, 25 December 1890, Pim Papers, Ca 2, William Cullen Africana Library, University of the Witwatersrand.
16. Khama made thirty-four laws and Tshekedi only five, as recorded in Isaac Schapera's *Tribal Legislation among the Tswana of the Bechuanaland Protectorate, a Study in the Mechanism of Cultural Change* (London: London School of Economics, 1943), pp. 84-86.
17. This situation did not change until 1933. See Sir Alan Pim, *Report on the Financial and Economic Position of the Bechuanaland Protectorate* (London: H.M.S.O., 1933) and Lou Picard, "Role Change among Field Administrators in Botswana" (Ph.D. diss., University of Wisconsin, Madison, 1977).
18. Quoted in "Tshekedi and Another v. the High Commissioner (Sir Herbert Stanley), 1936," *High Commission Territories Law Reports 1926-53*, p. 22.
19. The warnings are from 1885 (Sir Charles Warren to H.C., C.T.) and 1887 (H.C. to Administrator, British Bechuanaland), *High Commission Territories Law Reports*, pp. 23, 26.
20. Lord Knutsford to H.C., 15 May 1891, *High Commission Territories Law Reports*, p. 28.
21. Apparently there were few homicides tried in Ngwato. One was recorded in 1901-02, and in 1919 one Boteti sorcerer (*ngake*) was convicted of killing a woman for medicines. Q. N. Parsons, "Khama III, the Bamangwato and the British" (Ph.D. diss., University of Edinburgh, 1973), p. 406.
22. Record of the Proceedings at an Interview granted by His Excellency the High Commissioner to Certain Bechuana Chiefs at Government House, Cape Town, on the 21st and 22nd November, 1927, DO 9/7/12186, PRO.
23. Jules Ellenberger, 15 September 1904, evidence to the South African Native Affairs Commission, Cape Town, 15 September 1904, vol. 4, p. 237.
24. In 1946, the D.C. heard twenty cases, of which only one was an appeal from the *kgotla*. Ten years later he heard ten times the number of cases, including roughly the same proportion of appeals.
25. The 10 June 1891 proclamation had forbidden the chiefs to exercise jurisdiction over Europeans.

26. Lord Athlone to Lord Passfield, 21 February 1930, D.O. 9/7/D.10247, PRO.
27. "Financial and Economic Position of the Bechuanaland Protectorate: Report of the Commission Appointed by the Secretary of State for Dominion Affairs," *Parliamentary Papers,* Cmd. 4368, 1933.
28. Lord Hailey's *African Survey,* quoted in Chanock, *Law, Custom and Social Order,* p. 52.
29. Proclamations nos. 75 and 74 of 1934, in Bechuanaland Protectorate, *High Commissioner's Proclamations and the More Important Government Notices from 1 January to 31 December 1934,* vol. 19. Mafeking: The Mafeking Mail, 1935.
30. Charles Rey, *Monarch of All I Survey, Bechuanaland Diaries, 1929–37,* ed. Neil Parsons and Michael Crowder (Gaborone: Botswana Society, 1988), p. 84 (entry for 11 September 1931).
31. Rey to H.C., 25 June 1931, William Ballinger Papers, A3.1.28, William Cullen Africana Library, University of the Witwatersrand.
32. Plaintiffs' Heads of Argument, Chief Tshekedi v. the High Commissioner, Chief Bathoen v. the High Commissioner, n.d., Tshekedi Khama Papers (private collection), Pilikwe.
33. Bathoen Gaseitsiwe, personal communication to author, 1981.
34. Michael Crowder, *The Flogging of Phinehas McIntosh, a Tale of Colonial Folly and Injustice, Bechuanaland, 1933* (New Haven: Yale University Press, 1988), p. 195.
35. The lineage and ward *kgotlas* would continue to adjudicate in civil matters between their members, but they could not enforce their decisions. If the parties refused their judgment, the case would have to go to the junior tribunal. Assistant D.C., D.C., and Tshekedi Khama, Notes of a Discussion at Serowe, box 12, BTA, file R-S1, BNA.
36. Rey, *Monarch,* p. 4 (entry for 20 October to 17 November 1929).
37. R.M. (G. E. Nettelton), Notes of proceedings at the Serowe *kgotla,* 4 September 1935, box 12, BTA, file R-S1, BNA.
38. G. O. Mathiba, ibid.
39. Rey, *Monarch,* pp. 138, 191 (entries for 1–7 September 1933, and 8 November 1935).
40. In their earlier tactic of writing directly to the H.C. they requested permission to travel to London where they could present their case directly to the Secretary of State for the Dominions; they also suggested the appointment of a royal commission to investigate the proclamations, drew up petitions, engineered the asking of awkward questions in the British Parliament, and simply refused to implement the decrees.
41. Five years earlier, when first sending a draft of the proclamation to the H.C., Rey had anticipated Tshekedi's opposition and had enclosed a copy of the Foreign Jurisdiction Act. Rey to H.C., 25 June 1931, Ballinger Papers, A3.1.28, Witwatersrand.
42. Isaac Schapera, *Praise Poems of Tswana Chiefs* (Oxford: Clarendon, 1965), p. 239.
43. Death and life imprisonment were in effect excluded from the chief's powers. The 1934 proclamations were effectively adopted in 1961 as the African Courts Proclamation, with an amending act in 1968. Lord

Hailey, *Native Administration in the British African Territories,* part 5, *The High Commission Territories: Basutoland, the Bechuanaland Protectorate and Swaziland* (London: H.M.S.O., 1953), pp. 226–28.

44. Chanock argues for central Africa that the repugnancy clause did not conflict with the logic of the colonial system, which was support for local hierarchies. Chanock, *Law, Custom, and Social Order,* pp. 73–74.
45. Seboko Mokgosi of the Bamalete, 28 June 1935, S. 436/12, BNA.
46. Chief Kgari speaking in the Native Advisory Council, 1936, S. 387/5, BNA.
47. Councillor R. Gaseitsiwe, ibid.
48. Tshekedi speaking in the Dominions Office on 27 March 1930 to Lord Passfield and others, p. 3, Ballinger Papers, A3.1.3, Witwatersrand.
49. Chanock, *Law, Custom, and Social Order,* p. 238.
50. I. Schapera, *Migrant Labour and Tribal Life* (London: Oxford University Press, 1947), appendix H, "Direct Imports by Natives."
51. Mokgalo Selepeng to author, 17 June 1981.
52. The paucity of available wage-paying jobs in the Ngwato chiefdom is illustrated by the correspondence from a royal relative who, having fallen out with Tshekedi, begged the British to provide him with employment; he suggested being made Ngwato tax collector on the Rand or a school organizer. Edirilwe Seretse to Government Secretary, 23 December 1933, DCS 18/11, BNA. The only other paid employment available locally was limited mainly to being a clerk at a trader's store, a teacher, or a stock inoculator.
53. Oonetse and MmaLeetile, appeal against Serowe *kgotla* decision, 1939.
54. Schapera, *Handbook,* p. 23.
55. Ibid., pp. 191–92.
56. The D.C. did allow MmaLeetile to keep one wagon, which he regarded as her personal property, but he upheld the principle of joint property in all other matters.
57. K 401/56, Ngwato Kgotla Records (*kgotla* case records formerly kept in the D.C.'s storeroom in Serowe, now transferred to the BNA, Gaborone).
58. D 2/45, box 2, Ngwato Kgotla Records, BNA, and MN 6/47.
59. K 45/46, Ngwato Kgotla Records.
60. K 540/40, box 1, Ngwato Kgotla Records, BNA.
61. K 16/9/1948, box 4, Ngwato Kgotla Records, BNA.
62. This point was made by several informants, inter alia, Bathoen Gaseitsiwe, interview with author, Gaborone, 9 June 1981.
63. Schapera, *Handbook,* p. 33.
64. The following discussion of these facets of Ngwato society as they were defended in the *kgotla* is based on a collection of case records—160 synopses and 30 verbatim transcripts—selected from the period 1937 to 1965. My sample was drawn according to the care with which the transcript had been prepared and to the apparent importance of the case; i.e., longer cases tended to be selected. The synopses were made systematically of every case I could find for one year in each of four decades—1937–38, 1946, 1956, 1965—so that I could categorize them and see if there had been any change in types of cases brought to the *kgotla* over

time. All *kgotla* records are in Setswana. My excellent translator was James Mpotokwane, to whom I am deeply indebted.
65. Schapera, *Handbook*, p. 28.
66. Ibid., p. 203.
67. Oonetse and MmaLeetile, Appeal against Serowe *kgotla* decision, folio 14, DCS 40/7 BNA.
68. Schapera, *Handbook*, p. 161.
69. Ramasimo and Sekgarametso, K 536/40, box 1, Ngwato Kgotla Records, BNA.
70. Oatile Mabole and Mokapana Oatile, K 29 April 1938, box 1, Ngwato Kgotla Records, BNA.
71. Nchaben and Makube, Madinare, 25 October 1940, Ngwato Kgotla Records, BNA.
72. R.M.S. (G. E. Nettelton) to Tshekedi, 21 October 1935, BTA, box 15, file R1-M1, BNA.
73. Bakgomohi and Baitshenyetsi, K 23/44, box 2, Ngwato Kgotla Records, BNA.
74. Chanock noted the same phenomenon in Zambia and Malawi in *Law, Custom, and Social Order*, p. 233.
75. Gabosimologe v. Ramee and Rakokame, K51/47, BNA.
76. Tshekedi's annotation to Schapera's *Handbook*, p. 69.
77. Schapera, *Handbook*, p. 30.
78. The D.C.'s court records reveal a limited set of privileged people bringing cases to him concerning divorce, money debts, and breach of contract.
79. Chanock, *Law, Custom, and Social Order*, p.63.

4. "Lesser Breeds without the Law"

1. Tshekedi distinguished between "subordinate tribes" such as the Kgalagadi and Tswapong and the "allied tribes" or "clans" whose headmen Khama had allowed his daughters to marry. Tshekedi's notes on Isaac Schapera's *A Handbook of Tswana Law and Custom* (London, 1938), p. 74, photocopy in African Collection [uncatalogued], Manuscripts and Archives, Sterling Memorial Library, Yale University.
2. Andrew Roberts, "The Sub-Imperialism of the Baganda," *Journal of African History* 3, no. 3 (1962): 435–50; Gwyn Prins, *The Hidden Hippopotamus, Reappraisal in African History: The Early Colonial Experience in Western Zambia* (Cambridge, England: Cambridge University Press, 1980); John Iliffe, "The Creation of Tribes," in *A Modern History of Tanganyika* (Cambridge, England: Cambridge University Press, 1979), pp. 318–41; Terence Ranger, "The Invention of Tradition in Colonial Africa," in *The Invention of Tradition*, ed. Eric Hobsbawm and Terence Ranger (Cambridge, England: Cambridge University Press, 1983), pp. 211–62.
3. Among the Tswana chiefdoms, only the Tawana had a similarly diverse range of "subtribes," that is, eleven as opposed to twenty-one within the Ngwato chiefdom; like the Ngwato, the Tawana were greatly outnumbered by one of these "subtribes." The following figures of Ngwato

ethnic groups come from the 1946 census returns in Isaac Schapera's *The Ethnic Composition of Tswana Tribes* (London: London School of Economics, 1952), pp. 65, 94: Ngwato (17,850); Kalanga (22,777); Tswapong (11,237); Birwa (9,636); Sarwa (9,587); Khurutshe (5,441); Kgalagadi (3,963); Talaoate (3,538); Kaa (3,055); Pedi (2,572); Phaleng (2,409); Herero (1,013); Rotse (1,006); Kwena (892); Seleka (889); Nabja (844); Koba (724); Teti (435); Subia (274); Malete (240); Rolong (155); Tlokwa (141).

4. I am using the term *clan* simply because it occurs frequently in the literature and documentation on which this chapter is based. It was used by those writers to describe the putative descendants of an eponymous founder. See Adam Kuper's discussion of "the myth of the clan in southern Africa" in *Wives for Cattle: Bridewealth and Marriage in Southern Africa* (London: Routledge & Kegan Paul, 1982), pp. 43–49. The expression *BaNgwato* refers to the core clan—the high- and low-ranking royalty—within the chiefdom, while *Bamangwato* refers to all subjects within the chiefdom above the level of *malata* (hereditary servants). For the sake of simplicity, I have dropped the prefixes from ethnic nomenclature in the following discussion except where distinguishing between the Ngwato clan (BaNgwato) and the chiefdom (Ngwato).

In addition, the following prefixes have been omitted wherever possible, for the sake of simplicity.

Mo-: prefix signifying an individual, as Mongwato
Bo-: prefix signifying adherence to a group, or a region inhabited by a group, as in Bokalaka
Ga-: prefix signifying territory, as in Gamangwato, the land of the Ngwato state
Se-: prefix signifying language among Sotho-Tswana speakers, as in Setswana

5. According to the 1946 census, there were 17,850 Ngwato and 22,777 Kalanga out of a total of 100,987 people in the chiefdom. DCS 33/10, BNA.
6. By 1943 Ngwato wards had been sent out to the following regional communities: Shoshong, Bobonong, Mmadinare, Mahalapye, Sebina's, which was also known as Border Beacon One in Bokalaka. See Schapera, *Ethnic Composition*, p. 67.
7. Isaac Schapera, "Kinship and Politics in Tswana History," *Journal of the Royal Anthropological Institute* 93, no. 2 (1963): 159–73. In addition to the fourteen disputes explicitly concerning subject peoples, there were two schismatic church movements that may have played a similar role in the chiefdom's political life.
8. Ethnic separatism is emphatically not a divisive problem in contemporary Botswana. This chapter does not propose that the three incidents gave rise to enduring ethnic animosity; their interest lies, rather, in the way ethnicity was used by politicians to try to win advantages for themselves and their followers in the emerging social order.
9. During his thirty-three-year reign (circa 1834–1857, 1858–1866, 1873–1875) Sekgoma had vanquished the Malete near Ngwapa in 1848, the

BaKaa near Shoshong in c. 1849, and the Gananwa in Tswapong in 1859. Isaac Schapera, *Praise Poems of the Tswana Chiefs* (Oxford: Clarendon, 1965), p. 194; Schapera, *Ethnic Composition,* p. 70. For the BaKaa attempts in 1849 to secure refuge among the Kwena from the rule of Sekgoma, see David Livingstone, *Family Letters,* ed. Isaac Schapera, 2 vols. (London: Chatto & Windus, 1959), vol. 2, p. 25.
10. In 1887 Khama attacked the Seleka at Ngwapa because he feared that they were conspiring to admit the Boers to his country. Schapera, *Ethnic Composition,* p. 78. Khama's regiment, Mafolosa, was "blooded" in battle against the Birwa at the head of the Motloutse River c. 1850. Schapera, *Praise Poems,* p. 206.
11. This statement was made by an old Tswapong man during an interview conducted by Tjako Mpulubusi, then (1981) of the Botswana Museum.
12. Livingstone, *Family Letters,* vol. 1, p. 214.
13. Enclosure in D.C.S. (F. Mackenzie) to Government Secretary, 27 April 1945, S. 78/4/1, BNA. This tale is also told in Schapera's *Ethnic Composition,* p. 72.
14. John Mackenzie, *Ten Years North of the Orange River, a Story of Everyday Life and Work among the South African Tribes from 1859 to 1869* (Edinburgh, 1871; reprint, London: Frank Cass, 1971), pp. 293–98.
15. Schapera, *Praise Poems,* p. 212.
16. Macheng was the son of the nephew and widow of the late chief Kgari, and he was brought up by the Ndebele who had captured him as a youth and installed him in office in 1857. He was expelled twice by Sekgoma I, his classificatory brother, allegedly because his strict rule, modeled after that of the Ndebele, was unpopular with his people.
17. Mokakapadi, interview conducted by Tjako Mpulubusi, Lerala, Tswapong Hills, 1981.
18. Sechele Seabueng, interview conducted by Tjako Mpulubusi, Majwaneng Village, Tswapong Hills, 1981.
19. Isaac Schapera, *The Handbook of Tswana Law and Custom* (London, 1955; reprint, London: Frank Cass, 1984), pp. 118–20.
20. Ibid., pp. 96–98. Khama did not, for example, ban the payment of bridewealth among his subject peoples. Isaac Schapera, *Tribal Innovators: Tswana Chiefs and Social Change, 1795–1940* (London: Athlone, 1970), p. 138. He did, however, move a Birwa village to Bobonong because its residents were crossing into the Transvaal to hold circumcision ceremonies. Ibid., p. 210.
21. Julian Mockford, *Seretse Khama and the Bamangwato* (London: Staples, 1950), pp. 159–60.
22. Disang Raditladi, evidence to the Commission of Enquiry held at Serowe 15 November–1 December 1937 [Raditladi Enquiry], fo. 158, African Collection (uncatalogued), Manuscripts and Archives, Sterling Memorial Library, Yale University. (Hereafter, African Collection.)
23. Phethu Mphoeng, speaking at the Raditladi Enquiry.
24. Khama sent three relatives to become governors in the districts (Bobonong, Mmadinare, and Shoshong) between 1900 and 1913.
25. Modisaotsile Nkgomane, who was married to Khama's daughter, Mma-Khama, had been in exile with Sekgoma from 1899 to 1901, but he

returned and apologized to Khama and was then made governor of the Birwa at Bobonong.

26. E. H. Ashton, "Notes on the Political and Judicial Organization of the Tawana," *Bantu Studies* 11 (1937): 67–83.

27. W. C. Willoughby's version of Khama's address to the *kgotla* was given in a letter to the L.M.S., dated 21 April 1896. Q. N. Parsons, "Khama III, the Bamangwato and the British with Special Reference to 1895–1923" (Ph.D. diss., Edinburgh University, 1973), p. 215. All these peoples who wished to become independent were resident in Palapye. In 1898, Khama sent some back to the deserted capital at Shoshong and settled others on the Motloutse River.

28. By 1938 Tshekedi had placed six representatives in the hinterland; he increased their number to nine by 1949. In addition to these governors based in rural areas, both Khama and Tshekedi placed representatives at several railway sidings, a practice adopted in no other Tswana chiefdom.

29. In 1938, hut-tax collectors were earning between £30 and £84 per year, while the chief's representatives were earning between £7 and £60. See the 1938 Ngwato budget, BTA, box 16, file R1-N4, BNA.

30. Ngwako Thakgathi, interview with author, Mololatau, August 1986. The R.M. of Francistown described the same process in less violent terms: "When tax defaulters are brought before me I give them suspended sentences to enable them to obtain work," and then he arranged for a labor recruiter to proceed to where the defaulters were being tried. R.M.F. to General Secretary, 17 May 1934, S. 391/7, BNA.

31. From 1912 until 1932, 80 percent of the protectorate's budget was spent to pay central and district administrators and the police. David Massey, "Labor Migration and Rural Development in Botswana" (Ph.D. diss., Boston University, 1981), p. 71.

32. The 5-shilling surcharge payable to the protectorate's Native Fund was mandatory throughout the protectorate from 1929 until 1938. The Ngwato and Tawana chiefdoms had kept their rate at 3 shillings until 1929, five years longer than any of the other chiefdoms. Lord Hailey, *Native Administration in the British African Territories*, part 5, *The High Commission Territories: Basutoland, Bechuanaland Protectorate and Swaziland* (London: H.M.S.O., 1953), p. 303.

33. According to Tshekedi, the tax was to pay specifically for "eradication of cattle disease and abatement of contagious disease, including compensation for stock destroyed, improvement of African stock, fencing of African areas." He went on to argue that since the eradication of lung sickness in 1928, Ngwato taxpayers received no compensation for this tax. Tshekedi Khama, Notes on Taxation for Sir A. W. Pim, 6 January 1932, BTA, box 14, file R1-E3, BNA. He was aggrieved because the large Ngwato contribution to the fund—i.e., 40 percent of its revenues—was used exclusively to eradicate lung sickness, and so the Ngwato chiefdom received no regular allocation from the fund until 1931. Like his father, Tshekedi was annoyed that the fund was being used to pay for general social services, which he believed the protectorate government should rightly have been providing. Quill Hermans, "Towards Budgetary Inde-

pendence: A Review of Botswana's Financial History," *Botswana Notes and Records* 6 (1974): 96–97.
34. This Ngwato fund spent its revenues in 1934, for example, on the upkeep of the tribal borehole, wages and uniforms of the tribal police, teachers' salaries and repairs to church and school buildings (BTA, box 18, file R1-T12, BNA).
35. Tshekedi had justified creating his own tribal fund by citing "the modern demands of administration." He argued that the commission paid to him for tax collection did not cover the costs incurred by sending out six wagons, drawn by ninety-six oxen, over his vast countryside to bring the proceeds back to Serowe. Tshekedi, Notes for Pim. The D.C., G. E. Nettelton, noted that Tshekedi saw his commission as a personal rather than a tribal emolument. G. E. Nettelton, evidence to the Tagart Commission, 14 December 1932, S. 294/6, BNA. Ad hoc chiefly levies had to be approved by the R.C. from 1934 on. Lord Hailey, *Native Administration,* pp. 303–04.
36. S. J. Ettinger, "South Africa's Weight Restrictions on Cattle Exports from Bechuanaland, 1924–41," *Botswana Notes and Records* 4 (1972): 21–29.
37. 1938 Ngwato budget, BTA, box 16, file R1-N4, BNA.
38. Julian Mockford, *Seretse Khama and the Bamangwato* (London: Staples Press, 1950), p. 152.
39. E. Gluckmann, "The Tragedy of the Ababirwas and Some Reflections on Sir Herbert Sloley's Report" (reprinted from the *Rand Daily Mail* by Central News Agency, Johannesburg, 1922), p. 17. Gluckmann did not specify which "revolution" Khama had in mind.
40. Birwa folklore names Zimbabwe as their place of origin, with the northern Transvaal and the Tuli Block as their subsequent places of residence. They never settled anywhere as a cohesive group. By 1895 when Khama ceded a strip of land along the Limpopo River to the British government, which turned it over to the British South Africa Company, many Birwa were living there at a place known as Lentswe-le-Moriti. Schapera, *Ethnic Composition,* p. 76. Ngwako Thakgathi and Sekwakwa Kgwatalala, interviews with author in Mololatau and Bobonong, respectively, 7 August 1986. The singular of BaBirwa is, properly, Mmirwa.
41. Khama to R.C., 7 August 1920, S. 40/7, BNA.
42. Eminent figures in Bobonong today believe that the conflict originated not in a British South Africa Company demand for Birwa expulsion from their land but in a quarrel between Khama and Malema over tax collection—that Malema refused either to collect or to pay. Chief Mmirwa Malema, Member of Parliament Mosweu, and Headmaster of Bobonong Secondary School K. Morake, interviews with author in Bobonong, 7 August 1986.
43. H. S. McNeill to F. B. Philip (local secretary of the British South Africa Company, Cape Town), 12 November 1920, S. 40/7, BNA.
44. They first hired a black lawyer from the Transvaal, Paul Malatlane, who recommended that they hire a white lawyer instead, allegedly because he was afraid as a black foreigner to sue Khama. Simon Malema, interview with author, Mololatau, 7 August 1986.

45. Malema's grandson, the present Chief Malema, suggests that this money probably came from cattle sales and a £1 tax levied on labor migrants. He spoke of Malema as having only one major expenditure, the education of his daughter in a South African school before 1921. Another informant, Simon Malema, says that Malema often sold cattle to a "Scottish" store in the Tuli Block, so he could easily have lost that amount. The money had been buried, and Khama's regiments dug it up. Interviews in Bobonong and Mololatau, respectively, 7 August 1986.
46. Gluckmann, "Tragedy," p. 18.
47. Ibid., p. 5.
48. According to Ngwako Thakgathi, they had taken refuge at Gananwa in the Transvaal under Malebogo rather than in the Ngwato chiefdom under Khama. Interview, 7 August 1986.
49. The imperial secretary refused to allow Malema to have legal representation even though none of the sections of the proclamation establishing the Bechuanaland protectorate denied him that right (Proclamation by H. E. Sir Henry Brougham Loch, 10 June 1891).
50. Gluckmann, "Tragedy," p. 2.
51. Khama to H.C., 21 August 1922, quoted in Parsons, "Khama III," p. 397.
52. Thomas Tlou and Alex Campbell, *History of Botswana* (Gaborone: Macmillan, 1984), p. 199; Mockford, *Seretse Khama*, p. 178.
53. As might be expected, there were relatives who disputed Malema's claim to seniority, advancing their own instead. Malema was older in years than his brothers but he had been born to his father's junior wife. Simon Malema stressed in conversation with me that success in power and loyalty can make a junior more senior than a genealogical senior. Interview, 7 August 1986.
54. Unlike the BaNgwato, Birwa had no regiments, and they had retained initiation rites as well as ancestral spirit worship. Their Tswana dialect has become closer to that of the Ngwato over time. Ngwako Thakgathi admitted, after detailing these differences in conversation with me, that Serowe's displeasure did not curtail their practices. He said that the main issue was really taxation for which they reaped no rewards such as schools or hospitals. Interview, 7 August 1986.
55. The quotations are respectively from Mockford, *Seretse Khama*, p. 152, and from Khama to the R.C., 8 July 1920, S. 40/7, BNA.
56. When Malema returned, Tshekedi ruled that his son should give him twenty head of cattle. The fact that a B.P. police camp was established at Fort Motloutse after this incident was probably not decisive in keeping the peace, but was more a reflection of British fears, as well as the need to control the smuggling of stolen cattle into the Transvaal. Malema's followers were settled at Mololatau, some 25 kilometers southeast of Bobonong so that their rebellious spirit would not affect other Birwa. Even in the 1980s, the name of Modisaotsile carries such opprobrium among the Birwa that a public outcry recently scotched plans to name a new school there after him. Joseph Legwaila, personal communication to author, July 1988.

57. Isaac Schapera, "The Native Land Problem in the Tati District," *Botswana Notes and Records* 3 (1971): 224.
58. Richard Werbner, "Land and Chiefship in the Tati Concession," *Botswana Notes and Records* 2 (1970): 6–13.
59. From 1899, the Tati Company and the Bechuanaland Protectorate government had put Rauwe in charge of rent and later hut-tax collection from the Kalanga of Habangaan and Sebina and the Rolong under Moroka. See Schapera, "Native Land Problem," and Werbner, "Land and Chiefship."
60. James Mpotokwane, interview with author, Gaborone, 9 October 1981.
61. Schapera, *Praise Poems*, p. 241. This praise was composed by Seitshiro Mosweu in about 1936. See also James Mpotokwane, "A Short History of the Bahurutshe of King Motobele," *Botswana Notes and Records* 6 (1974): 37–45; Henderson Tapela, "Movement and Settlement in the Tati Region" (Paper presented to the Symposium on Settlement in Botswana, Gaborone, 1980).
62. Tshekedi Khama to R.M.S., 16 September 1927, DO 9/7/11141.
63. Remarks made by the chief's men—Edirilwe Seretse and Gaofhetoge Mathiba—at a meeting held at Serowe, 7 January 1927, DCS 43/8, BNA.
64. Ibid., remarks made by acting R.C.
65. Leburu Maifhala to R.M., Francistown, 8 July 1927, BTA, box 13, file R-C2, BNA.
66. From an unsigned draft of an official message filed in DCS 43/8, BNA.
67. Tshekedi Khama to R.M.S. (G. E. Nettelton), 16 September 1927, DO 9/7/11141, PRO.
68. Notes from *kgotla* meeting, 6 July 1934, BTA box 13, file R-C2, BNA. No Khurutshe attended, although invited by Tshekedi.
69. Oitsile Mosweu meant that the British, by arguing for freedom of worship, were allowing the Khurutshe to defy Tshekedi's orders. He was speaking in the *kgotla* meeting held at Serowe on 7 January 1927 to discuss the Khurutshe trouble at Tonota, DCS 43/8, BNA. The transcript reveals that only one Khurutshe spoke one sentence during that hearing.
70. The Kalanga terms for the following Tswana or English words are as follows: *She* for *kgosi* or *chief*, *BuKalanga* for *Bokalaka* or the country of the Kalanga, and *BakaNswazwi* for the followers of Mswazi. Mbako D. K. Mongwa argues that the "Baka-Nswazwi" became assimilated to the Bakalanga when they settled in the Maitengwe area, the Pedi language diminishing with each generation. Mbako D. K. Mongwa, "The Political Struggle between Baka-Nswazwi under John Madawo Nswazwi and the BaNgwato under Tshekedi Khama (1926–32)" (B.A. diss., University of Botswana and Swaziland, 1977), p. 5.
71. Martin Flavin, *Black and White, From the Cape to Cairo* (New York: Harper, 1950), pp. 62–63.
72. V. Posselt of Francistown, memorandum, 24 September 1943, S. 195/9, BNA.
73. The R.C. (A. D. Forsyth Thompson) wrote a reply to Posselt (27 July 1944), which was based on the Ngwato version as told to him by Phethu Mphoeng. S. 195/9, BNA.
74. Some Kalanga defended Mswazi by saying "Tshekedi was inferior to him,

as Nswazi had ruled during the life of Tshekedi's father so [he] didn't see why he should be ruled by this young boy, as Nswazi was an old man." Justice Siku, interview conducted by Carol Kerven, Tsamaya Village, 6 May 1976. I am grateful to Ms. Kerven for the opportunity to read and quote from her field notes.
75. Schapera, *Praise Poems*, p. 244.
76. In December 1930, when the Mswazis first tried to ask for independence from the Ngwato state, they specifically stated "that the Mangwato should not hold cattle posts in Mosetse and Thlalolan [sic]." Mswazi's people to R. MacFarlane, a Tsessebe trader, 29 December 1930, S. 195/8, BNA. *Mosetse* refers to the cattle-post area due west of Mswazi's hamlet on the Mosetse River. "Thlalolan" refers to the nearby Tlhalogang River. Ngwato suspected Kalanga of buying stolen Ngwato cattle from Sarwa and of trading for stolen cattle with poor Ngwato. R.M., Francistown, to Government Secretary, 2 May 1930, DCF 2/11, BNA.
77. M. Monyako at meetings held in the Serowe *kgotla* to investigate Headman Mswazi's complaints, 30 June to 2 July 1930, S. 77/8, BNA.
78. Ibid.
79. Nkhutelan v. Baliki et al., Bokalaka, 7 July 1943, K./Bok. 22/43, BNA. [Translated from Setswana by James Mpotokwane.]
80. Tshekedi Khama to D.C.S., 24 April 1940, DCS 29/6, BNA. In Bokalaka, the number of cattle collected for tax purposes leapt up to thirty-four in 1938–39 from none in 1936–37 and 1937–38.
81. John Mswaze [sic] to H.C., 5 October 1929, DCS 12/10, BNA.
82. Tshekedi Khama, Memorandum dealing with medical facilities in the Ngwato territory, 6 March 1935, BTA, box 16, file R1-M7, BNA.
83. G.S. (G. E. Nettelton) to Hill and Fraenkel, Mswazi's lawyers, 23 May 1945, S. 78/4/2, BNA.
84. One of the speakers at the regimental labor *kgotla* in 1930 remembered having queried the 2-shilling contribution being collected to send wagons to Bokalaka during the fence conflict; he said he was told by Gaofhetoge Mathiba, the tax collector, that he had no right to enquire. Golekanye, DCS 15/10, BNA. Nevertheless, in 1934, the British prohibited such levies without the written authority of the R.C.
85. Quotations from the testimony, respectively, of Phethu Mphoeng, Keeditse (the second two quotations) and Phethu Mphoeng again in the minutes of the Serowe *kgotla* meeting, 30 June and 1 and 2 July 1930, S. 77/8, BNA.
86. Even the formidable Margaret Hodgson admitted to her diary after visiting Mswazi that it was difficult to understand his case: "He himself gives a different statement every time you speak to him but he has legitimate grievances." Margaret Hodgson Ballinger, diary entry for 30 June 1931, Ballinger Papers, University of Cape Town.
87. Mswazi's people, c/o R. McFarlane, Tsessebe, to Resident Commissioner, 12 January 1932, S. 261/2, BNA.
88. R.M.S. (Captain J. W. Potts) to Assistant R.C., Mafeking, 29 February 1932, S. 78/3, BNA. R.C. (Charles Rey) to H.C., March 1932, S. 78/3; H.C. (Stanley) to R.C. (Rey), 18 March 1932, S. 78/3, BNA.

Notes to Pages 167–170   245

89. Notes of meeting at Serowe *kgotla* in connection with Mswazi's complaints, held on Thursday, 19 May 1932, S. 78/3, BNA.
90. R.M.S. (G. E. Nettelton) to General Secretary, 16 September 1932, S. 78/4/1, BNA.
91. Mongwa explains this quiet period by saying that the Mswazis saw the futility of the situation and paid the tax to obtain Mswazi's release. "Political Struggle," p. 62. The Acting R.C. (Captain Robert Reilly) felt Tshekedi had illegitimately obtained payment by acting as if the protectorate government backed his right to collect such levies. Reilly to H.C., 22 June 1932, S. 78/3, BNA.
92. Richard Werbner, "Land, Movement and Status among the Kalanga of Botswana," in *Studies in African Social Anthropology*, ed. M. Fortes and Sheila Patterson (New York: Academic, 1975), p. 111.
93. Keetile Malikongwa, speaking at the Commission of Enquiry: Mswazi and Makalaka, Palapye, March 1945, folio 5, S. 78/4/2, BNA.
94. Notes of a meeting held by the R.C. with the Government Secretary, D.C.S., and Tshekedi, 14 September 1944, S. 195/9, BNA.
95. Minute by Nettelton, 18 February 1945, S. 78/4/1, BNA.
96. R.C. (Forsyth Thompson) to H.C., 26 February 1945, S. 78/4/1, BNA.
97. The legal battle leading to the High Court's decision to allow the Ngwato to proceed against the Mswazis was protracted and complex. It reveals the British capitulating to Tshekedi's initiative. In September 1945, the Mswazis applied to the High Court for an interdict against the removal of the 150 recalcitrants from Bokalaka. The acting justice (Grindley-Ferris) rejected the appeal saying that Tshekedi was simply carrying out the H.C.'s lawful orders with the approval of the British government. In April 1946, Sir Walter Harragin, judge of the High Court, heard Tshekedi and the Mswazis state their cases through their respective advocates. Tshekedi's lawyer, Douglas Buchanan of Cape Town, argued that the Bechuanaland protectorate was governed under the Foreign Jurisdiction Act and that its inhabitants were not British subjects but foreigners. As a result, Tshekedi, "the chosen instrument of the Secretary of State," was not subject to British or protectorate courts. He submitted as proof a letter of minor importance from a junior official which referred to an order of the Secretary of State. The High Court accepted this position and rejected the Mswazis' contention that the Privy Council must hear the case because it was costly and a matter of public importance. The court set aside the interdict because Tshekedi's regiments had already arrived in Bokalaka. Buchanan had warned that, subject to Tshekedi's decision, the regiments would proceed with the removal without the administration's support because violence might occur if there were a delay. The above account is based on "Tribal Dispute in Bechuanaland," *Bulawayo Chronicle*, n.d. (1946), S. 79/1/4, BNA, and Mary Benson, *Tshekedi Khama* (London: Faber, 1960), p. 150.
98. Tshekedi and Douglas Buchanan, Ex Gratia Proposal for a Final Settlement of the Mswazi Situation, n.d., S. 79/1/3, BNA; R.C. (Anthony Sillery) to H.C. (Evelyn Baring), 9 December 1947, S. 79/1/3, BNA. In 1948 the Mswazis' cattle had been sold at public auction, realizing over £14,000, which was split equally between a fixed deposit account and

the expenses of the occupying forces. In 1958 John Mswazi asked the African Authority in Serowe whether his small band of stalwarts could return to Ngwato territory. By then, the chieftainship had been suspended. In the hope of provoking faith in the new political order, both the protectorate and tribal administrations allowed the Mswazis to reoccupy their former lands. R.C. (D. M. Robinson) to Deputy H.C., 9 September 1958, S. 79/5/2, BNA.

99. Charles Douglas-Home, *Evelyn Baring, the Last Proconsul* (London: Collins, 1978), pp. 172–73.
100. Evidence of Mmoshe Lesetedi in transcript of the Serowe *kgotla* proceedings, 1930, S. 77/8, BNA.
101. "The Mswazis" to H.C., via Hill and Fraenkel [their Mafeking law firm] 20 September 1945, S. 78/4/3, BNA.
102. The Mswazis to R. MacFarlane, a Tsessebe trader, 29 December 1930, S. 195/8, BNA.
103. Amos Dambe, Shoshong, to R.C., 17 February 1945, S. 78/4/1, BNA.
104. D.C.S. (F. Mackenzie) to Government Secretary, 25 October 1944, S. 195/9. In 1932 Tshekedi had been so opposed to his enemy K. T. Motsete's plans to establish a school in the Tati district that, in the words of the R.C., he threatened that "anybody who supports the said school by money or scholars must understand that the Chief would drive him or them out of the land." R.C. (Charles Rey) to H.C., 2 February 1932, S. 78/1, BNA.
105. The quotations come respectively from G. E. Nettelton to D. W. How, Government Secretary, 23 May 1932, S. 78/3, BNA, and R.M.S. to Government Secretary, 16 July 1932, S. 78/4/1, BNA.
106. Tshekedi, "Mswazi's Affairs, Notes for Discussion," 17 July 1945, S. 78/4/2, BNA; D.C.S. (F. Mackenzie) to G.S., 28 January 1946, S. 78/4/4, BNA; note by Chief Tshekedi at Sebina's [another Kalanga village] 15 October 1947, S. 79/1/2, BNA.
107. Enclosure in D.C.S. (F. Mackenzie) to G.S., 27 April 1945, S. 78/4/1, BNA. In 1947, H.C. Baring defended Tshekedi's confiscation of Mswazi property according to traditional law, that is, because the Mswazis were "illegally" absent from their homes. On the other hand, the R.C., Anthony Sillery, had cautioned the D.C.S. against "rid[ing] Native Law and Custom too hard." R.C. to D.C.S., 11 October 1947, and R.C. to H.C., 13 and 15 October 1947, S. 79/1/1, BNA.

5. "Things Fall Apart"

1. These views were held, respectively, by Mary Benson, *Tshekedi Khama* (London: Faber, 1960), and Michael Scott, *A Time To Speak* (New York: Doubleday, 1958); Mosinyi, as quoted in Harold Robertson, "From Protectorate to Republic: The Political History of Botswana, 1926–66" (Ph.D. diss., Dalhousie University, 1979); Tshekedi Khama; Lenyeletse Seretse, as quoted in Bessie Head's *Serowe: Village of the Rain Wind* (London: Heinemann, 1981), p. 82; and V. F. Ellenberger, First Assistant Secretary of the High Commissioner.

Notes to Pages 176–186   247

2. D.C.S., *Annual Report* (referring to 1931), 6 January 1936, DCS 21/9, BNA.
3. I. Schapera, *Migrant Labour and Tribal Life* (London: Oxford University Press, 1947), p. 34.
4. D.C. (W. F. Mackenzie), *Annual Report* (1943), 1 February 1944, DCS 24/24, BNA.
5. Ibid.
6. The D.C.S. provoked an investigation of the traders' alleged habit of charging higher prices from African than from European customers. D.C.S., *Annual Report* (1945), 2 February 1946, DCS 24/24, BNA.
7. D.C.S., *Annual Report* (1946), n.d., file number missing, BNA.
8. V. F. Ellenberger, report on 20–25 June 1949, meetings in the Serowe *kgotla*, 29 June 1949, Ellenberger Papers, Rhodes House Library.
9. The D.C.'s *Annual Reports* reveal that from 1942 through 1952, there were only one excellent harvest (1948), two average ones (1943 and 1944), and one that was fair (1951); the rest ranged from poor to almost total failures, leading to near starvation. BNA.
10. Gabolebye Marobela, interview with author, Serowe, 1981. Marobela also told this story in the Serowe *kgotla* while defending Tshekedi's intentions during the succession debacle. The shopping trip had occurred while Seretse was studying in Britain.
11. Tshekedi to J. P. Proudfoot, District Supt. of the Native Recruiting Corporation, 18 December 1946, DCS 32/14, BNA.
12. Benson, *Tshekedi Khama*, p. 175.
13. Ibid., p. 177.
14. Phethu Mphoeng, notes of the November 1948 *kgotla* meetings, BTA, box 20, file "SSK," BNA.
15. The quotations are, respectively, from Lecheko Madikwe, Oabona Nthobatsan, Tshekedi, transcript of the 28 and 29 December 1948 *kgotla*, BTA 20, "SSK," BNA.
16. The quotations are respectively from Seretse and Joel Baitswi, ibid.
17. Charles Douglas-Home, *Evelyn Baring, the Last Proconsul* (London: Collins, 1978), p. 179.
18. Ellenberger report on June 1949 *kgotla*.
19. Ibid.
20. John Redfern, *Ruth and Seretse: A Very Disreputable Transaction* (London: Gollancz, 1955), pp. 50–51.
21. Ellenberger report on June 1949 *kgotla*.
22. Lenyeletse Seretse, quoted in Head, *Serowe*, p. 82.
23. Serogola Seretse, quoted in chap. 2 of L. D. Raditladi's manuscript, "The Destiny of Seretse Khama, Royal Head of the Bamangwato People," kindly loaned to me by Zachariah Matumo, Gaborone.
24. "Tshekedi Tells of Duties Awaiting White Chieftainness," Johannesburg *Star*, 4 July 1949, Ellenberger Papers.
25. R. V. Selope Thema, Chairman of the African National Congress, told Harragin that Seretse had no right to marry without the tribe's consent and that if Seretse's child married a white woman too, then one day a white man would rule the Bamangwato (untitled newsclipping in Ellenberger Papers, n.d.).

26. The quotations are, respectively, from Phethu Mphoeng, quoted in Raditladi, "Destiny," and Manyapelo Osupile, BTA 20, "SSK," BNA.
27. Ironically, the ex-regent had justified his request by citing the 1943 Native Administration Proclamation, which he had so fiercely opposed in its initial stages. See chap. 3.
28. Douglas-Home, *Evelyn Baring*, pp. 184–85.
29. Jan Smuts to Winston Churchill, 16 March 1950, in *Selections from the Smuts Papers*, ed. Jean van der Poel (London: Cambridge University Press, 1973), vol. 7 (August 1945 to October 1950), pp. 348–49. As the grand design for *apartheid* began to take shape, it became clear that the three High Commission Territories were intended to become the nucleus for the establishment of Bantustans; they would also increase the total land area within the Union that could be designated as African.
30. Sir Walter Harrigan, "Report of the Judicial Enquiry Re Seretse Khama of the Bamangwato Tribe," *Botswana Notes and Records* 17 (1985): 53–64.
31. Malan had in September 1949 telegrammed to the British government an unequivocal statement of the Union's position, and he made several speeches through October in which he threatened to demand the High Commission Territories in 1950. See also the Southern Rhodesian Legislative Assemblies Debates, 7th Parliament, 2d session, 30 #46, pp. 2511–15.
32. Johannesburg *Star*, 16 November 1949, Ellenberger Papers.
33. Harragin, "Re Seretse," p. 58.
34. Tshekedi Khama, memorandum to Harragin, n.d. (November 1949), pp. 12–13, South African Library, Cape Town.
35. Tshekedi, quoted in Redfern, *Ruth and Seretse*, p. 89.
36. Harragin, "Re Seretse," p. 62.
37. Harrigan's report was finally published in 1985 as the "Report of the Judicial Enquiry Re Seretse Khama." See n. 30.
38. Minutes by Attlee, 21 December 1949 and 22 January 1950, prime minister's office papers, PREM 8/1308, PRO, quoted in Ronald Hyam, "The Political Consequences of Seretse Khama: Britain, the BaNgwato and South Africa, 1948–52," *The Historical Journal* 29, no. 4 (1986): 931.
39. Diary entry in April 1950, quoted in ibid., p. 936.
40. *Parliamentary Papers*, Commonwealth Relations Office, "Succession to the Chieftainship of the Bamangwato Tribe," March 1950, Cmd. 7913, pp. 5 and 6.
41. Ibid., p. 7.
42. Doris Bradshaw to H. Lovell, 22 March 1950, Mss. 6/9, BNA.
43. Ramarula Mathodi, quoted in Sethare Jack v. Rex, 13 September 1951, Criminal Appeal Case No. 6/1951, BNA.
44. L. M. Seretse, quoted by Mokakapadi Ramosoka, 10 July 1951, BTA, box 1, file J. 6, BNA.
45. Rajaba Monaheng, quoted in Rajaba Monaheng and others v. Rex, 3–6 October 1950, Criminal Appeal Case No. 7/1950, BNA.
46. Ramarula Mathodi, quoted in ibid.

Notes to Pages 194–200   249

47. Patrick Gordon Walker, quoted in Robertson, "Protectorate to Republic," p. 317.
48. *Parliamentary Papers,* "Report of the Observers on the Attitude of the Bamangwato Tribe to the Return of Tshekedi Khama to the Bamangwato Reserve," December 1951, Cmd. 8423, p. 5. Macmillan was director of colonial studies at St. Andrews University, Bullock the former president of the Trade Union Congress, and Lipson once the Independent M.P. for Cheltenham. See Michael Crowder, "Professor Macmillan goes on Safari: The British Government Observer Team and the Crisis over the Seretse Khama Marriage" (Paper delivered at the Institute of Commonwealth Studies Conference to mark the centenary of the birth of W. M. Macmillan, October 1985).
49. The village was Sefhare in the Tswapong Hills. Ever ready to defend himself on the basis of "traditional" legal principles, Tshekedi explained the Sefhare people's acceptance of his supporters in terms of "the seniority enjoyed by their foremost leader." Cmd. 8423, p. 9.
50. To fund their trip, Keaboka Kgamane, Peto Sekgoma, and four others had borrowed in the name of the tribe £2,500 from Serowe traders against future cattle sales.
51. Redfern, *Ruth and Seretse,* p. 203.
52. The prosecuting attorneys in this case were masters at the inept phrasing of questions: "If [the royal headmen] are removed, then one of the main planks in the set-up of the tribe would be removed?" "Can you explain whether the same inspiration descended upon another 800 people in Serowe?" Regina v. Keaboka Kgamane and 40 others, Criminal Case No. 6/1952, BNA.
53. Oitsile Mosweu was quoted by Constable Galebowe as having made this remark, but Galebowe later retracted his testimony. Ibid.
54. D.C.S. (W. F. Mackenzie), *Annual Report for 1951,* n.d., S. 541/11, BNA.
55. Tshekedi Khama, memorandum furnished to the Secretary of State, Commonwealth Relations Office, December 1951, DCS 42/12, BNA.
56. Tshekedi noted four cases of his supporters being dismissed from office: G. Kolonyane, as schoolmaster at Bobonong; Molwa Sekgoma as housemaster from Moeng College; Ofhentse as foreman of the Moeng College cattle; Moonwa as the head of church activities at Sefhare. DCS 42/12, BNA.
57. Abel Sikunyana, interview with author, Serowe, 1980.
58. Tariso Modimotsile, quoted in Sethare Jack v. Rex.
59. G. D. Marobela, quoted in Head, *Serowe,* p. 98. Not all of Tshekedi's supporters left with him for Rametsana; some feared the damage they would cause to their herds by leaving. Lenyeletse Seretse, a senior member of the royal family and later vice president of Botswana, believed that Tshekedi's fatal flaw was to withdraw from Serowe with his followers; his initial promise was to go alone. Interview with author, Gaborone, April 1981.
60. Casalis Goletilweng, Regina v. Keaboka Kgamane and 40 others.
61. W. M. Macmillan, quoted in Crowder, "Professor Macmillan," p. 9.
62. In 1953 L. D. Raditladi tried to found a party representing educated

young men. Called the Bamangwato National Congress, this short-lived party included K. T. Motsete and M. T. Chiepe among its members. Neil Parsons, "The Central District: The BaNgwato Crisis, 1948–1956," in *Birth of a Nation, The Making of Botswana*, ed. J. Ramsay and R. F. Morton (Gaborone: Longman, 1987).

63. Testimony of a forty-five-year-old Serowe man, BTA, box 3, file BD/1/53, BNA.
64. For example, the British Government Observer Team met one afternoon in Serowe with a thousand women who were vehemently opposed to Tshekedi. Crowder, "Professor Macmillan," p. 9.
65. The women of Mahalapye petitioned the R.C. in favor of Seretse in 1949, "we are women, and we also put forward our request as such because a chief is for us all and not for men only who speak in *kgotla*." Neil Parsons, "Seretse Khama and the Bangwato Succession Crises, 1948–53" (Paper presented at the 29th African Studies Association Annual Conference, New Orleans, November 1985), p. 10.
66. On his return in 1956, Seretse stated that he hoped women would *not* attend the *kgotla*; his "scrupulously correct" attitude dissatisfied some Ngwato. D.C.S. (N. B. Rutherford), *Annual Reports for 1956 and 1957* (15 March 1957 and 20 March 1958), S. 564/10 and S. 568/5, BNA.
67. "A Denial of Tshekedi's Allegations by the Madinare People," English version of an article submitted to the newspaper *Naledi*, 1951, BTA, box 20, file A, BNA.
68. Quoted in C. C. McLaren for D.C., drafted by J. A. Germond, to Government Secretary, 21 January 1951, S. 442/8, BNA. W. M. Macmillan, attending only one *kgotla* during a week devoted to divining opinion in the hinterland, quoted the Kgalagadi headman of Rakops, "If a regent has caused as much trouble as Tshekedi Khama has, he can say nothing. The Regent ate Seretse.... We don't want Tshekedi or his property." Crowder, "Professor Macmillan," p. 7.
69. Quoted in District Officer, Bokalaka (H. Murray-Hudson) to D.C.S., 19 September 1956, DCS 42/2, BNA.
70. The cattle-post area in dispute was called Gogwane. In addition to plowing there without permission, Seretse's overseers were grazing more cattle than Tshekedi thought was good for the soil. After Tshekedi expelled these errant overseers, two court cases were heard—one in the Subordinate Native Authority court by Oteng Mphoeng, and one by David Robinson, the assistant district officer. Both ruled in Tshekedi's favor; Robinson frankly admitted, "the actions of Tshekedi must be judged in the light of whether they strengthened or weakened [the structure of the new regime with Rasebolai Kgamane as Native Authority]." David Robinson, Assistant District Officer, to D.C.S., 1 January 1954, DCS 42/13, folio 26, BNA.
71. Ibid., folio 24.
72. Isaac Schapera, *Handbook of Tswana Law and Custom* (London, 1955; reprint London: Frank Cass, 1984), p. 222.
73. Tshekedi wrote to the chiefdom's agricultural and livestock adviser in 1949: "The few herds of my cattle which you saw at Mamosarwane are the result of over ten years of hard work and colossal expenditure, and

it is only now that I am beginning to see results and even then, the stock I have is nowhere near in quality to what Chief Khama possessed. I calculate that it will take me at least another ten years of concentrated work to bring it to what it used to be." Tshekedi to B. B. Murcott, 7 April 1949, BTA, box 2, file A1/M1, BNA. Accurate statements of herd size are nearly impossible to acquire, even for chiefs. Just prior to 1950, Tshekedi said that he had more or less 2,500 cattle and 2,000 goats (Tshekedi Khama Papers). A local rancher estimated for me that Tshekedi probably owned 25,000 head of cattle at his peak.

74. Ntsemanato Rancholo, evidence, 29 December 1953, Gogwane Dispute, folio 20, DCS 42/13, BNA.
75. Tradition states that he should have rewarded them for their services as herders by presenting them with an occasional calf. Schapera, *Handbook,* 1955, p. 253; and F. B. H. Watermeyer, Animal Husbandry Officer, to D.C.S., 31 July 1950, S. 170/2, BNA.
76. Tshekedi Khama, "Memorandum on the Productive Development of the B.P.," 18 September 1945, S. 400/6, BNA.
77. Tshekedi Khama to High Commissioner, 3 December 1948, Tshekedi Khama Papers, Pilikwe.
78. Martin Flavin to Mrs. Ballinger, 6 March 1948, Ballinger Papers, A3.1.54, William Cullen Africana Library, University of the Witwatersrand.
79. Redfern, *Ruth and Seretse,* p. 101.
80. Tshekedi Khama, "The Principles of African Tribal Administration," *International Affairs* 27, no. 4 (October 1951): 455. In the second passage, he was quoting with approval the Nigerian politician O. Awolowo.
81. Notes on the meeting of the D.C. and Tshekedi at Seruli, 22 April 1952, DCS 42/12, BNA. According to the D.C.S., the British government wanted neither Seretse nor Tshekedi as African Authority, but it failed to interest Tshekedi in an alternative post—adviser on the protectorate's economic development. D.C.S. (N. B. Rutherford), *Annual Report,* 1954, n.d., S. 556/14, BNA.

6. Conclusion

1. The quotations are from, respectively, Bathoen Gaseitsiwe and Mokgalo Selepeng, author's interviews, Gaborone, 1981.
2. Gabolebye Marobela, interview with author, Serowe, 1981.
3. Sheila Rule, "In Botswana, a Democracy in Full Voice," *New York Times,* 31 July 1988, p. 17.
4. The Sebe brothers who ruled the Ciskei phrased their political quarrels in these terms in the early 1980s.
5. J. Lefela to D. Hammarskjöld, 18 December 1957, and Basutoland National Council, 44 Session (1948), quoted in Robert Edgar, *Prophets with Honour, a Documentary History of Lekhotla la Bafo* (Johannesburg: Ravan, 1987), p. 12.
6. William Beinart, "Chieftaincy and the Concept of Articulation: South Africa ca. 1900–1950," *Canadian Journal of African Studies* 19, no. 1 (1985): 94.

7. Jean Comaroff, personal communication to author, and *Body of Power, Spirit of Resistance, the Culture and History of a South African People* (Chicago: University of Chicago Press, 1985), p. 234.
8. Union of South Africa, "Summary of the Report of the Commission for the Socio-Economic Development of the Bantu Areas within the Union of South Africa" (Tomlinson Commission Report), U.G. 61/1955, p. 58.
9. Hugh Macmillan, "Swaziland: Decolonisation and the Triumph of 'Tradition,'" *Journal of Modern African Studies* 23, no. 4 (1985): 666. In 1989, Chris Lowe of Yale University was conducting historical research into this issue in Swaziland.
10. Shula Marks, "Natal, the Zulu Royal Family and the Ideology of Segregation," in *The Societies of Southern Africa in the Nineteenth and Twentieth Centuries*, vol. 9, Collected Seminar Papers, no. 24, University of London, Institute of Commonwealth Studies, 1977–78, p. 116.
11. William Beinart and Colin Bundy, *Hidden Struggles in Rural South Africa, Politics and Popular Movements in the Transkei and Eastern Cape, 1890–1930* (London: James Currey, 1987), pp. 10–11, 28–29.
12. John Holm, "Rural Development and Liberal Democracy in Botswana," *African Studies Review* 25, no. 1 (1982): 83–102.
13. Barry Streek and R. Wicksted, *Render unto Kaiser: A Transkei Dossier* (Johannesburg: Ravan, 1981).

Sources

Oral Sources

Serowe: Arthur Barnard, Gwen Blackbeard, Marge McQuirk, Maletemengwe Makabole, Molebatsi Makoloba, G. D. Marobela, Patiko Mathodi, P. M. Mazile, Rajaba Monageng, G. O. Motsokono, John Palmer, Mrs. H. C. Pretorius, Sr., Baropi Ratshosa, O. F. Resheng, Tsogang Sebina, Linda Sekgoma, Radiphofu Sekgoma, A. C. Sikunyana, J. J. Tebape, Mrs. George Watson, William Woodford, and the residents of Ramoseki ward.
Palapye: D'Arcy Henry, Rra Shashane, Mrs. Minnie Shaw.
Gaborone: Bathoen Gaseitsiwe, Vernon Gibberd, Zachariah Matumo, James Mpotokwane, Mokgalo Selepeng, Lenyeletse Seretse, Palatse Tshoagang.
Lerala: Serathi Magama and forty other villagers.
BoBirwa: Ngwako Thakgathi, Sekwakwa Kgwatalala, Chief Mmirwa Molema, M.P. Mosweu, Headmaster Morake, Simon Malema.

Archival Sources

BOTSWANA:

Botswana National Archives, Gaborone: Bamangwato Tribal Archives; Ngwato Kgotla Records, 1937–65; High Court Records, Lobatse; District Commissioner, Serowe—correspondence and annual reports; miscellaneous correspondence written and received by the Resident and High Commissioners' offices.
Mrs. Ella Khama, Pilikwe: Tshekedi Khama Papers (private collection).
Mrs. Minnie Shaw, Palapye: Serowe Chamber of Commerce minutes (private collection).
District Commissioner's Office, Serowe: miscellaneous contents of storeroom.

GREAT BRITAIN:

Public Record Office, Kew: selected Dominions Office files regarding the Bechuanaland Protectorate.
School of Oriental and African Studies, University of London: London Missionary Society Papers.
Congress for World Mission, London: London Missionary Society Papers, 1940–1950.
Rhodes House: Anthony Sillery Papers
      N. V. Redman Papers
      V. F. Ellenberger Papers

Royal Commonwealth Society, London: Rev. François Coillard Papers

SOUTH AFRICA:

William and Margaret Ballinger Papers, University of Cape Town, University of the Witwatersrand.
Rev. Ernest Baker Papers; 1949 Memorandum by Tshekedi Khama to Sir Walter Harragin, South African Library, Cape Town.
Howard Pim Papers, University of the Witwatersrand.
G. E. Nettelton Papers, University of Cape Town.

UNITED STATES:

Manuscripts and Archives, Sterling Memorial Library, Yale University: Raditladi Enquiry, 1937; Tshekedi Khama's annotated version of Schapera's *Handbook of Tswana Law and Custom.*

Official Publications

Bechuanaland Protectorate. *Annual Reports.* London, 1888, 1896–97, 1902–03, 1903–04, 1919–1938
———. African Advisory Council. *Minutes.* Mafeking, 1924–1928, 1930–1960.
———. *High Commissioner's Proclamations and the More Important Government Notices from 1 January to 31 December, 1934.* Vol. 19. Mafeking: The Mafeking Mail, 1935.
Cape of Good Hope. Commission of the Griqualand Labour Question. *Report.* Government Notice No. 102, 1876.
———. South African Native Affairs Commission. *Report, 1903–5.* 6 vols. Cape Town, 1905.
Great Britain. *Parliamentary Papers.* "Further Correspondence Respecting the Affairs of South Africa." C. 2220. London, 1878–79.
———. "Further Correspondence Respecting the Affairs of the Transvaal and Adjacent Territories." C. 4588. London, 1885.
———. "Financial and Economic Position of the Bechuanaland Protectorate: Report of the Commission Appointed by the Secretary of State for Dominion Affairs," March, 1933 (Pim Report). Cmd. 4368. London, 1933.
———. "Bechuanaland Protectorate: Report of the Observers on the Attitude of the Bamangwato Tribe to Tshekedi Khama of the Bamangwato Reserve, Dec. 1951." Cmd. 8423. London, 1951–52.
———. "Succession to the Chieftainship of the Bamangwato Tribe, March, 1950." Cmd. 7913. London, 1950.
Transvaal. Transvaal Labour Commission. *Report.* Johannesburg, 1903.
Union of South Africa. Bechuanaland Protectorate. *Confidential Reports,* 1910.

Books, Pamphlets, Articles, Theses

Alverson, Hoyt. *Mind in the Heart of Darkness: Value and Self-identity among the Tswana of Southern Africa.* New Haven: Yale University Press, 1978.
Ashton, E. H. "Notes on the Political and Judicial Organization of the Tawana." *Bantu Studies* 11 (1937): 67–83.
Ballinger, William, and Margaret Hodgson. *Britain in Africa*, no. 2, *The Bechuanaland Protectorate.* Alice, South Africa: Lovedale, 1932.
Barnes, Leonard. *The New Boer War.* London: Hogarth, 1932.
———. "Tshekedi and After." *Nineteenth Century* 114 (1933): 573–82.
Bates, Robert. *Essays on the Political Economy of Rural Africa.* Berkeley: University of California Press, 1983.
Bawden, M. G., and A. R. Stubbs. *The Land Resources of Eastern Botswana.* Surrey: Directorate of Overseas Surveys, 1963.
Behnke, Roy H., Jr. "Production Rationales: The Commercialization of Subsistence Pastoralism." *Nomadic Peoples* 14 (1983): 3–33.
Beinart, William. *The Political Economy of Pondoland, 1860 to 1930.* Johannesburg: Ravan, 1982.
———. "Chieftaincy and the Concept of Articulation: South Africa ca. 1900–50." *Canadian Journal of African Studies* 19, no. 1 (1985): 91–98.
Beinart, William, and Colin Bundy. *Hidden Struggles in Rural South Africa, Politics and Popular Movements in the Transkei and Eastern Cape, 1890–1930.* London: James Currey, 1987.
Benson, Mary. *Tshekedi Khama.* London: Faber, 1960.
Best, Alan. "General Trading in Botswana, 1890–1968." *Economic Geography* 46, no. 4 (1970): 598–611.
Bonner, Philip. *Kings, Commoners and Concessionaires, The Evolution and Dissolution of the Nineteenth Century Swazi State.* Johannesburg: Ravan, 1983.
Booth, Alan R. *Swaziland: Tradition and Change in a Southern African Kingdom.* Boulder: Westview Press, 1983.
Brown, J. Tom. *Among the Bantu Nomads.* London: Seely, Service, 1926.
Burchell, William J. *Travels in the Interior of South Africa*, 2 vols. London, 1822–1824. Reprint. Cape Town: C. Struik, 1967.
Burman, Sandra, and B. Harrell-Bond. *The Imposition of Law.* New York: Academic, 1979.
Campbell, John. *Travels in South Africa, Undertaken at the Request of the Missionary Society.* London, 1815. Reprint. Cape Town: C. Struik, 1974.
Casalis, Eugene. *The Basutos or Twenty-Three Years in South Africa.* London, 1861.
Chanock, Martin. *Law, Custom, and Social Order, the Colonial Experience in Malawi and Zambia.* Cambridge, England: Cambridge University Press, 1985.
Chapman, James. *Travels in the Interior of South Africa 1849–1863: Hunting and Trading Journeys from Natal to Walvis Bay and Visits to Lake Ngami and Victoria Falls.* Ed. Edward C. Tabler. 2 vols. Cape Town: A. A. Balkema, 1971.

Sources

Child, Graham. "Ecological Constraints on Rural Development in Botswana." *Botswana Notes and Records* 3 (1971): 157–64.

Chirenje, J. Mutero. *Chief Kgama and His Times, c. 1835–1923: The Story of a Southern African Ruler.* London: Rex Collings, 1978.

———. *A History of Northern Botswana 1850–1910.* Rutherford, N.J.: Fairleigh Dickinson University Press, 1977.

Cobbing, Julian. "The Mfecane as Alibi: Thoughts on Dithakong and Mbolompo." Unpublished seminar paper, given at the University of Witwatersrand, 1987.

Colclough, Christopher, and Stephen McCarthy. *The Political Economy of Botswana: A Study of Growth and Distribution.* Oxford: Oxford University Press, 1980.

Comaroff, Jean. *Body of Power, Spirit of Resistance, the Culture and History of a South African People.* Chicago: University of Chicago Press, 1985.

Comaroff, John L. "Talking Politics: Oratory and Authorship in a Tswana Chiefdom." In *Political Language and Oratory in Traditional Society,* edited by Maurice Bloch. London: Academic, 1975.

———. "Rules and Rulers: Political Processes in an African Chiefdom." *Man* 13 (1978): 1–20.

———. "Dialectical Systems, History and Anthropology: Units of Study and Questions of Theory." *Journal of Southern African Studies* 8, no. 2 (1982): 143–72.

Comaroff, John L., and Simon Roberts. *Rules and Processes: The Cultural Logic of Dispute in an African Context.* Chicago: University of Chicago Press, 1981.

Comaroff, John L., and Jean Comaroff. "Christianity and Colonialism in South Africa." *American Ethnologist* 13, no. 1 (1986): 1–22.

——— and ———. "On the Founding Fathers, Field Work and Functionalism: A Conversation with Isaac Schapera." *American Ethnologist* 15, no. 3 (1988): 554–65.

Crowder, Michael. "Resistance and Accommodation to the Penetration of the Capitalist Economy in South Africa: Tshekedi Khama and Mining in Botswana, 1929–1959." Paper for discussion at the University of London, Institute of Commonwealth Studies Decolonisation Seminar, 10 October 1985.

———. *The Flogging of Phinehas McIntosh, a Tale of Colonial Folly and Injustice, Bechuanaland, 1933.* New Haven: Yale University Press, 1988.

———. "Professor Macmillan Goes on Safari: The British Government Observer Team and the Crisis over the Seretse Khama Marriage." Paper delivered at the University of London, Institute of Commonwealth Studies Conference to mark the centenary of the birth of W. M. Macmillan, October 1985.

———. "Tshekedi Khama and Opposition to the British Administration of the Bechuanaland Protectorate, 1926–1936." *Journal of African History* 26 (1985): 193–214.

———. "The Succession Crisis over the Illness and Death of Kgosi Sekgoma II of the BaNgwato, 1925: Western versus Traditional Medicine." Unpublished paper, n.d., given to me by the author.

Sources 257

Crush, Jonathan. *The Struggle for Swazi Labour, 1890–1920.* Kingston and Montreal: McGill-Queen's University Press, 1987.
Dachs, Anthony. *Khama of Botswana.* London: Heinemann, 1971.
Davenport, T. R. H. *South Africa, A Modern History.* 3rd ed. Toronto: University of Toronto Press, 1987.
Delius, Peter. *The Land Belongs to Us, the Pedi Polity, the Boers and the British in the Nineteenth Century Transvaal.* Berkeley: University of California Press, 1984.
Denbow, James R., and Edwin N. Wilmsen. "Advent and Course of Pastoralism in the Kalahari." *Science,* 19 December 1986, 1509–15.
Dornan, S. S. "The Tati Bushmen (Marsarwas) and their Language." *Journal of the Royal Anthropological Institute* 47 (1917): 37–112.
Douglas-Home, Charles. *Evelyn Baring, the Last Proconsul.* London: Collins, 1978.
Duggan, William. *An Economic Analysis of Southern African Agriculture.* New York: Praeger, 1986.
Edgar, Robert. *Prophets with Honour, a Documentary History of Lekhotla la Bafo.* Johannesburg: Ravan Press, 1988.
Ettinger, S. J. "South Africa's Weight Restrictions on Cattle Exports from Bechuanaland, 1924–41." *Botswana Notes and Records* 4 (1972): 21–29.
Exton, H. "The Bojala: A Bechuana Ceremonial; and Some Affinities of Native Customs." *Cape Monthly Magazine,* 2nd ser., 1 (1870): 281–89.
Flavin, Martin. *Black and White, From the Cape to the Congo.* New York: Harper, 1949.
Gardner, R. "Some Sociological and Physiological Factors Affecting the Growth of Serowe." *Botswana Notes and Records* 6 (1974): 77–88.
Gerth, H. H., and C. W. Mills, eds. *From Max Weber: Essays in Sociology.* New York: Oxford University Press, 1958.
Gluckman, Max. "The Kingdom of the Zulu in South Africa." In *African Political Systems,* edited by Meyer Fortes and E. E. Evans-Pritchard. London: Oxford University Press, 1940.
Gluckmann, Emmanuel. *The Tragedy of the Ababirwas and Some Reflections on Sir Herbert Sloley's Report.* Johannesburg: Central News Agency, 1922.
Goody, J., ed. *Succession to High Office.* Cambridge, England: Cambridge University Press, 1966.
Hailey, William Malcolm. *Native Administration in the British African Territories. Part 5, The High Commission Territories.* London: H.M.S.O., 1953.
Hall, Martin. *The Changing Past: Farmers, Kings and Traders in Southern Africa.* London: James Currey, 1988.
Hamnett, Ian. *Chieftainship and Legitimacy: An Anthropological Study of Executive Law in Lesotho.* London: Routledge & Kegan Paul, 1975.
Harragin, Sir Walter. "Report of the Judicial Enquiry *re* Seretse Khama of the Bamangwato Tribe." *Botswana Notes and Records* 17 (1985): 53–63.
Harris, John C. *Khama, the Great African Chief.* London: Livingstone, 1922.
Head, Bessie. *Serowe, Village of the Rain Wind.* London: Heinemann, 1981.
Hepburn, J. D. *Twenty Years in Khama's Country and Pioneering among the Batuana of Lake Ngami.* C. H. Lyall, ed. London, n.d.
Hermans, Janet. "Official Policy towards the Bushmen of Botswana: A Review, Part I." *Botswana Notes and Records* 9 (1977): 62–63.

Hermans, Quill. "Towards Budgetary Independence: A Review of Botswana's Financial History, 1900–1973." *Botswana Notes and Records* 6 (1974): 89–115.

Hinchey, Madalon, ed. *Proceedings of the Symposium on Drought in Botswana.* Hanover, N.H.: Botswana Society in Collaboration with Clark University Press, 1979.

Hitchcock, Robert. *Kalahari Cattle Posts: A Regional Study of Hunter-Gatherers, Pastoralists, and Agriculturalists in the Western Sandveld Region, Central District, Botswana.* 2 vols. Gaborone: Ministry of Local Government and Lands, 1978.

Hodson, Arnold. *Trekking the Great Thirst: Sport and Travel in the Kalahari Desert.* London: T. Fisher Unwin, 1912.

Holm, John. "Rural Development and Liberal Democracy in Botswana." *African Studies Review* 25, no. 1 (1982): 83–102.

Hubbard, Michael. "Desperate Games: Bongola Smith, the Imperial Cold Storage and Bechuanaland's Beef, 1931." Paper presented to the History Departmental Seminar, University College, Botswana, March 1981.

Hyam, Ronald. "The Political Consequences of Seretse Khama: Britain, the BaNgwato and South Africa, 1948–1952." *The Historical Journal* 29, no. 4 (1986): 921–47.

Jennings, A. E. *Bogadi: A Study of the Marriage Laws and Custom of the Bechuana Tribes of South Africa.* Vryburg, South Africa: London Missionary Society, 1933.

Jousse, P. [pseud. "Inquisitor"]. "The Truth about the Bechuanas, Khama the King." Johannesburg: Central News Agency, 1914.

Joyce, J. W. "Report on the Masarwa in the Bamangwato Reserve, Bechuanaland Protectorate." League of Nations, Advisory Committee of Experts on Slavery, Geneva, 1938. *League of Nations Publications.* 6. B. (Slavery) C 112, M98, Annex 6, 57–76.

Kerven, Carol. *Botswana Mine Labour Migration to South Africa.* Gaborone: National Migration Study, Central Statistics Office, 1979.

Khama, Tshekedi. "Native Standpoint against Transfer." *Race Relations* 2, no. 3 (1935): 152–56.

———. *A Statement to the British Parliament and People.* London: Headley Brothers, 1935.

———. "The Principles of African Tribal Administration." *International Affairs* 27, no. 4 (1951): 451–56.

———. *Bechuanaland and South Africa.* London: African Bureau, 1955.

———. *Political Change in African Society: A Study of the Development of Representative Government.* London: African Bureau, 1956.

Kimble, Judy. "'Clinging to the Chiefs': Some Contradictions of Colonial Rule in Basutoland, c. 1890–1930." In *Contradictions of Accumulation in Africa, Studies in Economy and State,* edited by Henry Bernstein and Bonnie K. Campbell. Beverly Hills: Sage, 1985.

Knight-Bruce, Louise. *The Story of an African Chief.* London: K. Paul, Trench, Trubner, 1895.

Kuper, Adam. *Wives for Cattle. Bridewealth and Marriage in Southern Africa.* London: Routledge & Kegan Paul, 1892.

Kuper, Hilda. *An African Aristocracy, Rank Among the Swazi.* London: Oxford University Press, 1965.
———. *Sobhuza II, Ngwenyama and King of Swaziland.* New York: Africana, 1978.
Legassick, Martin. "The Sotho-Tswana Peoples before 1800." In *African Societies in Southern Africa,* edited by Leonard Thompson. New York: Praeger, 1969.
Leonard, A. G. *How We Made Rhodesia.* London: K. Paul, Trench, Trubner, 1896.
Lestrade, G. P. "Some Notes on the Bogadi System of the Bahurutshe." *South African Journal of Science* 23 (1926): 937–42.
———. "Some Notes on the Political Organization of the BeChwana." *South African Journal of Science* 25 (1928): 427–32.
Livingstone, David. *Family Letters, 1841–1856.* Edited by Isaac Schapera. London: Chatto & Windus, 1959.
———. *Missionary Correspondence, 1841–1856.* Edited by Isaac Schapera. London: Chatto & Windus, 1961.
Lloyd, E. *Three Great African Chiefs: Khame, Sebele, Bathoeng.* London: T. Fisher Unwin, 1895.
London Missionary Society, South Africa District Committee. *The Masarwa (Bushman): Report of an Inquiry by the South Africa District Committee of the London Missionary Society.* Lovedale, South Africa: Lovedale, 1935.
Mackenzie, John. *Ten Years North of the Orange River, a Story of Everyday Life and Work among the South African Tribes from 1859 to 1869.* Edinburgh, 1871. Reprint. London: Frank Cass, 1971.
———. Reply to questionnaire, 29 November 1881. *Report of the Government Commission on Native Laws and Customs.* Cape Town, 1883, appendix C (vol. 2, part 2), 231–48.
———. "Native Races of South Africa and Their Polity." *British Africa.* Vol. 2 of *The British Empire Series.* 2. London: Kegan Paul, Trench, Trubner, 1899, 168–94.
Macmillan, Hugh. "Swaziland: Decolonisation and the Triumph of 'Tradition.'" *Journal of Modern African Studies* 24, no. 4 (1985): 643–66.
Marks, Shula. "Natal, the Zulu Royal Family and the Ideology of Segregation." *The Societies of Southern Africa in the Nineteenth and Twentieth Centuries.* Vol. 9 of Collected Seminar Papers, no. 24, University of London, Institute of Commonwealth Studies, 1977–78.
Massey, David. "The Development of a Labor Reserve: The Impact of Colonial Rule on Botswana." Boston University, African Studies Center, Working Papers, no. 34, 1980.
———. "Labor Migration and Rural Development in Botswana." Ph.D. diss., Boston University, 1981.
Maylam, Paul. *Rhodes, the Tswana and the British, Colonialism, Collaboration and Conflict in the Bechuanaland Protectorate 1885–1899.* Westport, Conn.: Greenwood, 1980.
———. *A History of the African People of South Africa: From the Early Iron Age to the 1970s.* London: Croom Helm, 1986.
Miers, Suzanne, and Michael Crowder. "The Politics of Slavery in Bechuanaland: Power Struggles and the Plight of the Basarwa of the Bamangwato

Reserve, 1926–40." In *The End of Slavery in Africa*. Edited by Suzanne Miers and Richard Roberts. Madison: University of Wisconsin Press, 1988.

Mockford, Julian. *Khama, King of the Bamangwato*. London: J. Cape, 1931.

———. *Seretse Khama and the Bamangwato*. London: Staples, 1950.

Moffat, Robert. *Apprenticeship at Kuruman, Being the Journals and Letters of Robert and Mary Moffat, 1820–28*. Edited by Isaac Schapera. London: Chatto & Windus, 1951.

Molema, S. M. *Montshiwa, 1815–1896, Barolong Chief and Patriot*. Cape Town: C. Struik, 1966.

Mongwa, Mbako D. K. "The Political Struggle between Baka-Nswazwi under John Madawo Nswazwi and the BaNgwato under Tshekedi Khama (1926–32)." B.A. diss., University of Botswana and Swaziland, 1977.

Moore, Barrington. *Social Origins of Dictatorship and Democracy: Lord and Peasant in the Making of the Modern World*. Boston: Beacon, 1966.

Moore, Sally Falk. *Law as Process, an Anthropological Approach*. London: Routledge and Kegan Paul, 1978.

Mountevans, E.R.G.R.E. *Adventurous Life*. London: Hutchinson, 1946.

Mpotokwane, James. "A Short History of the Bahurutshe of King Motobele, Senior Son of King Mohurutshe." *Botswana Notes and Records* 6 (1974): 37–45.

Mullagin, Kathleen. "Alfred Jennings: The Political Activities of the London Missionary Society in Bechuanaland, 1900–1935." Ph.D. diss., St. John's University, New York, 1974.

Nangati, Fanuel. "Early Capitalist Penetration: The Impact of Precolonial Trade in Kweneng (1840–76)." Paper presented to the Symposium on Settlement in Botswana, Gaborone, 1980.

Okihiro, Gary. "Hunters, Herders, Cultivators and Traders: Interaction and Change in the Kgalagadi, Nineteenth Century." Ph.D. diss., University of California, Los Angeles, 1976.

Packard, Randall. *Chiefship and Cosmology: An Historical Study of Politics and Competition*. Bloomington: Indiana University Press, 1981.

Parson, J. "The Working Class, the State and Social Change in Botswana." *South African Labour Bulletin* 5 (1980).

Parsons, Q. N. *The Word of Khama*. Lusaka: NECZAM, 1972.

———. "Khama III, the Bamangwato and the British with Special Reference to 1895–1923." Ph.D. diss., Edinburgh University, 1973.

———. "On the Origins of the Bamangwato." *Botswana Notes and Records* 5 (1973): 82–103.

———. "Shots for a Black Republic? Simon Ratshosa and Botswana Nationalism." *African Affairs* 73 (1974): 449–58.

———. "'Khama and Co.' and the Jousse Trouble, 1910–1916." *Journal of African History* 14, no. 3 (1975): 383–408.

———. "The Economic History of Khama's Country in Botswana, 1844–1930." In *The Roots of Rural Poverty in Central and Southern Africa*, edited by Q. N. Parsons and Robin Palmer. Berkeley: University of California Press, 1977, 113–43.

———. "Seretse Khama and the Bangwato Succession Crises, 1948–53." Paper presented at the 29th African Studies Association annual conference, New Orleans, November 1985.

Sources   261

Peires, J. B. *The House of Phalo, a History of the Xhosa People in the Days of Their Independence.* Johannesburg: Ravan, 1981.

———. "Continuity and Change in Ciskei Chiefship." *The Societies of Southern Africa in the 19th and 20th Centuries.* Vol. 8 of *Collected Seminar Papers, no. 22.* University of London, Institute of Commonwealth Studies, 1977.

Peters, Pauline E. "Cattlemen, Borehole Syndicates and Privatization in the Kgatleng District of Botswana: An Anthropological History of the Transformation of a Commons." Ph.D. diss., Boston University, 1983.

Picard, Louis A. "Role Changes among Field Administrators in Botswana: Administrative Attitudes and Social Change." Ph.D. diss., University of Wisconsin, Madison, 1977.

Plaatje, Solomon T. *Sechuana Proverbs with Literal Translations of Their European Equivalents.* London: K. Paul, Trench, Trubner, 1916.

Price, Elizabeth Lees (Moffat). *Journals Written in Bechuanaland, Southern Africa, 1854–83; with an Epilogue: 1889 and 1900.* Edited by Una Long Gill. London: E. Arnold, 1956.

Prins, Gwyn. *The Hidden Hippopotamus, Reappraisal in African History: The Early Colonial Experience in Western Zambia.* Cambridge, England: Cambridge University Press, 1980.

Quinlan, Tim. "The Perpetuation of Myths: A Case Study of Tribe and Chief in South Africa." *Journal of Legal Pluralism and Unofficial Law* 27 (1988): 79–115.

Raditladi, L. D. "The Destiny of Seretse Khama, Royal Head of the Bamangwato People." Unpublished ms. in the possession of Zachariah Matumo, Gaborone, n.d.

Ramokate. "Notes on the Khurutshe." *Botswana Notes and Records* 2 (1971): 14.

Ramashoana, D. M. "The Origin of Secwana." *Bantu Studies* 3 (1927): 197–98.

Ramsay, Jeffrey, and R. F. Morton, eds. *Birth of a Nation: The Making of Botswana.* Gaborone: Longman, 1987.

Redfern, John. *Ruth and Seretse: A Very Disreputable Transaction.* London: Gollancz, 1955.

Rey, C. *Monarch of All I Survey. Bechuanaland Diaries 1929–37.* Edited by Neil Parsons and M. Crowder. Gaborone: Botswana Society, 1988.

———. "Background to the Bamangwato." *Journal of Racial Affairs* 1, no. 3 (1950): 6–11.

Roberts, Simon. "The Tswana Polity and 'Tswana Law and Custom' Revisited." *Journal of Southern African Studies* 12, no. 1 (1985): 75–87.

Robertson, Harold H. "From Protectorate to Republic: The Political History of Botswana, 1926–66." Ph.D. diss., Dalhousie University, 1979.

Roe, Emery M. "The Development of Livestock, Agriculture and Water Supplies in the Eastern Areas of the Bechuanaland Protectorate, 1895–1965: A Short History and Policy Analysis." Ithaca, N.Y.: Cornell University, Rural Development Committee, 1980.

Rule, Sheila. "In Botswana, a Democracy in Full Voice." *New York Times,* 31 July 1988, p. 17.

Sandham, J. G. "Trade among the Tswana of the Nineteenth Century." M.A. thesis, School of Oriental and African Studies, University of London, 1969.

Sansom, Basil. "Traditional Rulers and Their Realms" and "Traditional Economic Systems." In *The Bantu-Speaking Peoples of Southern Africa.* Edited by W. D. Hammond-Tooke. London: Routledge & Kegan Paul, 1974.

Schapera, Isaac. "Economic Conditions in a Bechuanaland Native Reserve." *South African Journal of Science* 30 (1930): 633–55.

———. "Premarital Pregnancy and Native Opinion on Social Change." *Africa* 6 (1933): 59–89.

———. "Oral Sorcery among the Natives of Bechuanaland." In *Essays Presented to C. G. Seligman,* edited by E. E. Evans-Pritchard, R. Firth, B. Malinowski, I. Schapera. London: Routledge, 1934, 293–305.

———. *The Bantu-Speaking Tribes of South Africa; an Ethnographic Survey.* London: Routledge, 1937.

———. *A Handbook of Tswana Law and Custom.* London, 1955 [2d ed.]. Reprint. London: Frank Cass, 1984.

———. "The Political Organization of the Ngwato of the Bechuanaland Protectorate." In *African Political Systems,* edited by M. Fortes and E. E. Evans-Pritchard. London: Oxford University Press for the International African Institute, 1940.

———. *Married Life in an African Tribe.* New York: Sheridan, 1941.

———. *Native Land Tenure in the Bechuanaland Protectorate.* Lovedale, South Africa: Lovedale, 1943.

———. "The Work of the Tribal Courts in the Bechuanaland Protectorate." *African Studies* 2 (1943): 27–40.

———. *Tribal Legislation among the Tswana of the Bechuanaland Protectorate, a Study in the Mechanism of Cultural Change.* London: London School of Economics, 1943.

———. *Migrant Labour and Tribal Life, a Study of Conditions in the Bechuanaland Protectorate.* London: Oxford University Press, 1947.

———. "Kinship and Marriage among the Tswana." In *African Studies of Kinship and Marriage,* edited by A. R. Radcliffe-Brown and Daryll Forde, 140–65. London: Oxford University Press for the International African Institute, 1950.

———. *The Ethnic Composition of the Tswana Tribes.* London School of Economics Monographs on Social Anthropology, no. 11. London: London School of Economics, 1952.

———. *The Tswana.* Part 3 of *Ethnographic Survey of Africa, Southern Africa,* edited by Daryll Forde. London: International African Institute, 1953.

———. "The Sources of Law in Tswana Tribal Courts: Legislation and Precedent." *Journal of African Law* 1 (1957): 150–62.

———. "Agnatic Marriage in Tswana Royal Families." In *Studies in Kinship and Marriage,* edited by Isaac Schapera, 103–13. London: Royal Anthropological Institute, 1963.

———. "Kinship and Politics in Tswana History." *Journal of the Royal Anthropological Institute* 93 (1963): 159–73.

———. "Contract in Tswana Case Law." *Journal of African Law* 9 (1965): 142–53.

———. *Praise Poems of Tswana Chiefs.* Oxford: Clarendon, 1965.

———. "Tswana Legal Maxims." *Africa* 36 (1966): 121–34.

———. "Sorcery and Witchcraft in Bechuanaland." In *Witchcraft and Sorcery*, edited by Max Marwick, 108–20. Harmondsworth, England: Penguin, 1970.

———. *Tribal Innovators: Tswana Chiefs and Social Change, 1795–1940*. London: Athlone, 1970.

———. "The Native Land Problem in the Tati District." *Botswana Notes and Records* 3 (1971): 219–68.

———. *Rainmaking Rites of Tswana Tribes*. Leiden: Afrika-Studiecentrum, 1971.

———. "Contempt of Court in Tswana Law." *Journal of African Law* 21, no. 2 (1977): 139–52.

Scott, James. *Weapons of the Weak, Everyday Forms of Peasant Resistance*. New Haven: Yale University Press, 1985.

Scott, Michael. *A Time to Speak*. Garden City, N.Y.: Doubleday, 1958.

Sebina, P. M. "Makalaka." *African Studies* 8, no. 1 (1947): 82–96.

Shillington, Kevin. *The Colonisation of the Southern Tswana 1870–1900*. Johannesburg: Ravan, 1985.

Silberhauer, G. B., and A. J. Kuper. "Kgalagari Masters and Bushmen Serfs: Some Observations." *African Studies* 25, no. 4 (1966): 171–79.

Sillery, Anthony. *Founding a Protectorate; a History of Bechuanaland 1885–95*. The Hague: Mouton, 1965.

———. *Botswana; a Short Political History*. London: Methuen, 1974.

Smith, Andrew. *Journal of His Expedition into the Interior of South Africa, 1834–6; an Authentic Narrative of Travels and Discoveries, the Manners, and Customs of the Native Tribes, and the Physical Nature of the Country*. Edited by William P. Lye. Cape Town: A. A. Balkema, 1975.

Squires, Bernard T. "Malnutrition amongst Tswana Children." *African Studies* 2, no. 4 (1943): 210–14.

Stevens, Christopher, and John Speed. "Multi-Partyism in Africa: The Case of Botswana Revisited." *African Affairs* 76, no. 304 (1977): 381–87.

Streek, Barry, and R. Wicksted. *Render unto Kaiser: A Transkei Dossier*. Johannesburg: Ravan, 1981.

Tagart, E. S. B. *Report on the Conditions Existing among the Masarwa in the Bamangwato Reserve of the Bechuanaland Protectorate and Certain Other Matters Appertaining to the Natives Living Therein*. Pretoria: Government Printer, 1933.

Tapela, Henderson. "Movement and Settlement in the Tati Region: A Historical Survey." Paper presented to the Symposium on Settlement in Botswana, Gaborone, 1980.

Thompson, Leonard, ed. *African Societies in Southern Africa: Historical Studies*. New York: Praeger, 1969.

———. *Survival in Two Worlds: Moshoeshoe of Lesotho, 1786–1870*. Oxford: Clarendon, 1975.

Tlou, Thomas. "Melao Yaga Kgama: Transformation in the Nineteenth Century Ngwato State." M.A. thesis, University of Wisconsin, Madison, 1968.

———. "The Nature of the Botswana States: The Batawana Case." *Botswana Notes and Records* 6 (1974): 57–75.

———. *A History of Ngamiland 1750 to 1906, the Formation of an African State.* Gaborone: Macmillan, 1985.

Tlou, Thomas, and Alec Campbell. *History of Botswana.* Gaborone: Macmillan, 1984.

Truschel, Louis W. "Accommodation under Imperial Rule: The Tswana of the Bechuanaland Protectorate, 1895–1910." Ph.D. diss., Northwestern University, 1970.

———. "Political Survival in Colonial Botswana: The Preservation of Khama's State and Growth of the Ngwato Monarchy." *Transafrican Journal of History* 3 (1973): 71–92.

"Tshekedi Khama v. Simon Ratshosa and Another." *South African Journal of Law* 49 (1932): 246–55.

"Tshekedi Khama and Another v. the High Commissioner, 1936." *High Commission Territories Law Reports: "Decisions of the High Court and Special Courts of Basutoland, the Bechuanaland Protectorate and Swaziland, 1926–53."* Edited by Sir Harold William, C. M. G. Maseru, 1953.

Union of South Africa. *Summary of the Report of the Commission for the Socio-Economic Development of the Bantu Areas within the Union of South Africa* [Tomlinson Report]. U.G. 61–'55. Pretoria, 1955.

van der Poel, Jean, and W. K. Hancock, eds. *Selections from the Smuts Papers.* Vol. 7. London: Cambridge University Press, 1973.

Warwick, Peter. *Black People and the South African War, 1899–1902.* Johannesburg: Ravan, 1983.

Werbner, Richard. "Land and Chiefship in the Tati Concession." *Botswana Notes and Records* 2 (1970): 6–13.

———. "Land, Movement and Status among the Kalanga of Botswana." In *Studies in African Social Anthropology,* edited by M. Fortes and Sheila Patterson, 95–120. New York: Academic, 1975.

Willoughby, William C. *Native Life on the Transvaal Border.* London: Simkin, Marshall, Hamilton, Kent, 1900.

———. "Notes on the Totemism of the Becwana." *Journal of the Royal Anthropological Institute* 35 (1905): 295–314.

Wilson, Monica, and Leonard Thompson, ed. *The Oxford History of South Africa.* 2 vols. New York: Oxford University Press, 1969, 1971.

Wiseman, John A. "Multi-Partyism in Botswana." *African Affairs* 76, no. 302 (1977): 70–79.

Wood, J. G. *The Uncivilized Races of Men in all Countries of the World.* Vol. 1. Hartford: J. B. Burr, 1870.

Wynne, Susan. *Local Institutions and Development in Botswana.* Gaborone: Ministry of Agriculture, 1981.

Index

African Advisory Council, 14
African Auxiliary Pioneer Corps, 119, 176, 177
African National Congress, 200
age regiments. *See* regiments
agriculture and agricultural production
 and climate, 20–21, 118
 Kalanga methods of, 168
 and labor migration, 60–61, 119
 and Mswazis, 165
 neglect of, 98
 and social control, 118
Anglican Church, and Khurutshe case, 156, 157–161
Anglo-American Corporation, 207
Arden-Clarke, Charles, 116
Assistant Commissioners, 108, 110
Athlone, Lord, 85, 109–110, 112
Attlee, Clement, 190

Baboni Khama, 70, 75, 157
Bagakgametse, 94, 95
Baitshenyetsi, 131
Bakgomohi, 131
Ballinger, William, 78, 80, 122
Ballingers, 167
Bamangwato (citizens of the Ngwato chiefdom). *See* Ngwato chiefdom
BaNgwato. *See* Ngwato clan
Bantu-speaking peoples, 10–11
 cattle-wife exchanges of, 23
Bantustans, 15, 15–16, 211–212, 213–214, 215–216
Baring, Sir Evelyn, 170, 179, 185, 186–187, 190, 191, 192
Barnes, Leonard, 80
Barotseland, 40
Basutoland, 4, 12, 14
Bates, Robert, 31
Batho, P. G., 196
Bathoen Gaseitsiwe (chief of the Ngwaketse), 45, 113, 114, 115, 116
Bechuanaland Protectorate, 4, 14, 44–49
 as Botswana, 4, 15, 46 (*see also* Botswana)
 establishment of, 108
 political order of, 5, 7–8
 see also British colonial administration
Bechuanaland Soldiers Benefit Fund, 177
beer brewing
 and anti-Khama organizing, 144
 in divorce proceeding, 128
 by poor women, 177, 201, 208
 prohibition of, 51–52, 53, 102, 177, 200, 201
begging, 22, 30–31
Beinart, William, 212
Bessie Khama, 69
Birwa, the, 149–155, 241n.40, 242n.54
Bobonong, 151, 152, 153
Boers, 44, 140, 142, 143, 144, 148
Bokalaka, 166, 168, 176, 178, 201
boreholes, 65, 203
 chief alone able to sink, 119
 taxes for, 147
 in Tshekedi's development schemes, 204, 205
Botletle River, 202
Botswana, 4, 46
 democracy of, 211
 ethnic separatism in, 238n.8
 formation of, 15
 natural resources of, 215
 Seretse Khama, president of, 218n.6
 and Tshekedi Khama, 16
British colonial administration, 4, 13–14, 15, 44–55, 222nn.72, 73
 Bantustan policy contrasted with, 214
 courts of, 64
 and customary law, 74, 101, 107–117, 133, 134
 and fall of Ngwato chieftainship, 175, 207
 anti-European sentiments, 197
 direct rule, 192–193, 194–197
 and marriage of Seretse, 179–180, 183, 186–191

265

British colonial administration (cont.)
  and hereditary servants, 64
  and interference in tribal government, 46, 93
  and Khama III, 44–45, 46–49, 50, 51–53, 106–107
  and labor migration, 59–60
  and legal appeals, 77
  military force demonstrated by, 115, 169
  and regimental-labor controversy, 78–80
  and Sarwa servitude, 84, 85, 90
  and South Africa, 91
  and subject peoples, 136–137, 146, 148–149, 172–173
    and Birwa case, 151–155, 172
    and Khurutshe case, 156, 157–161, 172
    and Mswazi case, 162–172, 245n.97
  taxation by, 50, 67, 79, 146–147, 205 (see also taxation)
  and traditional political forms, 99
  and "tribe" as fundamental unit, 137
  and Tshekedi, 63–64, 84, 93, 172
  in Tswana/Ngwato factional conflicts, 68, 75, 77
  see also District Commissioner; High Commissioner; Resident Commissioner; Resident Magistrate
British South Africa Company, 45, 46, 150, 156, 163
Buchanan, Douglas, 180
Bullock, H. L., 194, 195
bureaucracies, 5
  Bantustan, 215–216
  of Tshekedi, 173
  under Tswana chiefs, 16, 50, 54–55, 61, 146
burial customs of Tswana, 33

capitalism
  growth of, 98–99
  patriarchy undermined by, 83, 118, 212–213
  and Ratshosas, 77
  and Tshekedi's development efforts, 208–209
cattle, 65
  British purchase of (turn of century), 40–41
  commercialization of, 76, 90, 120, 203, 214–215

  epidemics among, 13, 97, 144, 178
  exchanges of, 7, 23
  herding of, 21
  investments from sale of, 65, 90
  Kalanga attitudes toward, 165
  and *kgotla*, 197
  and labor migration, 60–61
  levy of, 178
  and power of early groups, 11
  and private vs. communal property, 194, 203
  sale of and labor migration, 98
  sale of for tax payment, 97
  Sarwa theft of, 85, 87, 88–89, 91, 130
  South African purchase and embargo of, 13, 55, 58, 66, 97, 120, 147, 177
  taxes to fight diseases of, 147, 240n.33
  in wealth of chief, 27, 120
  and white businesses, 66
Central African Federation, 189
Chadibe, Khama's gardens at, 51, 202
Chamberlain, Joseph, 45, 46, 59, 115
changes in Ngwato chiefdom. See Ngwato/Tswana chiefdom, changes in
Chanock, Martin, 101, 118
chiefdoms, Ngwato. See Ngwato chiefdom
chiefdoms, Tswana. See Tswana chiefdoms
chieftainship, 7
  autonomy lost by, 15
  in Bantustan, 211
  British rule over, 13–14
  changing of, 16–17
  traditionalist view of, 212
  and "tribal" identity, 16
  see also patriarchal order
chieftainship, Ngwato, 166
  agricultural wealth of, 119, 120
  in Birwa case claims, 151, 153, 155
  fall of, 175–176
    antipathies behind, 8
    economic context of, 176–179
    and marriage of Seretse, 179–191
    interim British rule, 192–193, 194–196
    effects of on communal activities, 192–193, 205–206
    mob violence, 193–198
    factions in, 198–204, 207–208
    Tshekedi on, 206, 211
    and return of Seretse, 207

and opposition to Tshekedi, 207–208
and capitalist relations, 208–209
and current state of affairs, 210
and southern Africa's industrial revolution, 216
mfecane impact on, 37, 38–39
Motsete on changes in, 81
and religion, 159
and South Africa transfer, 93, 113–114
and subject peoples, 172–174 (*see also* subject peoples)
as territorial monarchy, 172
Tshekedi's strengthening of, 146
chieftainship, Tswana, 18–19
and British vs. customary law, 107–111, 112, 113, 114, 115
and British overrule, 45–46, 49–50, 51–54
bureaucracy of, 50, 54–55, 61–62
development of, 18–19, 36–37, 61–62
gaining of, 30
and *kgotla* disputes, 104, 106–107
and patriarchal ideology, 31–36
patronage exchanges of, 23
power of, 27–29, 32–33, 105, 235n.43
and regency, 30, 127, 224n.1
as territorial monarchy, 46
trade benefits to, 42
and South Africa, 62
and wealth distribution, 28, 30, 32–33, 54, 62, 148
and wealth of people, 215
Christianity (Church)
adoption of, 44
and chiefly reforms, 52
competing elites of, 53
and Khama III, 44, 105–106
evangelizing as organizing against, 144
and Khurutshe case, 156, 157–161
levy in support of, 82
and political ambitions, 161
see also London Missionary Society; missionaries
Churchill, Winston, 187, 191
collective responsibility, 5
acceptance of, 124, 129
vs. Botswana politics, 211
and breakdown of law, 197
in *kgotla*, 103
labor migration as threat to, 118

Tshekedi asserts, 97, 172, 173
Tshekedi's definition of resented, 200
Colonial Development and Welfare funds, 205
Comaroff, Jean, 105, 212
Comaroff, John, xii
Communism, and Mswazi complaints, 172
courts, of British administration, 64
customary law. *See under* law

democracy or accountability
of Botswana, 211
chiefs' reforms lacking in, 146
development of among Ngwato, 192, 196
and *kgotla*, 25
late-colonial shift to, 214
Sertese favors, 207
and Seretse-marriage *kgotla*, 183, 184
and Tshekedi on role of chiefs, 206
and Tshekedi's innovations, 205
and Tswana politics, 31, 50
development, economic. *See* economic development
diamond mining, 12–13, 58
and labor migration, 120
See also migration, labor
Disang Raditladi, 95–96, 122, 131–132
District Commissioner/Resident Magistrate, 14
and closer government, 146
direct rule by, 192, 193
and law, 111, 113, 116, 121, 123
and marriage of Seretse, 190
and post-suspension unrest, 196, 197
on post-WWII employment expectations, 177
Raditladi on, 95
See also Resident Magistrate
divorce
and law, 106, 108, 110, 127–129
of Tshekedi, 94–96
drought
of *1932*, 13, 96
of *1942*, 13, 178
and public labor, 83
dynastic rivalries, 30, 180
Handbook on, 172
Khama's containment of, 144–145
Kwena interference in, 40
and legal innovation, 121
and patronage, 76, 77, 96
property as issue in, 95

dynastic rivalries (*cont.*)
  and Sarwa controversy, 84, 85
  and Sekgoma's death, 69–71
  seniority and, 26–27, 68, 121, 219n.15 (*see also* seniority)
  and territorial allocation, 49
  and Tshekedi's accession, 63, 69–77
  and Tshekedi's fall, 175, 180, 199
  Tshekedi's management of, 133–134
  as visible issue, 83, 98
  see also politics of Tswana; Raditladis; Ratshosa brothers

economic development
  for Botswana, 215
  by elite, 65, 76, 95–96, 214–215
  and Mswazi frustration, 166
  and privatizing of property, 203
  of South Africa, 4, 12, 55, 57–60, 134, 216
  Tshekedi's projects for, 147, 204–205, 206, 208
education
  as expected for son, 96
  Moeng College, 178, 206
  and Mswazis, 166, 171
  of Ratshosa brothers, 76
  and royalty, 55
  of Seretse, 179
  taxes for, 147, 166
  vs. traditionalism, 215
  of tribal bureaucracy, 55
  of Tshekedi, 69
  Tshekedi's apprehension over, 81–82, 125
Ellenberger, Jules, 70
Ellenberger, Vivien, 95
entrepreneurship
  of anti-regimental labor petitioners, 82
  and Ratshosas, 77
  see also capitalism
Evans, Admiral E. R. G. R., 92
exchange alliances, 7–8, 22, 23–24
  vs. British-encouraged reforms, 51
  and cattle, 23–24
  and decline of chieftainship, 216
exploitation, 31

family law, 106, 108, 110
  Disang inheritance case, 122–123
  and gender, 127–128
  Khama's reform of, 126, 131
  Sekgarametso case, 128–129

female inheritance, Khama's introduction of, 106
females. *See* women
firearms
  and Ngwato, 38, 39, 41, 141
  shotguns regulated, 109
flogging of Phinehas McIntosh, 91–93, 111, 115
Foreign Jurisdiction Act (1890), 115
Forsyth, Douglas, 187
Francistown, 158

Gaborone, 211
Gamangwato. *See* Ngwato chiefdom
Gaseitsiwe, Bathoen (chief of the Ngwaketse), 45, 113, 114, 115, 116
Gasetshwarwe (illegitimate son of Sekgoma II), 75, 81, 227n.31
George V (king of England)
  and Tshekedi's banishment, 92
George VI (king of England)
  soldiers recruited for, 176
German possessions in Africa, 45, 148
Gluckmann, Emmanuel, 151, 152, 153–154
gold mining, 4, 12–13, 58
  and labor migration, 60, 120
Gorewang Kgamane, 70–71
Griqua hunters, 40
guns. *See* firearms

Hailey, Lord, 112, 133
Handbook of Tswana Law and Custom (Schapera), xii, 100, 112, 121, 123, 172
Harragin, Sir Walter, 188, 189–190, 206
hereditary servants. *See* Sarwa
Hertzog, J. B. M., 93
hierarchy in Tswana society, 22, 24–26
  and *kgotla*, 25, 102
  ranks-to-classes transformation, 91
  reverence for, 35
  See also seniority; status
High Commissioner, 14, 49
  and Birwa case, 154
  and flogging incident, 92, 111
  and law, 107, 108, 113, 115
  and marriage of Seretse, 179, 182
  and regimental-labor controversy, 80
  and Sarwa controversy, 85
  and tax monies, 147
High Commission Territories, 4, 14, 15, 93, 191. *See also* British colonial administration

Index 269

hinterland. *See* subject peoples
Hodgson, Margaret, 80

Ikalanga/Sekalaka, 171
immigrants (refugees), acceptance of, 26, 37, 38, 60, 138, 221n.50
incwala (Swazi harvest ritual), 16, 213
Indian state, Ngwato chiefdom compared with, 170, 173–174
Inkatha, 214

Jameson, L. S., 51
Joyce, J. W., 86

Kadalie, Clements, 80
Kalanga/Kalaka, 89, 137, 145, 157
   labor migration by, 59
   Mswazi clan of, 162–172, 178, 201, 245nn.97, 98
Keaboka Kgamane, 192, 193–194, 196
Keate award, 59
Kedikilwe (Talaote chief), 142
Keletlhokile Raditladi, 123
Kesebonye Sephekolo, 83–84
Kgalagadi, the, 42, 43, 61
   headman from killed, 141, 142
   and regimental-labor fracas, 79
Kgamane, Gorewang, 70–71
Kgamane, Keaboka, 192, 193–194, 196
Kgamane, Rasebolai, 167, 198
kgamelo (milk-bag cattle), 23, 51
Kgari (chief of the Bakwena), 117
Kgari (grandfather of Khama), 155
Kgatla, the
   and rainmaking, 53
   as South African labor, 50
kgosana (royal family member), 121
"*kgosi*" ("chief" or "rich man"), 27
kgotla (village forum), 8, 25, 31, 101–102, 103–104, 123
   acceptance of, 105
   and British law, 108, 109, 110, 111, 114, 116, 123
   and chief's house, 19
   as democratic foundation, 211
   and Khama III, 55
   and labor migration, 117, 118
   and law, 121, 130, 131
   and male supremacy, 129
   from political to political-and-legal, 134
   and property, 132–133
   and Sarwa, 87–88, 131
   Seretse's education on, 179
   and Seretse's marriage, 180, 181–182, 183–184, 185, 186, 189, 191, 216
   and social change, 209
   suspension of, 192, 196, 197, 198
   Tshekedi's view of, 189
   values displayed in, 124, 125–126, 181
   ward/section/supreme, 103–104, 114, 235n.35
   and women, 126, 127–128, 177, 181, 199, 201
Khama, Baboni, 70, 75, 157
Khama, Bessie, 69
Khama, Ian, 210
Khama, MmaKhama, 70
Khama, Ruth (formerly Ruth Williams), 180, 183, 185, 187, 190–191
Khama, Semane (Tshekedi's mother), 70, 94
Khama, Seretse, 70, 218n.6
   and accession of Tshekedi, 71
   British rejection of, 196
   chieftainship renounced by, 207
   exile of, 190–191, 192
   exile of ended, 207
   Jamaican job offered to, 195
   marriage of, 179–191
Khama, Tshekedi. *See* Tshekedi Khama
Khama III, 10, 41–42, 219n.15
   and Birwa case, 149–155
   and British overrule, 44–45, 46–49, 50, 51–53, 106–107
   and Christianity, 44, 105–106
   decisions of as precedent, 129
   funeral of, 52–53
   and Kalanga, 162–163, 164, 165–172
   Kgalagadi village burned by, 43
   and *kgotla*, 55
   and Khurutshe, 158
   and labor export, 59, 60
   peaceful expansion by, 140
   and property rights, 131
   and Ratshosa, 69
   reforms of, 105–106
   and the Sarwa, 87, 88, 130
   and section *kgotla*, 103
   and subject peoples, 136, 141, 143, 144–145
   and Tshekedi's land claims, 202, 203
   Tuli Block given by, 150
   wealth of, 41–42, 106
   and women's rights, 126, 127, 131
Khoisan people, 10, 11, 19, 24–25, 42–43, 61, 84
kholwa (Christian Africans), 214

Khurutshe, the, 89, 145, 156–162
Kirkham, Mr. (trader), 71
Kololo, the, 38, 140
Kuper, Adam, 23
Kwena, the, 38, 43, 50, 141, 156, 185
Kwena chiefdom, 39–40
  Tshekedi's plan for governance by, 189
Kweneng, the, 206

labor, public service. *See* public labor
labor migration. *See* migration, labor
land rights or loss
  and ethnic tensions, 149, 172–173
    Birwa case, 150, 151
    Khurutshe case, 161
    Mswazi case, 164
  and social change, 133
  see also property rights
law
  as customary, 100–101, 133
    vs. British law, 74, 77, 107–117, 133
  British use of, 172
  factors in forming of, 18, 118–119
  and Khama, 105–106
  and management of social change, 100–101, 124–133
  origins of (19th century), 101–107
  origins of (20th century), 107–124
  and Ratshosa cases, 74
  and royal marriage, 180
  and Seretse-Tshekedi conflict, 189, 194
  Tshekedi creates, 101, 107, 121–124, 133
  and Tshekedi's postexile property claims, 203
  and dominance of rich, 214
  limitations of, 135
  vs. patriarchal order, 5
  Seretse studies for, 179, 183
  and subject peoples, 172
  see also family law
law cases
  Baboni Khama, 75–76
  Birwa, 149–155
  Disang inheritance, 122–123
  Khurutshe, 156–161
  Mswazi, 162–172, 245n.97
  Ratshosa, 73–75, 77
  Sarwa (Baitshenyetsi), 131
  Sekgarametso, 128–129
  Seretse marriage, 188–189
League of Nations, and the Sarwa, 86

Lebang Raditladi, 95, 123
Leetile Raditladi, 94–95, 122
Lekhotla la Bafo, 212
Lenyeletse Seretse, 193–194
Lerala, xii
letsholo (compulsory meeting or hunt), 78, 176
lion, Tswana chief as, 32, 33, 138, 209
Lipson, D. L., 194, 195
"listener," for subject community, 144
Livingstone, David, 141
Lobatse, 188
Lobengula (chief of the Ndebele), 46, 153, 162
London Missionary Society, 105
  and Keletlhokile, 123
  and Khurutshe case, 156, 157, 158
  and levy, 82
  and Mackenzie, 44
  and marriage of Seretse, 180
  Masarwa report by, 86
  monopoly given to, 156
    breaking of, 205
  Semane takes refuge in, 70
  and Tshekedi's accession, 71
  see also Christianity; missionaries

MacDonald, Malcolm, 115
Macfarlane, Mr. (Witwatersrand Labour Organization representative), 60
Macheng, 142, 219n.15, 239n.16
Machuchubane, 142
McIntosh, Phinehas, flogging of, 91–93, 111, 115
Mackenzie, John, 26, 44
Macmillan, Hugh, 214
MacMillan, W. M., 194, 195
Madinare, 201
Mafeking, Cape Colony/Union of South Africa, 14, 49, 95, 167
mafisa (cattle-loan system), 23, 24
Mahalapye, 201
Malan, D. F., 187
malata (hereditary servants). *See* Sarwa
Malema (Birwa chief), 150–155
Marks, Shula, 214
marriage
  and low rank, 139
  of Seretse, 179–191
  among Tswana, 23–24, 26
Masarwa. *See* Sarwa
Matabele, the, 167
Matabeleland, 40

Metse-Mosweu River, concrete wall across, 82–83
mfecane (period of violence, 1820s and 1830s), 12, 37–39, 221n.50
  ethnic diversity from, 162
  and hinterland, 140
migration, labor, 13, 58–61
  attempt to control, 119
  and disaster years, 97, 98
  effects of increase in, 129–130
  and ethnic tensions, 173
    and Mswazi, 165
  as legal change catalyst, 117–121
  and precolonial social order, 215
  as radicalizing, 200
  and reforms, 134
  remittances from, 126, 177
  by Sarwa, 89
  social evils of, 117–118, 120
  during Tshekedi's regency, 64, 67
  WWII increase in, 176
missionaries, 44
  and British vs. local law, 112
  Khama praised by, 105
  and mfecane, 39
  on migrant laborers, 58–59
  and Mswazi hospital, 166
  Mswazi request for, 171
  as pawns, 161
  see also Christianity; London Missionary Society
MmaKhama, 70
MmaLeetile Raditladi, 122
Mmusi, Peter, 211
Moanaphuti Segolodi, 78–79, 80, 81
Modisaotsile, 151, 152, 154
Moeng College, 178, 206
Molefe, 158
Moloi, 94
Mololatau, 154
Monageng, Rajaba, 88, 230–231n.78
Moshoela, Ella, 94, 95
Moshoeshoe (chief of the Sotho), 12, 37, 44, 212
Motloutse, 153
Motsete, K. T., 81–82, 125
Mphoeng, Oteng, 169
Mphoeng, Phethu, 70, 71, 71–72, 73, 78, 129
Mswazi, John, 166, 167, 168, 169, 171
Mswazi, the, 162–172, 178, 201, 245nn.97, 98
Mzilikazi (chief of the Ndebele), 141

Nata, royal cattle posts at, 94, 202–203
nation-state
  and Bechuanaland, 15
  and Ngwato chiefdom, 209, 211
  and Tshekedi's fall, 175
Native Advisory Council, 14, 52, 147
Native Authority, 113, 192, 198
Native Fund, 147
Native Recruiting Corporation (N.R.C.), 119, 176
"Native Reserves," 14
Natives Administration Proclamation (1934), 112, 113, 115, 116
Natives Tribunal Proclamation (1934), 112, 114, 115, 116
Ndebele, the, 37, 38
  and Birwa, 153
  British expeditions against, 40
  and British-laid boundaries, 148
  final British defeat of, 141, 145
  and Kalanga labor migration, 59
  and Khama, 140
  and Khurutshe, 156, 160
  and mfecane, 37, 38, 140
  and Mswazi, 162, 163
  and rise of Ngwato, 38, 139, 140, 141
  and subject peoples, 141, 143
Neale, Captain H. B., 70
Nettelton, G. E., 78, 79, 114–115
newcomers, acceptance of, 26, 37, 38, 61, 138, 221n.50
Nguni, the, 10, 11, 20, 29
  Ndebele, 37, 38 (see also Ndebele, the)
Nguni chiefs, 36
Ngwato (clan founder), 11
Ngwato chiefdom (Gamangwato), 3, 12, 221n.50
  British rule over, 4, 44–53, 106–107 (see also British colonial administration)
  dynastic rivalries within, 30, 180 (see also dynastic rivalries)
  economic development in, 65, 95–96, 147, 204–205, 206, 208 (see also economic development)
  economic independence sought for, 204–205, 208
  ethnic diversity in, 137–139, 237–238n.3
  ethnic tensions in, 148–149, 173, 238n.8
    and Birwa case, 149–155
    and Khurutshe case, 156–162

Ngwato chiefdom (Gamangwato) (cont.)
  and Mswazi case, 162–172,
    245n.97
  and Sarwa labor, 89
  (see also subject peoples)
  long-distance trade of, 39–41, 120,
    143
  migration from, 59–61 (see also migration, labor)
  nation-state and, 209, 211
  19th-century Ngwato clan hegemony
    in, 139–145
  vs. other southern African chiefdoms,
    213–214
  and South Africa, 12–13, 15–16 (see
    also South Africa)
  standing army or police lacking in,
    119, 138
  white chieftainness as threat to, 185–
    186
  See also chieftainship, Ngwato;
    Tswana chiefdoms
Ngwato/Tswana chiefdom, changes in,
  18–19, 67, 209
  bureaucratization, 4–5, 16, 50, 54–55,
    62, 146, 173
  centralization, 36–37, 39, 49, 61–62,
    107, 146
  group leadership to territorial monarchy, 46
  patronage/patriarchy to capitalist investment, 61–62, 77, 83, 90, 96,
    98–99, 208, 212–213
  in property rights, 51, 61, 67, 202–
    203
  status to contract, 89, 134
  tribute to taxation, 50, 136, 145
Ngwato clan, 137–138
  beginnings of, 37–38, 139
  hegemony of, 38, 139–145 (see also
    subject peoples)
  ox-killing ceremony by, 35–36
Ngwato Reserve, 4
Northern Rhodesia, Tshekedi sees as
  market, 205
Nswazi. See Mswazi

Oonetse Raditladi, 122
Oratile Sekgoma (later wife of Simon
  Ratshosa), 69, 72
Order-in-Council (1891), 108
Oteng Mphoeng, 169

Palapye, 50, 154

Palapye Road, 41
Panzera, F. W., 60
Passfield, Lord (Sidney Webb), 9, 74–75,
  86, 112
patriarchal order, 4–5, 7, 8
  acceptance of, 105
  adaptation of (hereditary servants),
    130–131
  adaptation of (women's rights), 126–
    130
  in Bantustans and South African townships, 211, 216
  and capitalism, 83, 118, 212–213
  changed form of, 61–62
  and class interests, 214
  crisis in, 67–68
  decline of, 204, 209, 213, 216
  and labor migration, 61, 118
  principles safeguarding, 124
  and Sarwa, 86
  seniority in, 8, 25, 121, 219n.10 (see
    also seniority)
  traditionalist defense of, 212
  and transformation of dominance relationships, 173
  and "tribes," 137
  and Tshekedi, 10, 134, 206
  and Tswana chiefs, 31–36
  undermining of, 96
  and wealth of people, 215
  see also chieftainship
patronage, 7, 20–31, 42
  adherence to, 99, 120, 134
  and chieftainship, 23, 28, 54, 62, 148,
    215
  and exploitation, 31
  and kgotla, 104, 132
  and labor migration, 61, 134
  and political protest, 83
  and Ratshosas, 76, 77
  and regiments' loyalties, 29
  and regional separatism, 173
  and seniority, 25 (see also seniority)
  and Tshekedi's fall, 207, 208
  undermining of, 83, 90, 96, 99, 208
  and vassals, 43
Pedi, the, 162
Phaleng, the, 145
Phethu Mphoeng, 70, 71, 71–72, 73, 78,
  129
Phuting, the, 38, 140
Pim, Alan, 112
Pioneer Corps, African Auxiliary, 119,
  176, 177

Pirow, Oswald, 92
pitsos (assemblies), 127
Plumtree, Southern Rhodesia, 163
political systems, patriarchal vs. bureaucratic, 4–5. *See also* bureaucracies; patriarchal order
politics of Tswana. *See* Tswana society, politics of
Pondoland, 212
Potts, Captain (Resident Magistrate), 80
praise poets, 31, 138
prefixes, in ethnic nomenclature, 238n.4
primogeniture
  and succession struggles, 68–69
  and Tswana chiefs, 30
Privy Council, London, 14, 49–50, 64, 74, 75, 111
Proclamation of *1891*, 92
proletarianization, 13
  and irresponsibility, 117
property
  and Ngwato elite, 95
  private
    in capitalist transformation, 98–99, 213
    cattle as, 203
    and dominance of rich, 214
    growth of, 99
    and Tshekedi's fall, 175
  and the Sarwa, 87
property rights and relations
  changes in, 51, 61, 67, 202–203, 208
  and legal reform, 131–133
  and loyalty to Tshekedi, 84, 173
  and political rights (Tshekedi), 203
  Seretse partisan on, 194
public labor service
  Khama's use of, 42
  as paid vs. unpaid, 83
  and regimental labor fracas, 77–84
  Tshekedi's demand for (post-WWII), 178

Raditladi, 49, 122
Raditladis, 70, 81, 94, 127
  and British vs. customary law, 111
Raditladi, Disang, 95–96, 122, 131–132
Raditladi, Keletlhokile, 123
Raditladi, Lebang, 95, 123
Raditladi, Leetile, 94–95, 122
Raditladi, MmaLeetile (Ratshosa sister), 122
Raditladi, Oonetse, 122
rainmaking, 34, 34–35

abolition of, 105–106
and conservatism of commoners, 214
end of decreed, 51
as expected chiefly duty, 53, 54
and low rank, 139
Rajaba Monageng, 88, 230–231n.78
Ramasimo, 128
Rametsana, Tshekedi in exile at, 184–185, 198, 206
Ramosenyi (chief of the Khurutshe), 158
Rasebolai Kgamane, 167, 198
Ratshosa brothers, 55, 76–77, 72, 73, 78, 85, 94, 122
  and advisory council, 71
  and British vs. customary law, 111, 113, 116
  and regimental labor controversy, 81
  Sarwa of freed, 85
  and Sarwa killing, 88
  and treatment of Sekgoma, 70
Ratshosa brothers (individually)
  Johnnie, 69–70, 71, 72–73, 74, 74–75, 76, 77
  Obeditse, 70, 73, 74–75
  Simon, 69, 69–70, 72, 73, 74–75, 76, 85, 93
Ratshosa Motswetle, 69–70
Rauwe (chief of the Khurutshe), 156
refugees. *See* newcomers, acceptance of
regent(s), 30, 224n.1
  Tshekedi as, 4, 63, 71, 217n.2 (*see also* Tshekedi Khama)
  and women, 127
regiments, 29, 102
  and anti-Tshekedi resentment, 178
  and chiefs' power, 53–54
  as enforcement, 104
  labor fracas over, 77–84
  and labor migration, 117–118
  and Swazi regiments, 16, 213
  wages of requisitioned, 59
Reilly, Captain Robert O'Malley, 74
"Report on the Conditions existing among the Masarwa," 86
"Report on the MaSarwa in the Ngwato Preserve, Bechuanaland Protectorate," 86
Resident Commissioner, 14, 49
  and Birwa case, 150, 153–154
  on drought, 96–97
  and Khurutshe case, 159
  and law, 112, 113
  and marriage of Seretse, 179
  and Mswazi case, 169

Resident Commissioner (*cont.*)
  and regimental-labor fracas, 78, 79
  and Sarwa controversy, 85, 86
  and Seretse return request, 196
  and Tshekedi's accession, 71
Resident Magistrate, 14, 49, 64
  and flogging incident, 91, 92, 93
  and Khurutshe case, 159
  and law, 109, 114, 116
  and regimental-labor fracas, 78
  and tax defaults, 97
  and Tshekedi's accession, 72–73, 74, 77
  see also District Commissioner
Rey, Lieutenant Colonel Charles, 75–76, 78, 80, 91, 93, 112–113, 114
Rhodes, Cecil, 45, 144. *See also* British South Africa Company
Rhodesia, and Bechuanaland railway rates, 57
"Road to the North," 39, 40, 139, 141
Roberts, Simon, xii, 101

sacred powers, and Tswana chiefs, 33–34, 36, 53, 54
Salisbury, Lord, 195–196
Sansom, Basil, 28
Sarwa (hereditary servants), 24, 73, 84–90, 130
  and British vs. customary law, 109–110
  civil liberties granted to, 126
  control of, 118
  evasion by, 43
  hired out by Khama, 41
  and Kalanga, 164
  litigation over, 104
  as migrant laborers, 59
  and Ratshosas, 72, 76, 78, 85
  and reform of patriarchal order, 130–131
  and regimental labor controversy, 79
  slighting of, xiii
  socialists' inquiry into, 80
  subject peoples contrasted with, 138
  tribute from ended, 51
  and Tshekedi, 63–64, 84, 85–86, 204
  and wage-labor relations, 65
  and WWII absence of men, 177
Schapera, Isaac, xii, 100, 104, 112, 121, 123, 138, 172, 203
schooling. *See* education
Sechele (chief of the Kwena), 45
Segolodi, Moanaphuti, 78–79, 80, 81

Sekalaka. *See* Ikalanga
Sekgarametso, 128
Segkoma, Oratile (later wife of Simon Ratshosa), 69, 72
Sekgoma I (Khama III's father), 41, 70, 129, 140, 141, 142, 219n.15
Sekgoma II (Khama III's son), 51, 55, 69, 70, 144, 145, 158, 185
Selepeng, 156
Semane (Tshekedi's mother), 70, 94
seniority, 8, 25, 64, 121, 219n.10
  and Bantustan politics, 211–212
  and fall of chieftainship, 175, 207
  and Khama's freeing of Birwa, 153
  Ngwato vs. Khurutshe claims of, 156, 160
  as obedience rationale, 204
  signifying of, 35, 35–36
  and pro-Seretse faction, 199, 199–200
  and succession struggles, 26–27, 68–69, 121, 219n.15
  and Tshekedi's ruling, 123
  and Tshekedi's taking refuge with Kwena, 185
  wistful memory of, 210
Sephekolo, Kesebonye, 83–84
Seretse, Lenyeletse, 193–194
Seretse, Serogola, 184, 185
Seretse Khama. *See* Khama, Seretse
Serowe, xii, 41, 64, 137–138, 166, 218n.3
  British military force to, 115
  current condition of, 210
  and Khurutshe case, 159–160
  riots in, 193
  Seretse's marriage testimony at, 188
  white traders in, 65–66, 122, 177
Serowe church, 59
Serowe dam, 77, 79–80, 82–83
servants, hereditary. *See* Sarwa
sexual conflict, and "songs of the law," 105
Shaka (Zulu chief), 12
Shona, the, 40, 153
  Kalanga speak dialect of, 162
Shoshong, 40, 41, 141, 142
Sikwa (Tswapong chief), 143
slavery
  and Khama's removal of Birwa, 151
  and regimental labor controversy, 78, 79
  and Sarwa, 84–85, 86, 109–110 (*see also* Sarwa)
Sloley, Sir Herbert, 154

Smuts, Jan, 187
Sobhuza (Swazi king), 16
social control, among Tswana, 29, 102–103, 104
socialists, British, and regimental-labor rebellion, 80
"songs of the law," 105
Sotho, the, 10, 11, 13, 213
Sotho chiefdom, 37
South Africa
  apartheid policy of, 15–16, 216
  Bantustans of, 15, 15–16, 211–212, 213–214, 215–216
  Bechuanaland's dependence on, 186
  and British annexation of Bechuanaland, 45
  and British policy, 46, 91
  and capitalist development, 208
  cattle purchase and embargo by, 13, 55, 58, 66, 97, 120, 147, 177
  chief as protector against, 61, 93
  chiefs compared to, 172
  economic independence from sought, 204
  and flogging incident, 92–93
  incorporation in expected, 14, 223n.75
  incorporation in feared, 44, 45, 93, 113–114, 114–115, 185, 189, 231–232n.93
  incorporation in resisted, 50
  industrial development of, 4, 12, 55, 58–61, 134, 216 (see also diamond mining; gold mining)
  Kwena and Kgatla labor sent to, 50
  and marriage of Seretse, 186–188, 189–190, 191
  segregation policy in, 14–15
  transfer of Tati and Tuli to proposed, 66
Southern Rhodesia
  Mswazis seek haven in, 168, 170
  and Seretse marriage, 188, 189–190, 191
South West Africa
  and British annexation of Bechuanaland, 45
  railway to Walvis Bay proposed, 204
Soviet Union, and British decision on Seretse, 191
Special (High) Court of the Bechuanaland Protectorate, 14, 64, 74, 111, 115, 196–197
Stanley, Sir Herbert, 92

status
  and *kgotla* drama, 102
  seniority as, 25 (*see also* seniority)
  significance of, 139
  strategies to improve, 25, 26, 219n.10
  of subordinate tribes, 143
status-to-contract transition, 134
  and Sarwa, 89
stock. *See* cattle
subject peoples (under Ngwato), 24, 136
  and Birwa case, 149–155
  and British-imposed boundaries, 148–149
  and closer government, 146, 172
  and Khurutshe case, 156–162
  "lesser breeds" description of, 170
  and *mfecane*, 38
  and modernization, 174
  and Mswazi case, 162–172, 245n.97
  and Ngwato hegemony, 138–145, 149
  and Tshekedi, 201–202
Swazi, the, 153
Swaziland, 4, 14, 213–214

Tagart, E. S. B., 86
Talaote, the, 142, 145
Tati, 49, 66, 89, 89–90, 92
Tati Company, 156–157, 157
Tati Concession, 164, 165
Tawana, the, 145, 237n.3
Tawana chiefdom, exile for founder of, 26
taxation, 50, 146–147, 205, 222–223n.74, 241n.35
  and Birwa, 150, 152, 242n.54
  and breakdown of chieftainship, 202
  and chiefs' rights, 109
  and disaster years, 66–67, 97–98
  evasion of, 232n.104
  at fall of chieftainship, 192–193
  of headman for ward, 124
  Khama III converts tribute to, 50, 136, 145
  and labor migration, 58, 59, 61, 118, 119
  and Mswazi case, 164, 166–167, 169
  and Ngwato chief, 141, 145
  and protest against change, 133
  and Sarwa, 87, 89
  and tribal treasuries, 14, 147, 148, 168, 178
  and Tshekedi, 79, 97, 147, 165–166
  uses of, 147–148, 166, 240n.33, 240–241n.34

Thompson, A. D. Forsyth, 169
Tile, Reverend (London Missionary Society), 71
Tlhaping
  engraving of chief of, 3
  labor migration by, 59
Tomlinson Commission, 213–214
Tonota, 158, 160
trade
  long-distance, 39–43, 120
  and subject peoples, 143
  Ngwato-white, 65
traditionalism, 212
  and class interests, 214
  and Seretse's marriage, 181–182, 185–186, 199
  and Tshekedi's fall, 207
  failure of among Tswana, 214–215
  see also patriarchal order
traditional law. See law, as custom
transformations in chiefdom. See Ngwato/Tswana chiefdom, changes in
Tshekedi Khama, xii, 3–5, 9–10, 63
  accession of, 69–74, 217n.2
  aims of, 16
  beer sales prohibited by, 177, 200, 201
  and British, 63–64, 84, 93, 172
  as capitalist rancher, 90, 215
  centralization by, 146
  on chief-headman relationship, 197
  chieftainship renounced by, 189, 207
  close control by, 200
  and current conditions, 210
  and customary law, 74, 100–101, 104, 107, 109–110, 115–116, 121–124, 126, 133
  death of, 211
  divorce of, 94–96
  education of, 69
  economic development plans of, 204–205, 206, 208
  exile of (1933), 64, 92, 93, 111
  exile of (1949), 184, 192, 194–195
  and fall of chieftainship, 175, 206, 207, 208–209, 211, 215
  and flogging of McIntosh, 91–93, 111
  as judge, 81–82, 125, 127, 128, 132
  and Khurutshe case, 156, 158–160
  on labor migration, 118
  legal/labor systems manipulated by, 203
  in mining-development battle, 9
  and mode of government, 55
  and Mswazi case, 162
  opposition to, 193, 194–195, 199–200, 207–208
  and patronage, 147–148, 207, 208
  people's fear of, 182
  post-WWII demands from, 178
  private and public property of, 50, 51, 202–203
  and Raditladis, 94, 122 (see also Raditladis)
  and Ratshosas, 76–77, 94 (see also Ratshosa brothers)
  regency surrendered by, 217n.2
  and regimental labor fracas, 77–84
  and Sarwa, 84, 85–87, 90, 131
  and Seretse, 70, 71, 179
  and Seretse's marriage, 179–190, 192
  and subject peoples, 136
  successes of, 133–134
  and taxes/wages, 79, 97–98, 147, 165–166
  view of toward the young, 181
  wealth of, 10, 148, 173, 202–203, 250–251n.73
  and WWII recruitment, 119, 176
Tswana chiefdoms
  British rule over, 4, 13–14, 44–55, 222n.73 (see also British colonial administration)
  disaster years for, 96–98
  see also chieftainship, Tswana; Ngwato chiefdom
Tswana chiefdoms, changes in. See Ngwato/Tswana chiefdom, changes in
Tswana society, 10–12
  basic principles of, 124
  begging within, 22, 30–31
  and Botswana/Bechuanaland, 4
  burial customs of, 33
  collective responsibility in, 124
  environment of, 20–21
  long-distance trade of, 39–43, 120
  marriage relationships of, 23–24, 26
  from ranks to classes in, 91
  and South African industrial development, 55, 57–60
  and status-to-contract transition, 134
  village life of, 19–20, 21–22, 218n.3
  ward organization in, 103
Tswana society, politics of, 22–23
  and British overrule, 4, 13–14, 49–51, 52, 53, 222n.73 (see also British colonial administration)
  bureaucratizing of, 16, 50, 54, 55, 61, 146, 173

centralization in, 36–37, 39, 49, 61–62, 146
dynastic clashes, 68–69, 180 (see also dynastic rivalries)
enforcement, 29, 102, 104, 119
ethnicity as tool in, 155
and exchange relationships, 7–8, 22, 23–24, 51, 216 (see also patronage)
and exploitation, 31
hierarchy in, 22, 24–26, 35, 102
household autonomy, 7, 22, 114
labor-migration effect on, 59, 61 (see also migration, labor)
maneuvering in, 26–27, 71, 219nn.10, 15
vs. other southern Africa chiefdoms, 213–214
and patriarchal ideology, 31–36
power-sharing in, 28–29
and rebellion, 138
and religious conversion, 161
resistance and influence by commoners, 29–31, 43, 53, 82–83, 173
survival of traditional forms (1930s), 99
territorial monarchy grows, 46
veld people as vassals, 42–43 (see also Sarwa; subject peoples)
and wealth, 27, 28, 30, 32–33, 62, 65, 76, 77, 96, 103
see also chieftainship, Tswana
Tswapong Hills, 142, 144, 178
Khama's gardens at, 51
Tuli Block, 49, 66, 150
and Birwa case, 150–155

vassals. See Sarwa; subject peoples
veld people. See Sarwa; subject peoples
Victoria (queen of England)
and Birwa, 152, 154
and Khama, 44

wage labor
in capitalist transformation, 98–99, 213
and ethnic tension, 172
increase in, 65
local development of, 8
and reforms, 134
and rights of women or hereditary servants, 126
and Sarwa, 87, 89, 90
scarcity of, 120, 236n.52

Tshekedi pleads for improvement of, 97–98
and waning of patronage, 133
wagon trade, 143, 145
Khama's wealth from, 106
see also trade, long-distance
Walker, Patrick Gordon, 191, 194–195
Walvis Bay, South West Africa, railway to proposed, 204
Warren, Sir Charles, 46, 108
Watermeyer, E. P., 115
Webb, Sidney. See Passfield, Lord
Weber, Max, 4–5
white traders, 65–66
cash earnings from, 41
Disang's debts with, 122
profiteering by, 177
Tshekedi breaks monopoly by, 205
Williams, Ruth. See Khama, Ruth
witchcraft
and law, 108, 109, 110
Mswazis accused of, 171
refugees from, 140
Tshekedi suspected of, 185
women, xiii, 5
and absence of men (WWII), 177
anti-Tshekedi activities of, 200–201
civil liberties granted to, 126
and customary law, 100, 101
vs. British law, 116
initiation, 35
and kgotla, 126, 127–128, 177, 181, 199, 201
Khama on rights for, 126, 127, 131
labor-migration effects on, 130, 201
and legal disputes, 106
migration of restricted, 119, 126
in patriarchal order, 33
status of, 25, 127–128, 129
traditionalist views of, 212
work of, 21, 33
work, 21, 23
changes in, 4
World War II
effects of recruitment for, 176–177
Keaboka "rumor" on, 192
and Mswazi case, 168–169, 171
Tshekedi's use of recruitment for, 119
and South African expansion, 231–232

World War II (*cont.*)
  uniforms from worn, 184

Xhosa chiefdom, 13

Zion Christian Church, 212
Zulus, 12, 13
  and Inkatha, 214
  and *mfecane,* 37, 39

ABOUT THE AUTHOR

Diana Wylie has taught history at Yale University since 1985. A graduate of Goucher College (B.A.), Edinburgh University (M.Litt.), and Yale University (Ph.D.), she has also taught in rural Kenya and at the University of Oran in Algeria. She has been studying Africa since 1970 and, from 1979 to 1981, lived in Botswana, conducting interviews and studying archival documents for this book. She lives in New Haven, where she is a resident fellow in Calhoun College of Yale.

ABOUT THE BOOK

A Little God was composed on a Mergenthaler Linotron 202 in Sabon. Sabon was designed by the late Swiss typographer, teacher, scholar, book designer, and type designer Jan Tschichold.

The book was composed by Brevis Press in Bethany, Connecticut, and designed by Kachergis Book Design in Pittsboro, North Carolina.

Wesleyan University Press, 1990

INSTITUTIONAL CHANGE 13